D0548302

*EMPEROR TO EMPEROR*

*By the same author*

Logan Pearsall Smith:
an anthology of his writing

# EMPEROR

# TO

# EMPEROR

*Italy before the Renaissance*

EDWARD BURMAN

*Constable · London*

First published in Great Britain 1991
by Constable and Company Limited
3 The Lanchesters, 162 Fulham Palace Road
London W6 9ER
Copyright © Edward Burman 1991
ISBN 0 09 469490 7
The right of Edward Burman to be
identified as the author of this work
has been asserted by him in accordance
with the Copyright, Designs and Patents Act 1988
Set in Monophoto Apollo by
Servis Filmsetting Limited, Manchester
Printed in Great Britain by
St Edmundsbury Press Limited
Bury St Edmunds, Suffolk

A CIP catalogue record for this book
is available from the British Library

# CONTENTS

# ILLUSTRATIONS

All illustrations are by the author unless otherwise credited. *AL* = Alinari. *EPT L'Aquila* = Ente Provinciale di Turismo, L'Aquila.

## *FIGURES*

*All figures drawn by John Mitchell*

# CHRONOLOGY

*Events cited in the book:*

| | |
|---|---|
| 876 | Gregorius captures Bari: beginning of Byzantine hegemony over southern Italy |
| 883 | Montecassino sacked and burned by Arabs |
| c.885–915 | Arab stronghold on the Garigliano menaces Rome |
| 887 | With the death of Charles the Fat, Carolingian imperial authority largely passes to the bishops |
| 902 | Arabs take Syracuse and Taormina: Sicily entirely under Arab rule |
| 909–48 | Fatimid rule of Sicily |
| 924 | Hungarian sack of Pavia |
| 925 | Genova attacked by Arabs |
| 948–86 | Third Foundation of Montecassino by Abbot Aligern |
| 948–1091 | Kalbite rule of Sicily |
| 963 | Saxon king Otto I crowned Emperor in Rome |
| c.975 | Byzantine Catapanate established with capital in Bari |
| 996 | Delegation of the citizens of Cremona travels to Rome to protest against episcopal privileges |
| 1004 | Henry II crowned in Pavia at San Michele |
| 1009 | Revolt of Melo in Bari |
| 1011 | Byzantine palace in Bari rebuilt by Catapan Basilius Mesardonites |
| c.1017 | First Normans arrive in southern Italy |
| 1024 | Sack and burning of *Palatium* at Pavia |
| 1046 | Robert Guiscard departs from Normandy |
| 1058–86 | Desiderius is Abbot of Montecassino |
| 1059 | Robert Guiscard becomes Duke of Apulia & Calabria |
| 1061 | Roger I invades Sicily |
| 1067 | Normans capture Bari |
| 1071 | End of Byzantine rule in southern Italy |
| — | New basilica of Montecassino consecrated |
| — | Palermo captured by Roger II: end of Arab rule |
| 1073 | Sant'Angelo in Formis rebuilt by Desiderius |
| 1076 | Investiture Crisis between Henry IV and Pope Gregory VII |
| 1077 | Cittanova founded at Cremona |
| 1085 | Robert Guiscard dies |
| 1091 | Arab presence in Sicily ends |
| 1095 | Proclamation of the First Crusade |
| 1098 | Cistercian abbey of Citeaux founded |
| 1099 | Jerusalem captured by the First Crusade |
| 1101 | Roger I 'the Great Count' dies |
| 1107 | Foundation of the cathedral of Cremona |
| 1118 | Foundation of the cathedral of Genoa |
| 1131 | Foundation of the cathedral of Cefalù |
| 1153–4 | Building of the *ripa maris* in Genoa |
| 1154 | Death of Roger II |
| 1154–63 | Second medieval wall of Genoa built |

| | |
|---|---|
| 1167 | Formation of the Lombard League against Frederick Barbarossa |
| — | Baptistery of Cremona built |
| 1174 | Cathedral of Monreale founded |
| 1183 | Peace of Constantine |
| 1184–5 | Ibn Jubayr visits Sicily |
| 1190 | Foundation of new cathedral in Cremona |
| 1191 | Cistercian abbey of Casanova founded in Italy |
| c.1191–6 | S. Maria del Monte founded |
| 1194 | End of Norman rule in Sicily |
| — | Frederick II born at Jesi, near Ancona |
| 1204 | Sack of Constantinople |
| 1206–36 | Building of Palazzo del Comune in Cremona |
| 1209 | First civic constitutions of Cremona |
| 1215 | Frederick II crowned King of Germany at Aachen |
| 1220 | Frederick II crowned Emperor in Rome |
| 1229 | Statues of the *societas populi* in Cremona |
| 1231 | Frederick II's *Constitutions of Melfi* |
| c.1240–6 | Castel del Monte built |
| 1250 | Death of Emperor Frederick II |

*Aftermath*:

| | |
|---|---|
| c.1260 | First recorded use of the adjective 'italiano' |
| 1260 | Nicolo 'de Apulia', later known as Nicola Pisano, sculpts his first signed work – the pulpit for the Baptistery in Pisa |
| 1266 | Charles of Anjou kills Manfred, illegitimate son of Frederick II at the Battle of Tagliacozzo, establishing the house of Anjou on the throne of Naples (until 1442) and ending the rule of the Hohenstaufen dynasty |
| 1282 | After the Sicilian Vespers, Sicily is offered to the house of Aragon (Aragonese and Spanish rule lasted until 1713) |
| 1284 | Battle of 'La Meloria' between Genoa and Pisa |
| c.1290 | The *Novellino* written |
| 1293 | Beginning of a series of wars between Genoa and Venice which led to the decline of Genoese power |
| 1303–4 | Dante cites the 'School of Sicily' in his *De Vulgari Eloquio* as a source of 'Italian' poetry |
| 1305 | Giovanni Pisano, son of Nicola, sculpts a Madonna for the Arena Chapel in Padua |
| 1306–9 | Giotto paints the Arena Chapel |
| 1308 | Duccio paints his *Maestà* for Siena cathedral |
| 1334 | Cremona passes under the control of the Visconti |
| 1338 | Beginning of the Hundred Years War |

| 1339 | Foundation of a new cathedral in Siena |
| 1339–40 | Famine in Italy |
| 1348 | Black Death decimates population of Italian cities |
| 1349 | Desiderius' basilica at Montecassino destroyed by an earthquake |
| 1359 | Pavia passes under the control of the Visconti |

*Later Repercussions*:

| 1573 | The last Greek episcopal see, at Bova in the old *theme* of Tursi, Latinized |
| 1806 | Demise of the title 'Holy Roman Emperor' |

Fig. 1. Italy about 700 AD, including major sites mentioned in the book

# PREFACE

Medieval Italy was the crucible of modern western civilization. In a memorable sentence Edward Gibbon observed that in the period from 840 to 1017 'the three great nations of the world, the Greeks, the Saracens, and the Franks, encountered each other on the theatre of Italy.' The ultimate consequence of this encounter, together with the base provided by the civilization of ancient Rome, was the Italian Renaissance.

Common wisdom has it that between the 'fall' of the Roman Empire, traditionally dated as 476 AD, and the Renaissance of the 15th century, there was a 'middle' or 'dark' age lasting some thousand years. Such a view implies a lack of continuity of social and cultural life during the 'Middle Ages' which the humanists and artists of the Renaissance then recovered. It is not of course quite as simple as that. Yet while the precise degree and nature of continuity between the Roman and the late medieval worlds, especially the transition from a slave economy to a serf economy, still generate controversy among scholars it is apparent that there was some kind of continuity in legal structure and administration. In an amusing phrase the British historian Chris Wickham has observed in an article fuelling the controversy that we often speak as though the various features of classical Roman life were all mixed up in 'some giant classical bran-tub' which suddenly disintegrated in 476. Various elements of what we think of as classical Rome – architecture, poetry, law, the senate, the toga, slavery – in fact enjoyed separate chronological existences and therefore demises. They did not all suddenly cease to exist in a given year. Furthermore the concept of Holy Roman Emperor which persisted from Charlemagne to Frederick II represented a search for legitimacy in past institutions which is evidence of what might be termed an a posteriori continuity. They saw it if we sometimes don't, and in no place is it more perceptible than in Italy. A city like Pavia incarnates the transition perfectly: in its history we can see the legal and administrative structures of the ancient world undergo change as Roman laws are Christianized under King Liutprand of the Lombards, and then adapted during the new process of urbanization which heralds the beginning of fresh growth throughout Europe. Each phase of this process is at the same time new and an addition to or improvement upon existing structures; at the very least

[15]

the present was measured and judged by the yardstick of the past. The title of this book is designed to emphasize the remarkable degree of continuity – to deny the existence of a seven-hundred-year hiatus – from the overthrow of Emperor Romulus Augustulus to the coronation of Frederick II as Holy Roman Emperor in 1220.

In fact the story of the Italian peninsula from the demise of the Roman Empire in the year 476 to around 1300 is essentially that of a search for a new social identity; for a model to replace the civil, legal and military order which had held sway for so long. Yet Rome was always massively there. That is why the Ostrogoth kings, the Lombard law-makers, the monks of Montecassino and legalist popes such as Innocent III all worked with ancient Rome as their standard; it is also the reason why the concept of re-birth – and its myth of sculptors and architects seeking to recreate the greatness of Rome – was at the heart of the movement which eventually provided a new model. At the same time, however, the contribution of the invaders – Lombard, Carolingian, Byzantine, Muslim, Norman and German – was vital.

It is a complex story, rarely told in works accessible to the general reader and even more rarely in English; there is certainly no claim to tell the full story in such a short book as this. But at the same time some idea of this story is essential for a full understanding of the later history of Italy, and especially of the Renaissance. The structure of this book is designed to avoid the problems of parallel chronology and geographical diversity which would bedevil a complete – and presumably multi-volumed – linear history of medieval Italy. It was suggested by one of the most distinctive traits of late medieval Italian society; its predominantly urban character. The history of the peninsula is necessarily a mosaic made up of the histories of individual cities, castles (in the sense of fortified villages) and monasteries (often seen as prototypes of urban development); so the idea is to provide a panoramic view of Italy during the period 600–1300 by means of a jigsaw made up of a series of representative places. The choice of five cities from the many Italian cities of historical and cultural importance together with two monasteries, a cathedral and a castle is naturally a matter of personal taste, and open to criticism. The first criterion was to include examples of the cultures of invading peoples which formed an integral part of post-medieval 'Italian' society, the Lombards, Carol-ingians, Muslims, Byzantines, Normans and Germans. To accommodate these, some of the most important Italian cities have been deliberately excluded: Rome, for example, is a case sui generis, covered in many monographs on medieval history, as is the history of the Church; Venice (together with the lesser republics of Amalfi and Pisa) was excluded because a single maritime republic (Genoa) was chosen to illustrate a

general pattern; some cities, like Cremona, are personal choices representative of a general situation which others could illustrate equally well; last
of all, cities such as Florence and Milan have been excluded because they
enjoyed their greatest prosperity and importance after 1300 – when the
Medici and Visconti/Sforza respectively rose to power. It was with the
development of a culture associated with the Tuscan cities that, as I hope
to show, the adjective 'Italian' began to assume a clear and useful meaning.
The attempt to create a new society in the fullest meaning of the term was
in fact accomplished in the city-states of the Renaissance. The seeds were
sown in northern and southern Italy but the harvest was reaped between
these areas, in cities such as Florence and Siena, whose history is well-
known, and others such as Perugia, Pistoia and Orvieto, which have
received detailed treatment in recent historical works.

The castle chosen, Castel del Monte in Apulia, represents the Holy
Roman Emperor Frederick II, whose role as the last great medieval
emperor is vital to the story while the complexity of his political role and
his multiple cultural interests – which anticipate the concept of
'Renaissance man' – render his life as impregnable as his own castles to
brief summary. Here his life is viewed from the perspective of a single
castle, which does however represent the essence of his being; he was for
much of his life an itinerant king and emperor, and never created a real
capital. The cathedral, Cefalù, stands as symbol to King Roger II of Sicily
just as Castel del Monte to his grandson Frederick II. The two monasteries
chosen, one world famous and one almost totally unknown and indeed in
ruins, illustrate the different function of the monastery in the two periods
into which the book is divided; to simplify, it would be possible to argue
that in the first period (600–1100) Montecassino (and the Benedictines)
had a predominantly spiritual function while in the second (1100–1250)
Santa Maria del Monte (and the Cistercians) had an equally important
economic function. The division of the volume into three parts also reflects
this shift: Part I deals with a series of invasions and influences, each of
which had to come to terms with Benedictinism in some way (two of the
invading peoples destroyed Montecassino and two contributed to its
splendour): Part II deals with the new forces which paved the way for the
economic achievement of Italy in later centuries. The cultural mosaic
created by the blend of so many apparently heterogeneous forces in Part I,
and the socio-political and economic thrust of the cities in Part II, together
constitute the foundation of the Italian Renaissance. Part III offers a brief
account of how they came together.

A consequence of this composite nature is that this book cannot be a
chronological survey, although some chapters do follow more or less
sequentially. It does not purport to be a complete history of medieval

[17]

Italy; neither does it use documentary or archival material. It is mainly based on secondary sources in English and Italian, printed primary sources where they illustrate the general argument, and personal observation of cities and works of art. A glance at the Select Bibliography will suffice to illustrate my debt to such works: books and articles listed by chapter in the first part form the essential working bibliography, including some very specific, specialized and rare items; those listed under 'General' in the second part have been consulted as a whole for general background, or in part for single chapters and arguments. Since it is a working bibliography with no claims to completeness, editions given are those which have been used, including translations from other languages into English and Italian. My aim has been to create from these often specialized texts a readable narrative by using the fresh point of view provided by the choice of places, and to link history as firmly as possible to place and existing artefacts.

The place and artefact crucial to post-medieval Italian culture are the *piazza* and *campanile*. In every city the antiquity, dimensions and aesthetic qualities of these urban features inform and define the culture of its inhabitants. The role of the piazza needs no explanation, but while the British refer to the abstract concept of 'patriot' in defining their loyalty, and the French to the name of a devotee of Napoleon, it is worth noting that Italians use the term *campanilismo* to mean local pride. Emblems of Italian cities often bear the representation of a campanile, and some places – like Cremona, with its famous 'Torrazzo' – are particularly associated with such a tower. Hence an event such as the sudden collapse of the thousand-year-old campanile of Pavia in March 1989 was a traumatic event for the people of that city, because their fundamental point of reference and symbol of their past had crumbled in a matter of seconds. It was more than just a tower.

Given this close identity between physical fabric and inhabitants, an attempt has been made to render medieval history tangible by anchoring it to what may be seen today. Maps, figures and other illustrations have been chosen with this in mind.

# PART I

## Benedictine Italy and its enemies
## 529–1100

# 1

# *LOMBARD PAVIA*

Tucked away just south of the Renaissance cathedral and Visconti castle, which are the most visited monuments of Pavia, closer to the River Ticino and the bridge which for centuries provided the city's *raison d'être*, is the basilica of San Michele Maggiore. Although there is a tradition which says that this church was founded by Constantine – based on a now-lost and much later inscription – San Michele was originally built by the Lombards soon after their arrival in Italy in the second half of the 6th century. Such a date is supported by its dedication to one of the dragon-slaying saints especially venerated by them (the other being St George), and invariably portrayed in arms by that warmongering people. The new church, a stone's throw from the palace the kings occupied near the river, soon became a symbol of Lombard rule. In succeeding centuries it was to be the site of a series of royal coronations which constitutes a link between ancient Rome and medieval Italy: probably the coronation of the Lombard Arioald in 626; certainly that of the Carolingians Charles the Bald in 876, and Berenger and Adalbert in 950; and that of the Saxon Emperor Henry II in 1004. No direct evidence of the original structure remains, save bits of ancient wall which archaeologists believe were re-used. But we may imagine a three-aisled basilica on the model of Sant'Ambrogio in Milan, built of moulded kiln-fire bricks and with the continuous blind arcading found both at Sant'Ambrogio and in fragments of other Lombard churches in Pavia. It would have been embellished by Roman columns and capitals like the near-contemporary San Salvatore in Brescia. The original church was destroyed by fire during a rebellion which followed Henry's coronation, as we shall see; the present basilica was rebuilt at some time in the next hundred years, and was to host a coronation as important as those of its predecessor. For on Sunday 24 April 1155 it was the scene of a crown-wearing festival and three days of feasting designed to legitimate the claims of Frederick Barbarossa as heir to the Lombard kingdom.

San Michele is therefore a tangible symbol of continuity between

Detail of the façade of San Michele Maggiore (Pavia)

Roman Empire and Holy Roman Empire, and in its present form a masterpiece of Romanesque architecture. Its magnificent sandstone façade is divided into three vertical sections by half-pilasters and crowned by suspended loggias; three portals corresponding to the vertical sections have finely-carved human and animal figures in relief, now badly eroded. Inside, the central nave is separated from the two aisles by pilasters which sustain a ladies' gallery. In one of the chapels inside is a marvellous silver foil crucifix made in the 10th century, a fine example of the quality of work in Pavia at that time commonly thought to have been a kind of 'dark age'. It gives some idea of the splendour of Pavia at the height of its power from the 8th to the 11th centuries.

Pavia is still today an elegant city, with fine medieval buildings and atmosphere. Yet it is odd to reflect that this was the capital of Italy for over 400 years, since at first sight neither the size nor the position seem to justify such a role. Ticinum, as it was known to the Romans, had been a city of some importance in the late Empire, due to its position on the route to Gallia and the bridge over the River Ticino. In 410 it was chosen as the rallying point for his legions by the Vandal mercenary Stilicho before defending Milan from Alaric, and we shall see that the rebel Orestes fled there from Ravenna. But just 20 miles to the north was the far more important city of Mediolanum, or Milan, which became the second capital of the Empire when Diocletian decided in 286 to divide his power and responsibility with Maximian: Mediolanum retained this role until a single capital was established at Ravenna in 410. As an ex-capital and seminally important Christian centre as the seat of St Ambrose, Milan would have made a more logical choice for the capital. Yet it was Ticinum which became the Lombard and later the Carolingian capital of the Italian 'kingdom', becoming known as Pavia in the early decades of the 7th century when the first Lombard kings made their residence there. A curious legend provides an explanation as plausible as any other, albeit fantastic.

The Benedictine chronicler Paul the Deacon, writing just over 200 years later at Montecassino, relates the legend – which he presents as fact – in his *History of the Lombards*. The tenth king of the Lombards, Alboin, who was also to become King of Italy, arrived on the northern plains of Italy from Pannonia (modern Hungary) in 568. Paul the Deacon describes him as 'a man able in war and in every other thing' and elsewhere as possessing a 'bold physique and body perfectly formed for battle'. These comments highlight the need for a Lombard king to be seen as a hero, a personification of the warrior values of a military society in addition to being a political leader. The Lombards never lost their fundamentally warrior attitude. Excavations in the Lombard cemetery at Nocera Umbra

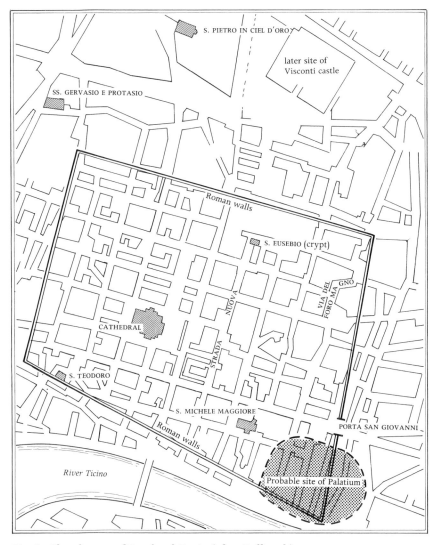

Fig. 2. Sketch map of Lombard Pavia (after Bullough)

showed that more than half the men were buried with full horseman's armour of sword, lance and shield, following pagan customs. All the men were buried with arms of some kind, and even male children had arrows in their graves.

As this warrior race passed westwards through northern Italy towards what was then known as Liguria and is now Lombardy, Alboin left a series of dukes representing him in major cities such as Cividale, Trento, Vicenza, Verona and Brescia. Ticinum was the first place to offer strong resistance to his progress, and in the year after his arrival in Italy he was forced to lay siege to the walled city. The siege lasted for three years, during which time a combination of famine, plague and military astuteness enabled Alboin to subdue much of northern and central Italy. Eventually, however, after 'three years and a few months', Pavia surrendered and Alboin returned there to occupy the city as victor. But as he was about to enter the Porta San Giovanni, Paul the Deacon tells us, the curious incident occurred. This gate was probably in the southern half of the eastern section of the late Roman wall, as little as 200 metres from San Michele – which would then have been the first building reached by a traveller entering from the south-east of the city. According to the legend Alboin's horse fell down exactly under the gate, and refused the prompting of both spurs and a royal marshal. Then, in the chronicler's words:

> ... one of the Lombards said to the King: 'Recall, my lord, the oath you have sworn. Break this cruel oath and you may immediately enter this city, because its people are Christian.' In fact Alboin had sworn to put the entire population to the sword, because they had not wished to submit. But now he broke his oath and promised mercy to the people who lived within the walls. Then the horse got up at once, and when the king entered the city he kept his word and caused harm to no one.

Next, in a decision which conveniently linked this sign from God with the evident strength of Pavia's walls and the courage of its citizens, he chose to stay in that city. This, according to Paul the Deacon, was the basis of the later adoption of Pavia as the Lombard capital of Italy.

But there were also more rational motives for choosing Pavia. The first concerns transport and communication in northern Italy. In Roman times these were guaranteed by the excellent network of roads, but political and economic decline had led to deterioration of the road system. In fact one of the most fascinating shifts which occurred in the early medieval period was that from road to river transport. Pavia, a strongly defended city sited at a road-crossing on the Ticino close to its confluence with the Po, was ideally situated to take advantage of Italy's most extensive river system (which again in 1990 Italian industrialists are seeking to revitalize in order to relieve the overloaded road system). We know from the late Roman author Cassiodorus Senator that in the first decade of the 6th century a party of the barbarian Eruli tribe travelled from Pavia to the capital at Ravenna in five days; some centuries later, in 969, Bishop Liutprand of Cremona made the journey from Pavia to Venice in three days. Salt merchants from Comacchio (in the south of the Po delta), and later

Venetian traders, were to play an important role in the commercial growth of Pavia; by the 11th century the fluvial ports along the Po at Ferrara, Cremona, Piacenza and Pavia rendered these cities centres of international trade.

The second motive may be found in one of the salient features of all medieval rulers in Italy: the constant search for historical continuity and the legitimacy which could be derived from demonstrating it. Alboin's first action on entering Pavia exemplifies this: he went directly to the *Palatium* or official residence built by Theoderic, the first Ostrogoth king of Italy, and occupied it. Apart from the symbolic significance of this gesture he may also have exploited the skill of administrative officials installed there; for although the history books speak of the 'fall' of the Roman Empire in the year 476 there was in fact a remarkable continuity of law, administrative practice, culture and land ownership. A subtle but unbroken thread guided the transition from the brief rule of Romulus Augustulus to the barbarian general Odoacer, who deposed the Emperor and then ruled himself from 476 to 490, and on to the Lombards. The youth Romulus, contemptuously nicknamed 'the little Augustus', had himself been placed on the imperial throne only the year before by his father Orestes. This Roman from Pannonia – like the Lombards – had been a secretary and favourite of Attila the Hun (d.453), and later *magister* of the militia of the reigning emperor Julius Nepos (473–80); he deposed Julius Nepos and forced him into exile in Dalmatia, then had Romulus acclaimed as emperor. But his schemes were destined to failure: Romulus was not recognized by the Eastern Emperor Zeno, who 'ruled' briefly in Ravenna while the legitimate emperor was in exile; furthermore, the troops who had made Orestes' coup possible were dissatisfied because their claim to one third of the land in Italy in exchange for services rendered was ignored.

It was a situation which invited usurpation. Odoacer, himself the son of a favourite of Attila, led the discontented army against Orestes and succeeded in defeating and killing him near Piacenza. Romulus was deposed from the imperial throne and sent into exile near Naples. This 'last emperor', in quotation marks because Julius Nepos actually survived until 480, seems to have been quite innocent amidst these machinations; the chronicler Valesian remarks that his life was spared 'because he was fair'. Be this as it may, Odoacer then took power himself, seeking legitimacy by recognizing the exiled Julius Nepos, and by suing for recognition and suzerainty from the Eastern Emperor Zeno (474–91). He sent the imperial insignia to Constantinople as a sign of loyalty, arguing that one emperor was sufficient. Although he never obtained the formal seal of approval, Odoacer was allowed to rule until Theoderic and an army of Ostrogoths came to Italy in 490. This event itself may have been Zeno's reply: some chroniclers state that Theoderic came on the invitation of Zeno; others that Zeno provided tacit assent. Whatever the case, Theoderic besieged Ravenna for three years, until Odoacer surrendered to the Ostrogoths on receiving assurances of safe conduct. After a few days imprisonment Odoacer was murdered, together with his wife, brother and son. In this way Theoderic became the first Ostrogoth King of Italy, ruling until 526. He established a line which continued for 80 years, and indirectly provided the legitimacy of the Lombard claim to the kingdom of Italy.

Under Theoderic, who first assumed the title *dominus* and later *rex*, and took the Roman name Flavius as if to emphasize the continuity he sought, Italy was ruled from two centres: Rome as the symbol of Empire and home to the wealthy senators who had ruled the country in previous years; and Ravenna, which had become the capital of the Western Empire with the Emperor Honorius in 403, as the effective administrative capital. In the latter city Theoderic achieved a political synthesis which is visually represented in the mosaics of the church he built, now known as San Apollinare Nuovo – for instance in the rather northern-looking magi on the right wall of the nave. He managed to maintain the kernel of Roman civilization while preserving the barbarian warrior values of the Goths; at the same time he enabled a strong Byzantine element to flourish in the visual arts. This synthesis was based on his own education and taste: son of an Ostrogoth king, temperamentally close to Roman ways, from the age of 8 to 18 he had lived and been educated under the protection of the Emperor at Constantinople, where he had been sent as a hostage by his father.

Certainly he was no 'barbarian' in the usual negative sense of the term – 'rough, wild or uncultured' as the *Concise Oxford Dictionary* has it. The historian Procopius informs us that he was a wise and enlightened king, qualities perhaps assumed at the Byzantine court; he may also have learned in Constantinople the art of surrounding himself with good scholars. For Theoderic surrounded himself with the best then available, including two of the most enlightened men of the period: Anicius Manlius Severinus Boethius (*c*.480–525), a learned Roman and son of a prefect under Odoacer, who had studied grammar, rhetoric and Greek and who as *magister officiorum* was responsible for the civil administration of Theoderic's kingdom; and Cassiodorus Senator (*c*.480–575), also son of a minister to Odoacer, who became *quaestor* or minister with responsibility for maintaining harmonious relations between Romans and Germans and served the kingdom in various capacities for much of his long life. Both these men managed to compose a large number of important works while managing the affairs of state: Cassiodorus' *Divine and Human Readings*,

[27]

used for the instruction of medieval monks, was every bit as influential as Boethius' *Consolation of Philosophy*. Their long-term presence in the royal court provides an insight into the character of Theoderic.

Royal patronage did not stop at these scholars, or even with the numerous buildings erected in his own honour. Theoderic repaired Trajan's aqueduct, encouraged land reclamation around Ravenna, and extended the city's walls. His own palace at Ravenna, as can be seen in the San Apollinare mosaics, was built on the model of the Roman villa with a fine portico sustained by three columns; but its decoration appears firmly Byzantine and delicate in detail. In contrast, the solidity of his surviving stone mausoleum is reminiscent of that of Hadrian in Rome, now the Castel Sant'Angelo.

Theoderic also maintained two further palaces, one in Verona and one in Pavia. It was in fact in the latter city, in the picturesquely named church of San Pietro in Ciel d'Oro, that his counsellor Boethius was buried after the tragic 'betrayal' which led to his imprisonment and execution, forced by circumstances in his prison tower there to seek consolation in philosophy. It was also in Pavia that we can see the pragmatic use of Christian bishops alongside pagan scholars, as these former spiritual leaders began to move out from their limited function to occupy the political stage – foreshadowing the future episcopal power which such cities as Cremona were forced to combat. For example, bishops Epiphanius (467–97) and Ennodius (513–21) of Pavia were employed both as envoys and as writers; the latter produced panegyrics in favour of Theoderic, and is commemorated by an epitaph in San Michele. Thus Pavia can be seen to have played an important role during Theoderic's reign.

But the synthesis he achieved depended as much on his powerful personality as anything else. Shortly after his death the Eastern Emperor Justinian (527–65) declared war on the Ostrogothic kingdom. Twenty years of conflict, known as the Gothic Wars, led to much of the country being ravaged by the combating Ostrogoths and Byzantine Romans. The eventual success of Justinian meant the end of the Goths as a nation, and the *Pragmatic Sanction* of 554 which marked the formal ending of these wars was designed to restore Italy to its place as the Western Province of the Empire of Constantinople. But the measures outlined in Justinian's *sanction* were insufficient to compensate for the weakening of Italy during the hostilities – which were in fact to continue on and off into the next century. No imperial decree could restore the *status quo* as it had been before the arrival of Odoacer and Theoderic, and the Western Province was never entirely dominated. For the process of change and integration could not be reversed, and in fact the *sanction* had limited real influence. In little over a decade was to begin a dynasty which with its Carolingian extension was to mark a real break with the Roman past and represent the beginning of what may be termed 'medieval Italy'; the synthesis suggested by Theoderic led the way to future developments, and in little more than a century the kingdom of Italy was to be subject to a substantially different sets of laws in the form of King Rothari's edict of 643. It should also be remembered in this context that the political changes between 544 and 568 were contemporary with another great innovation: the provision of the programme for a non-Roman way of life contained in the *Rule* of St Benedict, who died just three years after the issue of the *Pragmatic Sanction*.

The arrival of the Lombards under the leadership of Alboin filled a vacuum which had been created by the Gothic Wars. There was little dramatic change: the Lombards occupied the same territory and cities, and generally adopted policies little different from those of their predecessors. The similarity was such that in his *History of Florence* Machiavelli went as far as to state of the Lombards that 'there was nothing foreign about them except their name'. There were even blood-links, since Alboin's father Audoin had married a great-niece of Theoderic as his second wife; Alboin himself was therefore stepson to a direct descendent of the Ostrogoth king. Such a heritage must have influenced both his certainty in the legitimacy of his enterprise and his decision to occupy Theoderic's palace in Pavia. But in fact his rule was short-lived, for he was murdered soon after taking Pavia in a plot in which his own wife Rosmunda participated. His successor, Cleph (572–4), was summoned from Verona and became the first of a long series of kings of Italy to be crowned in Pavia. However a state of semi-anarchy prevailed in those early years of Lombard rule: King Cleph was also murdered and for the next ten years the newly established Lombard dukes ruled autonomously in the cities of northern Italy without electing a king.

When these dukes eventually agreed to choose a single ruler it was Cleph's son Authari (584–90) who became the third Lombard King of Italy, ruling over a kingdom which Paul the Deacon describes in terms of a golden age without crime, conspiracy, or violence of any kind. According to the same source each of the dukes gave half of his wealth and lands to the new king, thus providing the nucleus of the Italian kingdom for succeeding centuries. Their gesture was successful, for it was with Authari's rule that the kingdom was consolidated. His strategy was to strengthen his lands by resisting Frankish attacks from the north and attacking the Byzantine *themes* in the south; it was based on a double policy of controlling strategic points like alpine passes and key cities – such as Pavia itself – and maintaining separate, compact and therefore strong Lombard communities. Authari was the first of the Lombard kings

[29]

to assume the Roman honorific Flavius – following Theoderic's usage. During his six-year reign Lombard power was extended to much of northern Italy, with the semi-autonomous Lombard dukedoms of Spoleto and Benevento extending Lombard influence over more than half of the land area of the Italian peninsula. The Byzantines – as we shall see in the chapter on Bari – were left holding the heel and foot of Italy, Sicily, Sardinia and Corsica, and a strip which stretched across Tuscany from Rome to Ravenna. Authari further strengthened his position in the north by marrying the Bavarian princess Theodelinda, who had previously been engaged to the Merovingian king Childerbert II. She soon became a favourite of the Lombards. Her church of San Giovanni at Monza was one of their most celebrated monuments, and her political function important as regent to her son from her second marriage Adaloald (King: 616–26).

The immediate succession of Authari, who died in Pavia reputedly by poisoning, provides an intriguing illustration of the curious Lombard belief that royalty could be transmitted by means of non-procreative sexual intercourse. Already in the case of Alboin, we learn from Paul the Deacon that his wife Rosmunda had tricked the future murderer of her husband – a certain Perede – by waiting in the bed of a maid who he slept with; she allowed Perede to make love to her, and then announced that he must carry out the murder. Now Theodelinda was asked by the Lombard people to choose a new husband, to whom she would pass on Authari's royal power by means of intercourse. In fact there was rarely a normal succession in the line of Lombard kings of Italy. It was either through marriage or a political coup that a series of dukes moved to Pavia and assumed the throne: Arioald from Turin in 626, Grimoald of Benevento in 662, Alahis of Trent around 688, Rotarit of Bergamo around 702, Ratchis of Friuli in 744, and Desiderius of Brescia in 756.

It was perhaps with the first royal coronation in San Michele, that of King Arioald in 626, that Ticinum became capital of the Lombard kingdom of Italy; at the latest it achieved this status ten years later with the coronation of King Rothari. Lombard building began there during the longish period of peace which lasted through the reigns of Arioald and Rothari (ie. 626–52). In the same period or perhaps slightly earlier, roughly between 600 and 636, the name of the city was changed from Ticinum to Pavia.

Recent archaeological evidence has shown that the late Roman walls of Ticinum enclosed and fortified an area comprising an unequal square of approximately 750 by 550 metres, based on the *cardo* following the line of what is today confusingly known as the Strada Nuova running perpendicular to the river. These walls were five to six metres in width and were recorded as still very strong in the 5th century. By that time of course it was no longer a Roman city, and Christianity had begun to take root: it acquired a bishop as early as 375. In any case, by the end of that century Ticinum possessed two churches, both situated outside the Roman walls but already marking a shift in the focus of city life. The expansion of this city began with Theoderic and continued throughout the Middle Ages. A chronicler states that Theoderic 'built a palace (*palatium*), bath and amphitheatre', and Bishop Ennodius adds that in the years 489–90 both private and public Roman buildings were demolished to make room for the Ostrogoths. At the same time however, it is likely that older, Roman buildings were incorporated into the royal project. The complex indicated by the term *palatium* came to include the royal residence, administrative offices, the treasury, the chancery and law courts; later, during the reign of King Perctarit (672–88), a new gate known as the Porta Palatina was built into the Roman wall beside the *palatium*. At this time the first churches within the walls were built. The exact site of Theoderic's *palatium* is unknown, but is assumed to have been in the south-east corner of the ancient city – near to the river, and also to the future site of San Michele – where the Roman grid pattern that is still visible in Pavia's street plan is distorted into a curved corner. This distortion could have been made to accommodate the huge garden which Ennodius mentions.

It is known that King Arioald made his residence in Theoderic's restored or newly constructed *Palatium*, which thus became the royal residence until its destruction in 1024. To the north of the *palatium* was the area allocated to the *farae* or warrior clans of the Lombards, each *fara* being an extended family group of about 100 people. Such an area was known in medieval documents as *faramania*, a name which in Pavia is preserved by a curious instance of back-formation in the present Via di Foro Magno – where a Lombard word has been given a false Latin etymology. Thus it has been suggested that in this early part of Lombard rule the city was divided into two distinct communities: the Lombards to the East of the city, with royal palace, their own church and quarter; and the Romans to the West, with their place of worship, SS Gervasio and Protassio, outside the walls to the north-west of the city. For the early Lombards were from the Catholic point of view Arian heretics, and their first church in Pavia was that of the dualist Arian rite at San Eusebio within the *faramania*. San Eusebio is now destroyed, but the restored crypt can still be visited under one of the city's principal piazzas. Their heretical practices were however short-lived, since from King Arioald onwards all the Lombard kings were Catholic. From that moment dates the first great period of church building in Pavia, with a particular impulse after the formal abolition of Arianism by King Aripert I (653–61) and the consequent mass conversion of the Lombards.

[31]

It was in this period that the first basilica dedicated to San Michele was built, perhaps in time for Arioald's coronation in 626. Although the first undisputed evidence for its existence in fact refers to the year 662, the context suggests that the church already possessed a certain symbolic importance for the Lombards. Paul the Deacon relates how in that year King Grimoald was tricked by the rebel Perctarit and his right-hand man Unulf into believing that the imprisoned Perctarit was sleeping in his room while in fact he had escaped from Pavia to Asti. On asking his soldiers what had become of Unulf when the deception was revealed, Grimoald learned that 'he had sought refuge in the church of Saint Michael the Archangel'. Since San Michele was originally part of a monastery this seems to suggest that already in 662 it was a flourishing and powerful complex with walls and authority sufficient to offer sanctuary to an enemy of the king. That it was built some time before is further suggested by the fact that the deacon Tommaso and his immediate successors were responsible for *restoring* the church and having frescoes painted in the atrium during the bishopric of Bishop Damian, that is between about 690 and 710. We may imagine these frescoes to have been in the Byzantine style of the magnificent contemporary frescoes in the little Lombard church of S. Maria Foris Portas at Castelseprio, near Varese, or in the similar frescoes in S. Salvatore at Brescia.

It is also possible that the incident of Unulf's refuge, the transfer of Ennodius' epitaph, the many coronations, indicate a particular respect for San Michele and therefore a direct royal foundation: perhaps by Arioald. Certainly from the time of his successor Rothari (who founded San Giovanni *in Cimiterio*), royal foundations seem to have been the rule. They can be associated with Rothari's own widow (San Giovanni Domnarum), King Aripert (the oratory of San Salvatore), King Grimoald (Sant'Ambrogio), King Perctarit (convent of S. Agata), King Cunipert (San Giorgio), and the greatest of all Lombard kings Liutprand (San Pietro in Ciel d'Oro).

Whatever the reason, from this moment Pavia began a period of sustained growth, foreshadowing the urban growth which began throughout Europe in the 8th century. Clearly a city like Pavia had a head start, for urban decline in a continuously inhabited city had never been as great as that of the cities of northern Europe. It has been calculated by Ward-Perkins that in the period from about 300 to 800 AD as many as 116 of 372 Roman towns in Italy disappeared; but three-quarters of the northern Italian towns survived. There is evidence of remarkable continuity in his observation that 35 of the 50 modern provincial capitals in the area that was once the Lombard kingdom were Roman cities. Those that did survive – including, for instance, Cremona, as we shall see – enjoyed a period of renewed growth in the 8th century coinciding with the rising political power of the Church.

In fact the seminal event in the medieval urban history of Pavia was the transfer of the episcopal *cathedra* from SS Gervasio and Protassio outside the city walls to the twin churches of S. Stefano and S. Maria near the centre of the Roman city. This is thought to have occurred during the bishopric of Damian, thus around 700, even though archaeologists have found roof-tiles stamped Bishop Crispinus dating from the first half of the 6th century in a tower near the present cathedral. In the unusual arrangement to be found in many northern cities in early medieval Italy, S. Stefano (built by Damian's predecessor Bishop Anathasius and later known as S. Sirus), to the north of the complex, was the summer cathedral; S. Maria was the winter cathedral. The reasons for this arrangement are not known with absolute certainty: in part it was due to a symbolic representation of Old and New Testament, but it may also have reflected local climatic conditions in having the winter church to the south and thus warmed by sun. The fact that S. Stefano was a much larger, five-aisled church and S. Maria smaller would appear to substantiate this, but at the same time similar double churches in France and the absence of them in southern Italy would appear to contradict this hypothesis. In fact it seems more likely that they were designed to represent the liturgical change which came with the seasons, the move to the summer church usually taking place at Easter and that back to the winter church at Advent (although documentary evidence for the similar double cathedral at Milan specifies that the former move took place on Whit-Saturday, and the latter on the third Sunday of October – the anniversary of the church's consecration). The usual arrangement was in fact for the winter church, the *ecclesia maior*, to be named for the Virgin – as at Pavia, Milan and also Cremona – and the parallel summer church for a martyr, in this case St Stephen. This 'twin cathedral' – fragments of which have survived – was however much more than a church, or even double church: the concept embraced a complex of buildings, including a baptistery and in the case of Pavia the bishop's palace, buildings for other clergy, and a bath-house. Many similar cathedrals, as we shall see in Cremona, were later provided with walls and defensive towers which became the basis of power for the count-bishops of Carolingian Italy. Even at this early stage the symbolic importance of such an imposing complex at the heart of Pavia, just three decades after the conversion of the Lombards, must have been evident to the population. The open space in front of the new episcopal centre soon became a vital part of city life, in Donald Bullough's words 'the place where, except in moments of revolution, the Pavians expressed their corporate feelings'. In the centre of this piazza, the *platea atrii* on the site of the present Piazza del Duomo, stood a celebrated equestrian statue

The double cathedral of Pavia as represented by Opicinus de Canistris in his fourteenth-century description of Pavia, the *Liber de Laudibus civitatis Ticinensis*

probably brought from Ravenna in 751, known as the *Regisole*, which was destroyed in the 18th century. Thus Pavia may be said to have set the pattern for the medieval Italian city, with its cathedral, bell-tower and piazza with equestrian statue at the centre of civic life. Later, during the period of the *comune*, the extant municipal palace or *Broletto* was constructed on the same piazza. If piazza and campanile are accorded the crucial role in Italian culture outlined earlier, then 8th century Pavia was the model.

Apart from the two areas occupied by the *palatium* and the cathedral complex, the land within the Roman walls was far from being completely built up. Evidence suggests that there was much open land, and that private houses possessed large walled or hedged vegetable plots and orchards. Moreover the distribution of these houses was haphazard, since they were not aligned along the surviving Roman streets, as we imagine a modern town, but stood on isolated plots reached by paths which were considered common property. The more wealthy residents appear to have used two main types of home: the Lombard *sala*, which was a single-storied building with a post framework and wooden roof; and the more luxurious *casa solariata*, which was a two-storeyed building with the

[34]

main room on the upper floor – a predecessor of the later medieval Italian town-house. There were however probably few masonry and tiled-roof buildings, the majority being temporary structures made of wood with earthen floor and thatched roof. The poor probably lived in hovels or patched-up bits of ancient buildings. In fact much of the building that took place was probably a matter of re-building: sacking surviving Roman buildings for doorposts, lintels and other useful fragments, building against Roman walls, and in some cases adopting Roman forms – as in the case of the multi-apsed building thought to be a bath complex discovered during excavations near the church of San Tommaso in 1895. The fact that there was still a functioning Roman drainage system in Pavia in the 8th century means that one of the technical requirements for such a structure was fulfilled. In terms of religious architecture it seems likely that early Lombard churches did not differ much from those of the late Roman period: we must look to San Salvatore at Brescia, S. Maria-in-Valle at Cividale, or S. Maria Foris Portas for a precise idea of the architecture, sculpture and fresco decorations.

For the Lombard rulers did not initiate a wholly new building style. It has however been convincingly argued that in the later period of their rule, under King Liutprand (712–44), the highly ornamented decorative

The Lombard church of Santa Maria fuoris Porta, Castelseprio (near Varese), with an eighth-century fresco cycle rediscovered in the 1940s

[35]

Fresco detail: note the drama and movement

style of interlaced sculpture at Pavia was in the avant-garde of new artistic fashions. Endless scholarly debates on whether this style was Byzantine or Celtic in origin have not produced a conclusive answer. Whatever the distant origin, it seems evident that stone and marble sculptors indigenous to Lombardy developed this style, in which ornament and interlacing are clearly and symmetrically arranged in the space available; another feature is that the architectonic frame is an integrated part of the design, not just an arbitrary termination of the space to be decorated. Two examples suffice to illustrate the style: the sarcophagus of the Abbess Theodota in the Civic Museum of Pavia, whose sides are completely covered in ornate detail but never cluttered; and the equally decorated but elegant screen pillars of San Pietro in Ciel d'Oro.

The real achievement of the Lombard kings was not aesthetic, but consisted in the success of their legal and administrative organization. Indeed, one of the most surprising features of a reading of the chronicles and histories of the period from the end of the Roman Empire to the 12th century, the so-called 'Dark Ages', is the remarkable bureaucratic continuity. Just as today the legal system and the civil service perpetuate

[36]

Fresco detail: note the 'Renaissance'-like figure looking in

their own conditions irrespective of change in government, so the substructure of Roman law and territorial organization underwrote the success of the so-called barbarian kingdoms. This is nowhere as evident as in the history of Pavia.

The first vehicle of this continuity with the Roman Empire was the law. On 22 November 643 the series of laws known as Rothari's *Edict* were promulgated by a public assembly in Pavia. King Rothari defines himself in the opening remarks as the 17th king of the Lombards and of the

[37]

A contemporary representation of King Rothari issuing his edict (643)

'province of Italy', listing his ancestors as if to justify the writ of his laws. He states that his compendium of laws has been made so that 'each man may live in peace, in respect of law and justice', and in return for this peace be willing to do voluntary service to protect it against the enemies of the country. Yet in the midst of this almost 'modern' proclamation it must be remembered that these laws applied mainly to the free man, for the slaves were less protected. The distinction between free man and slave is fundamental throughout the *Edict*. Respect for the person of the former was paramount, so that obstructing the passage of a free man was considered a crime while obstructing that of a slave was not. Even in cases where offences against both were recognized – such as in the case of personal injury – it was nevertheless a more serious matter against the free man; fines and financial compensation value the life of a free man as worth 20 times that of a slave. For instance, chapter XXVII, on the right of passage of free men, specifies that a fine of 20 *soldi* should be paid in the case of the free man being blocked without wound; in the case of injury the same fine of 20 *soldi* is to be paid in addition to compensation for the injuries caused. An offence against the social order is considered as far more serious. Such a distinction between material and moral damage on the one hand, and infractions of social order on the other, demonstrate the importance of social order as perceived by the Lombards. In what might be described as a curious instance of ethnic objectivity the distinction between free man and slave was applied equally to Lombards, native Romans and others.

Evidence of Lombard survivals from their time in Pannonia – and before that in northern Europe – is discernible in the use of Lombard words in some of the chapter headings which are then translated into Latin as if many Lombard subjects of Rothari would no longer understand them: for example *mordh* (in chapter XIII), *grabworfin* (XV), *malapautzo* (XXXI), *waregang* (CCCLXVII). Often these Lombard words concern traditional procedures, such as the public declaration of intent known as *gairethinx* which is mentioned in several chapters. Survivals of a pagan and warrior ethic can also be seen in the chapters which emphasize the importance of the horse in Lombard society, and in the section which lists the rights and responsibilities of the hunter. Similarly the stress on individual dignity reflects barbarian usage, for the worth of the dignity and inherent truthfulness of the free man as conceived by the Lombards meant that he was always believed unless there was proof to the contrary. The accused was bound to provide evidence, not the accuser, and if the accused countered with the affirmation of *his* dignity then the credibility deriving from the comparative dignity of the two men was of greater weight than the facts of the case. Family history, past life, reputation and character were thrown on to the balance. But on the whole the detailed prescriptions

[39]

and punishments of the *Edict* are evidence of a highly ordered society ruled by law and precise administrative order. The 388 chapters represent a summation of Lombard law and society in the 7th century, and consist of a combination of Roman law, Ostrogoth laws, enquiries about ancient customs made amongst the elders, and the practical experience of King Rothari – who had then ruled for seven years.

Some of the most impressive chapters are those which guarantee the rights of the poor and of women, or of foreign visitors such as merchants who temporarily come under the protection of the king's laws. Another interesting category concerns the chapters which contain provisions made to avoid corruption, specifying that officials were not able to accept gifts without royal consent. Thus the king was always behind the law in the guise of the supreme guarantor of society: the position of the king was legitimized by the law, while at the same time his royal descent guaranteed the law itself. Thus law and king together were the essence of Lombard society; even the *iudex* who decided on minor matters in a provincial court had been appointed in person by the king, and thus personified the royal judgement. The necessity of providing a specialized body of *iudices* to fulfil this function, as we shall see, ultimately led to the creation of the school of law that must be considered one of the most extraordinary features of Carolingian Italy, when Pavia led the way for the whole of Europe.

The second vehicle of continuity with the Roman Empire was the administrative division of the kingdom. The invaders, Ostrogoth and Lombard, maintained the Roman system and employed its administrators: partly because they possessed no such structured system of their own; and partly because they inherited a system that still functioned in spite of economic decline and political changes. As the imperial residence or *palatium* had transferred from Rome to Pavia, so the 17 administrative provinces of late imperial Rome were organized into circumscriptions largely identical to the dioceses and cities which previously formed the base of civil and legal jurisdiction. Imperial responsibilities such as minting coins and providing for the maintenance of city walls were assumed by the Lombard kings; similarly, Roman offices such as *maiordomus*, *vesterarius*, *camerarius* and *notarius* were retained. The circumscriptions themselves were known as *iuiciariae* or duchies and were supervised by the officers known as *gastaldi* – from the Lombard 'gastald', or royal administrator – who lived in the cities. The main changes were due to the fact that the Lombard kingdom did not correspond precisely to the Roman province of Italia: duchies such as Friuli in the north-east and Spoleto in the south gained their importance from their position as border territories; smaller *castra* were built at the approaches to the alpine passes against the Franks – like the Castelseprio mentioned above – and in the Tuscan Apennines against the Byzantines. The use of passports was introduced in order to control movement of non-Lombards into the kingdom, and allow the application of the safe-conduct specified by Rothari. Military command, especially in the frontier areas, was held by dukes who often operated together with the gastalds responsible for civil administration. But the distinction between these two offices was often rather vague; some cities never had dukes, and gastalds often fulfilled their roles – for instance in the case of betrayal of the king's trust by a duke.

Under King Liutprand (712–44) a process of rationalization and centralization took place. The kingdom was thereafter divided into districts known as *civitates* which were based on the cities rather than on the ancient provinces, with the political and administrative power in them controlled by the *iudices* chosen by the king who assumed the real power of gastalds and dukes directly in his name. Smaller sub-districts like villages and rural areas were ruled over by *decani* and *saltari*, who were directly answerable to the *iudex*. The system was held together by means of an annual council of *iudices* which took place in Pavia, where the judges brought together their experiences and problems and discussed such matters as the interpretation of the law. Ultimate arbiter and court of appeal was the king in person, who thus maintained strict control over what happened distant from his capital. At that time the kingdom assumed a new stability and definitive physiognomy, being divided into three regions which became the basis of the Carolingian empire later in the century: Neustria (including modern Lombardy, Piemonte and Liguria), Austria (modern Friuli, Trentino, Alto Adige and part of the Veneto), and Tuscia (modern Tuscany). In addition there were the semi-autonomous southern duchies of Spoleto, which Liutprand declared part of the kingdom in 727 (including the modern region of the Marche, E. Umbria and N. Abruzzo), and Benevento (modern S. Abruzzo, Molise, Campania except Naples and Amalfi, Basilicata, N. Puglia and N. Calabria).

The adoption of Roman customs, together with residence beside the indigenous population, also modified the everyday life of the Lombards. Paul the Deacon, who had been a royal tutor in Pavia, found it necessary to explain that scenes from Lombard history in the frescoes painted for Theodelinda in Monza showed how they used to dress and cut their hair: 'In fact,' he writes, 'they shaved the central part of the neck up to the back of the head, and parted their hair on either side from their foreheads so that the hair fell down as far as the mouth'. These early Lombards wore their clothes loose; usually they were of linen 'like the Anglo-Saxons' and decorated by coloured bands. They only later began to wear trousers, and

[41]

their footwear then consisted of simple open sandals tied with leather laces. The process of detachment from original Lombard customs – or integration into Italy – can be observed in the excavations of their cemeteries, where it is possible to note a gradual loss of the custom of burying warriors with their arms. At the same time there is an increasing presence in the graves of Byzantine and Roman artefacts, gold, ivory and precious tableware. Literacy and the use of money were other important acquisitions from the Romans.

The most dramatic move away from Lombard customs occurred with Liutprand. For it was under the inspiration of that devout king that a Christian interpretation of the pagan body of laws codified by Rothari transformed Lombard society. Barbarian precedent was superseded by the commands of the scriptures; a warrior society dominated by weapons, horses and hunting was changed into a profoundly religious society underpinned by canon law. Such evidently Christian features as the concept of sin were added to the chapters of the earlier edict; the introduction of the notions of clemency and mercy profoundly changed the spirit of the laws. More revolutionary still was the idea that each member of the society had a *duty* to defend God's cause in the world. This affirmation was to inform the later medieval concept of kingship, and pave the way to the crusading ideal.

Other changes introduced by Liutprand involved personal and economic life, accelerating the rapid evolution which Lombard society was undergoing. Legislation against superstition and surviving pagan cults characterized the religious aspect of these changes; catholicism was more than a mere veneer. Equally important was a series of laws governing family relationships which indicated an attitude quite different from that of the warrior ethic and *farae*. The traditional custom of concubinage with maids and slaves was abolished, and emphasis was placed on legitimacy with the result that natural children lost the rights they had always possessed. Laws of inheritance were further modified so that a woman could inherit her father's property in the absence of a male heir – perhaps in the place of the natural son who would once have inherited. Severe laws against sexual abuse and crimes of various kinds shows a new kind of respect for women and the individual. The introduction of prisons, and punishments such as whipping and branding, demonstrate an attempt to move away from the ancient system and its ambiguous concept of dignity. Increased respect for the individual also entailed respect for salaried labour. In contrast with a society whose warrior ethic excluded such work, the new territorial division into *civitates* recognized the right of workers to move between these districts for the purposes of work or trade. War was no longer the only activity which necessitated travel. This fact was explicitly recognized in the law which stated that an absence of three years was permitted before an individual lost his rights to inheritance. Trade in slaves, salt, cloth and luxury goods, together with the consequent adoption of a monetary economy, led to the accumulation of personal wealth among citizens of the later Lombard kingdom. These changes in turn fostered a new, urban and monetary, society which spurred the growth of cities like Pavia in the 8th century.

Yet Liutprand's ambition contained the seeds which were to lead to the destruction of the kingdom within 30 years of his death in 744. Together with his nephew Hildebrand, in 740 the king attacked both the Exarch in Ravenna and the Byzantine-protected duchy of Rome; in the following year he re-united Spoleto and Benevento to his kingdom by personally quelling rebellions. His attempt to expand the kingdom was continued by his successors, Ratchis (744–9) and Aistulf (749–56), and in 751 the exarchate of Ravenna fell definitively to Aistulf after two centuries of existence. Thus Byzantine rule in northern and central Italy was ended, and their power-broking role in the peninsula truncated. But these apparent victories upset a well-established and delicate equilibrium: one of the first actions of Pope Stephen II (752–7) was to dispatch envoys to the newly crowned king of the Franks, Pippin, with letters complaining about the violence which the Church was suffering from Aistulf. Two years later he personally travelled to France to meet the king, stopping on the way at Pavia in an atmosphere whose tension we can only imagine. Then Pippin made a momentous decision: he promised to obtain lands from the Lombards and give them to 'St Peter'; in exchange for this promise he was named 'Roman patrician'. This action not only heralded the coming of Pippin and then his son Charlemagne to Italy, and thus the replacement of the Lombard kingdom by that of the Carolingians. It was also the origin of the papal state, or Patrimony of St Peter, which came into being in 754.

Three sieges of Pavia punctuate the last years of Lombard rule. In 754 King Pippin, in the company of Pope Stephen, led an army over the Mont Cenis pass into Italy. Aistulf was defeated in battle at Susa and retreated to his stronghold at Pavia. Pippin followed him, besieging the capital and laying waste to the surrounding countryside until Aistulf was forced to surrender. After Aistulf had consigned hostages to the French king and agreed to provide the land which had been promised to the pope, Pippin returned to France. But as soon as he departed, Aistulf reneged the agreement and resumed his attacks on the duchy of Rome; once again Pope Stephen sent letters of complaint to France. Two years after his first invasion Pippin returned in a carbon copy raid: he again beat Aistulf at Susa, and again laid siege to Pavia when the Lombard king retreated there. Aistulf was forced to provide further hostages when he surrendered this time, and also to give Pippin one third of the royal treasure. The plan was to destroy his will – and means – to continue to fight. But this time the negotiations were never allowed to be finished because Aistulf fell from his horse and died. He was succeeded as king by his duke in Tuscany, Desiderius (757–774), who inherited a disastrous situation.

In September 773 Pippin's son Charlemagne began the third and definitive siege of Pavia. It lasted until the following June, when Desiderius surrendered and was sent into exile in France. Thus the Lombard kingdom of Italy came to an end in its capital city of Pavia, and it was within the city walls that Charlemagne himself was crowned King of Italy. There was in fact a kind of legitimacy to this succession parallel to the tenuous link between Alboin and Theoderic: a few years earlier Charles Martel had sent his son Pippin to the court of Liutprand for a ritual hair-cutting ceremony, and, in Paul the Deacon's words, 'with the cutting of his hair he entered into a paternal relationship with him'. Liutprand then sent the young prince home to France laden with royal gifts. The relationship between the two kingdoms had been developed further during the Arab incursions into France, which culminated when the invaders were defeated at Poitiers in 732. At one point, when it seemed the Arabs would overrun his entire kingdom, Charles had made an appeal to all the Christian forces for aid against the infidel. 'Without hesitation,' Paul the Deacon writes, 'Liutprand rushed to help him with the entire Lombard army.' The partisan chronicler adds that the Arab invaders then fled, as though the mere announcement of Liutprand's arrival was enough; in fact, the Lombards never engaged in battle because the Franks had already defeated the Arabs at Arles. But the episode is interesting in showing us how the threat of Islam created allies from previous enemies, and how the Lombard and Frankish kingdoms were seen to have joint interests. Fusion, or absorption of the weaker kingdom into the stronger, was only a step away, and it may be that these events led indirectly to one of the greatest changes in medieval Italian history. For at the end of the century Charlemagne was able to re-establish a version of the Western Empire and have himself crowned Emperor, in Rome on Christmas Day 800.

Charlemagne spent several brief periods in Pavia on his four successive visits to Italy, but never made it his residence; the concern of the Frankish kings of Italy was their empire beyond the Alps – of which Italy was a kind of sub-kingdom. Frankish counts replaced the dukes, and *missi* or king's messengers presided over the courts in place of the royally appointed *iudex*; otherwise social and administrative structures remained more or less unaltered, with the tolls and services once paid to the Lombards simply changing destination. In fact during the next two centuries a king was rarely present in Italy, and from 884 Charles the Fat nominated a palatine count to run the kingdom for him. This was also the time, as we shall see in the chapter on Cremona, when bishops began to assume a political role and function as count-bishops with judicial powers, collecting taxes, maintaining militia, and turning their episcopal palaces into centres of temporal power. Pavia itself appears to have been semi-autonomous, with its own council, officials and property, directly dependent upon an emperor who was in effect an absentee landlord.

Yet within this apparent autonomy there was a high degree of centralized financial and commercial organization. The best example of this with regard to Pavia is a famous early 11th century document known as the *Honorantiae civitatis Papiae*. This shows how the royal administration, or *camera regia*, was then overseen by a director known as the *magister* who presided over a series of 'ministers' each with his own *ministeria*. These ministries were directly responsible for the organization of all trades and commercial activity within their mandate: they established privileges and duties, controlled entry to the categories of artisan, and collected taxes. They included the important ministry of the *negotiatores*, or merchants, and that of the *monetarii* who gained concessions for the mints of Pavia and Milan. Other ministries included that of the tanners and soap-makers, that of the gold-hunters, and that of the river fishermen – whose obligations included the provision of fish for the royal table on Friday when the king was in Pavia. It has often been argued that the *ministerium*, from which the modern Italian word *mestiere* or trade derives, was the basis of the 'corporazione di mestiere' or guilds which played such an important rule in the development of Italian cities during the Renaissance and which were themselves forerunners of trade unions.

Another of the most interesting consequences of this centralization under Lombard and Carolingian rule was the growth of a group of judges, the *iudices*, into a class of literate professional men upon whom both court and administration depended. For the presence of such a body of influential and highly trained men implies the existence of a royal 'law school' or centre of legal training which must rank as the first of its kind in post-Roman Europe. In the early 11th century members of this school made a compilation of Lombard and Carolingian law known as the *Liber papiensis*, which attempted a synthesis of Roman and later laws. This was followed by a companion interpretative work called the *Expositio ad librum papiensem* which included annotations, cross-references and case histories just like a modern legal compendium. These works marked an important shift from the simple *reading* of laws to their *interpretation*. They were the model for the revival of Roman and canon law which was one of the main factors in the so-called 12th century Renaissance. Indeed while it is often claimed that the school of law of the *studium generale* of Bologna was the origin of the earliest university in Europe – for instance during the grandiose celebrations of the 1,000th anniversary in 1989 – a similar 'school' existed at Pavia throughout the period of Lombard and Carolingian rule. It might even be argued that such a school presupposes continuity with the Roman world, from a Roman-born servant of Ostrogoth administration like Boethius to the *Liber Papiensis* 500 years later. In addition to the formation of *iudices*, the school provided the necessary professional training for notaries, clerks and chancery officials both for Pavia itself and for cities elsewhere in the kingdom; its programme of studies included grammar, reading and writing, and rhetoric. It was here that Paul the Deacon acquired both his narrative skill and the information necessary to compose his *History of the Lombards* – and, we may assume, other useful knowledge which was passed on to fellow scholars at Montecassino.

The provisions of the *Honorantiae civitatis Papiae* and the presence of a law school imply a thriving city, and in fact during the 9th and 10th centuries the area within the Roman walls of Ticinum seems to have been filled up with new buildings. The Magyars who attacked Pavia in 924 were said by one chronicler to have burned as many as 44 churches, a claim which gives some idea of the extent of recent building. In his *Antapodosis* Bishop Liutprand of Cremona left a vivid description of the destruction, given here in the translation of F.A. Wright:

> Our fair Pavia falls consumed in fire,
> And Vulcan rising high in windy ire
> Through all the city runs his deathly race
> And grips our churches in his fierce embrace,
> And maids unwed who now shall ne'er be brides.
> . . .
> The gold that we in chests had stored away,
> Lest any strangers on it hands should lay,
> Runs through the sewers, mixed with mud and mire.

Even allowing for the hyperbole of the occasion, these verses suggest a thriving city. A further sign of the wealth of the city at that time is provided by the fact that many of the churches and other buildings destroyed by the Magyars were soon rebuilt. All the stored gold had not run to waste. At the same time, the increased commercial importance of the city led to bishops, abbots and cities wishing to set up a *cella*, *curtis* or house in the city. Monasteries like Bobbio and Nonantola in Italy, and St

[46]

Martin of Tours and Cluny in France, established such bases; the cities with permanent representatives included Milan, Lodi, Bergamo, Piacenza, Reggio, Tortona and Genoa. The bishop of Cremona, who as we shall see controlled an important part of the river traffic on the Po, owned the church of S. Silvestro, three houses each with a mill, extensive gardens and the right of passage on the river. The Venetians seem to have had their own market near the monastery of S. Martino outside the city walls. The resulting building activity soon cluttered Pavia. Bullough cites the mention of building *supra viam publicam* in royal privileges as evidence of the saturation of urban land; use of public roads and even parts of the city walls suggests that powerful men or institutions would do anything to create their foothold in Pavia. Other buildings must have included quarters for merchants and warehouses, and also hostels for pilgrims to Rome from northern Europe as Pavia became a major stopping place on that route.

The market became one of the most important in Europe, maintaining close relations with Venice, Comacchio and Ferrara, and through Venice with Amalfi, Gaeta and Salerno; Frankish and Anglo-Saxon merchants were also regular visitors to the market. As in most Italian cities in this period there were really two markets. The first of them, the *forum*, was essentially a local market often held on Sunday so that people from nearby villages could combine purchases and sales with church attendance. For although prayers could be said in the minor churches and oratoriums, mass and special ceremonies like baptism could only be carried out in the *plebs*; this was strictly speaking the religious district based on the cathedral, but came to be used for the cathedral itself as the centre of religious life (*plebs* survives today in Lombard place-names as 'pieve'). This *forum* was held inside the city walls, and was mainly a market of direct commerce between producer and purchaser. Its presence led to the development of permanent shops nearby, and the well-known phenomenon of streets near the market specializing in certain trades; later these markets tended to become daily and no longer on Sunday. The second kind of market was the *mercatum*: this was at first a periodical market held outside the city walls on religious feast days – hence 'fiera' or fair – and later weekly. It was a larger and more complex affair, with merchants rather than producers selling their wares: these included luxury goods like silk and spices from the East which came via the sea ports; products of the great ecclesiastical estates maintaining a *cella* in Pavia – which also bought products from the first category such as incense, cloths and objects in gold and silver; and agricultural produce brought to the city by river. The success of this latter market may be judged from the fact that coins minted in Pavia from about 800 to 1000 were amongst the most widely distributed in Italy, until the rising power of Milan replaced them.

The fairs also attracted passing pilgrim traffic, since Pavia stood on the main pilgrim route from Canterbury via Lyons to Rome. Several important and even royal Anglo-Saxon pilgrims are known to have stopped there. In 688 the recently converted King Caedwalla of Wessex was given hospitality in Pavia by King Cunipert on his way to be baptized by the pope – and then to die almost immediately in Rome. Relations between the Lombard kings of Italy and the Anglo-Saxon kings of Britain were at that time particularly close: when King Perctarit planned to sail into exile it was to Britain that he headed – although changed circumstances meant that he turned back; his successor Cunipert, host to Caedwalla, had himself married the Anglo-Saxon princess Ermelinda. It is likely that King Cenred of Mercia, who travelled to Rome in 709, and King Ethelwulf, in 855, also stopped at Pavia. Certainly Archbishop Sigeric of Canterbury did so in 990; his contemporary Queen Ethelswitha, sister of King Alfred, actually died in Pavia on her way to Rome. The presence of these later pilgrims shows that the route continued to be used throughout Carolingian times.

But the Carolingians themselves, while maintaining Pavia as their formal capital, when they came to Italy actually ruled from Milan and Verona as much as from Pavia. Coronations and burials of Carolingian kings tended to take place elsewhere: Louis II (840–75), who spent the last 25 years of his life continuously in Italy and was the only king of his line to rule in practice as well as theory, was buried in Milan – as recorded by an epitaph in Sant'Ambrogio. Under the later Saxon emperors (i.e. from 963 to 1024) there was no real capital at all. Otto I introduced the Germanic concept of a mobile court in Italy, using Ravenna and Verona as much as Pavia.

The symbolic end of Pavia's period as capital of Italy came with the burning of the *Palatium* in 1024. After the last Saxon emperor Emperor Henry II had been crowned in San Michele in 1004, his German troops had wrought havoc in the city – the first of many signs of underlying distrust between Italian subjects and German rulers. When news of his death came 20 years later the citizens of Pavia rushed through the city in joy and burned the imperial palace to the ground. A further sign of protest was that from about this time dates recorded in documents in Pavia were based on the birth of Christ rather than using the imperial chronology. Yet in spite of this rebellion Pavia's role as legitimizing rule over Italy was not ended, for a new palace was soon built – significantly outside the city walls in tangible sign of the loosening of imperial power in Italy. Just as Alboin had occupied Theoderic's palace and Charlemagne had had himself crowned in Pavia, so in 1155 Frederick Barbarossa sought to legitimize *his* and the Hohenstaufen's claim to the Italian 'throne' by his crown-wearing ceremony at San Michele. That this search for legitimacy in Empire through association with the Lombards was not merely a medieval phenomenon is demonstrated by Napoleon's action in wearing the Lombard iron crown now in Theodelinda's chapel in the cathedral of Monza as recently as 1805, more than 1,000 years after the disappearance of the Lombard Kings of Italy.

Pavia itself continued to flourish without the *Palatium*, albeit bereft of its former glory and power. In the 12th and 13th centuries it played an important role in the development of the Lombard communes, as we shall see in the chapter on Cremona. In 1359 it passed under the control of the rampant Visconti family of Milan, and then of their successors the Sforza, becoming one of many subservient cities within the Duchy of Milan. The castle built by the Visconti, started in 1365, and the new cathedral, started in 1488, belong to the Italian Renaissance. The story of these buildings is not only quite beyond the scope of this book, but incarnates a new spirit of Pavia distinct from that represented by San Michele.

# *MONTECASSINO*

To enter the dank, gloomy Benedictine oratory of San Pellegrino at Bominaco is to step back through the centuries. Excavations at Montecassino show us that its dimensions and rough limestone blocks are similar to those of the oratory built there by St Benedict in 529 AD, and dedicated to the inspirer of early monasticism, St Martin of Tours. The St Pelegrinus for whom this oratory is named was himself a hermit. Tradition has it that he was an Irish prince who after visiting the Holy Land led an austere hermit's life in these mountains; according to a 13th century inscription on a stone inside the altar he was buried here. The chapel nestles into a remote hillside 50 miles north of Benedict's now disappeared chapel under a wood of Mediterranean pines and spruce firs, its altar below ground level like those of many primitive shrines dug into a hillside or built on the site of a natural cave. But what little light enters as the door swings open reveals an unexpected and overwhelming chromatic effect, as of bright colour spinning through the barrel-vaulted roof. It is only as eyes adjust to the gloom that the fresco cycle painted over the ceiling and walls comes into focus.

On the lateral walls, above scenes of Christ breaking the bread and – not irrelevantly in the Benedictine context – St Martin cutting his cloak with a dagger to give half to a beggar, and beneath a group of the Old Testament prophets Moses, Job, Jonah and Isaiah, are frescoed representations of the 12 months of the year – just above head-height where they can easily be read. The six on the left are in near-perfect condition, albeit restored; those from July to December on the right are badly eroded by time and humidity, and scarcely legible. Each of the months from January to June has two panels: the first has a symbolic representation of the season; the second shows the days of the month, with the seven days of the week represented by the letters *a* to *g*, following the Roman custom of using letters of the alphabet but omitting the '*H*' of Roman calendars. Thus January has four groups of *a* to *g*, plus a final short series of *a, b, c*. Important liturgical events and saints' days are clearly indicated: for

The exterior of the church of San Pellegrino at Bominaco

instance, in January, epiphany, various saints' days, and the conversion of St Paul. Above these calendar panels, in simple but beautiful small designs are representations of the signs of the zodiac – with each of the names written as well to avoid possible ambiguity.

The decorated panels present an eloquent testimony of the Benedictine year, which, as we shall see, was a fundamental reference point for both religious and lay calendars throughout the early medieval period. Six human figures performing tasks appropriate to the season illustrate the scansion of the monastic year. The first, representing January, is in fact a seated monk, his dark brown cowl dropping on to his shoulders. He is often said to be drinking from a flask, but no drinking vessel is visible and it is in fact a traditional winter image of a man warming his hands over a

[51]

The first six months of the Bominaco calendar

fire. He sits on a Byzantine throne-like chair, with his elongated hands palms upward to the flames of an invisible fire. The cycle modulates into the next month with the figure of a man standing with a simple axe in his hands, about to cut a strange snake-like tree with three thin branches. He is probably pollarding, a typical February task in this area, making supports for vines or other crops; he could even be trimming the vines themselves – though that is usually a later job. He is dressed in a high-collared pinkish cloth tunic, gathered at the waist, with green hose. His headgear (a strange curving hat) and simple costume suggest he is a layman.

[52]

The figure representing March is the most enigmatic of all. One school of thought holds that it is a man sleeping, although he in fact appears quite awake; another theory is that he is a personification of the wind. He is wearing a simple white full-length gown; but it has richly decorated cuffs and is thus not working dress. He seems to be suspended in a strange lack of perspective on a richly embroidered cloth like the borders of the cloaks worn by Byzantine saints. The strangest thing is the tight hood, rather like a modern bathing cap, into which his hair has been gathered. He is barefoot, and has crossed his left leg over the right, firmly holding the upper leg at the knee, moreover, he is clearly outdoors, with grass

[53]

carefully painted beneath his feet. He is in fact extracting a thorn from his foot, a common feature of Roman sculpture and visible in the calendar on the mosaic floor of the cathedral at Otranto, in Apulia. The symbolic significance of this ancient image in the medieval world is not clear. The year continues with the simplest of all the figures: a young man in a pink tunic with embroidered cuffs standing, apparently contemplating a white flower in each of his hands. In fact these flowers represent the renewal of nature, the young nobleman (with the same hat as the February figure) being a symbol of the vitality of youth, spring and nobility in contrast to the peasant figure representing June and agricultural work. In this case, the flowers appear to be lilies, the lily being the symbol of purity, and also the flower of the Virgin Mary – possibly to provide a Christian connotation to an overtly pagan allegory of spring. The young man seems to be looking into the next panel, where the figure representing May could be read as an older version of the same youth.

It is in fact the most interesting allegory: a well-dressed man in fine brown cloak and tunic sits on horseback, with a single flower – again, apparently a white lily – in his hand, looking out from the picture with enviable certainty. The horse, a horizontal animal squeezed into a vertical space, overflows this panel and encroaches on to the panels to left and right. The horse's tail is well combed, and he is wearing the finery of a noble's palfrey: a broad piece of embroidered cloth suspended across his belly from the saddle, fine reins, and a cord stretched back from the saddle round the rump, under the tail, decorated with tiny pompons. The rider sits on an embroidered cloth over the saddle, which is shaped like a seat with back support visible behind him – either wooden or of stiff leather. He is elegant, with neat shoes and a brooch clasping his cloak at his throat, a head-band, and fine whip in his left hand. He is in fact a knight off to war, for in 755 King Pippin the Short of France postponed the annual departure for war from March (the *campus martius*) to May (the *campus maius*) so that there would be more time to gather forage. Not only, as we shall see, was the Carolingian influence on the calendar fundamental, but Pippin's own brother Carloman retired to the abbey at Montecassino.

The horse seems to be looking forward, as if eager to reach June. This final legible month of the calendar is represented by a hatless rustic in red knee-height boots and yellowish tunic with a wicker basket, poised before a tree with one leg lifted as if to support the basket on his knee while gathering its curious lily-shaped fruit; in other medieval calendars in Italy this fruit is usually the cherry. The cuffs of this working tunic are not embroidered, although there is some decoration around the neck. Yet even this simple panel is exquisite in execution, for the grass between the gatherer's feet is carefully bent to fill the uneven space created by the lifted knee, and his left hand is beautifully entwined in the branches of the tree.

The extreme simplicity and solidity of these figures, and the smaller ones representing the zodiac – the bull at rest, the entwined twins – is stunning. The focus is on agricultural work, and the zodiac itself is linked to the work cycle by the Chaldean-Babylonian language which provided its names. For instance Aries meant 'hard worker', while Cancer derived from a term meaning wood-worker or carpenter; furthermore, the symbolic animals chosen to display agricultural origins were similar to those of the medieval representations. In these frescoes it is especially interesting to note how the months of the zodiac are slightly shifted so as to correspond with the solar months. Similarly the rustic origin and purpose of these frescoes may also be seen in the solid, tranquil aspect of the human figures: each one has the same serene expression, looking to the right – towards the altar – except the knight, who gazes confidently out from the wall; each has long hair and elegantly arched stylized eyebrows which descend in long Byzantine noses. The colours enhance this effect. They are faded now, predominantly pinks and light blues, with a background of greenish blue for the sky and a faded brown for the earth. Once they must have been richer, primary colours.

Nothing is known of the painters, although three separate hands have been identified in the oratory. The 'master' of the calendar is quite distinct, perhaps drawing his inspiration from illuminated manuscripts in the library at Montecassino and enlarging his model on the walls of the chapel; in fact the northern, possibly French, influence of miniatures is tempered by evident Byzantine touches – especially in the details of cuffs, brooch, and the trimmings of the horse – which suggest the Benedictine training of the painter. Above all, both northern and Byzantine influences are conditioned by the very real solidity of the figures, whose personality seems to confer solidity although they still float within their panels in pre-Giotto fashion. Bominaco was, and still is, remote, preserving the idea of the hermit life of St Pelegrinus in its rustic architecture. Originally known as Momenaco, the monastery of which San Pellegrino was part passed under the protection of the diocese of Valva in 1093, and was destroyed by the *condottiere* Braccio da Montone in 1423 during the war between Angevins and Aragonese for the Kingdom of Naples. Today, San Pellegrino and the basilica of Santa Maria Assunta 100 paces further up the same hill are all that remain.

The calendar of this fresco cycle is known as the Valva Calendar, from the name of the medieval diocese in which Bominaco stood. In their extreme beauty and simplicity the images represented in it provide an entry point to the mind of medieval man in Central and Southern Italy. For the measure of time was to a large extent determined by St Benedict and the Order he founded.

Time, both microscopic and macroscopic, was based upon the Christian liturgy. There was however no sudden adoption of such a calendar, and no universally accepted calendar until well after the medieval period. The Christian calendar developed slowly and irregularly from about the 4th century, fusing the months and leap year of the solar Julian calendar with non-Roman elements such as Easter and the seven-day week of the Hebrew calendar. Thus the Christian month was distinct both from the Greek month with its three equal decades and the Roman month with its irregular divisions based on the calends, ides and nones. Saturday, the *sabbata*, and Sunday, the *dies dominicus*, were added to the Roman days of the week, and a new and distinctive rhythm imposed on the month. In the 6th century a Paschal calendar with a complex 19-year cycle was introduced at Rome, with the twin novelty of fixing the beginning of the year on 25 December and dating the Christian era from the birth of Christ. These changes were sustained by the authority of the Venerable Bede – also a Benedictine – in the 8th century; thereafter they were gradually accepted.

The real break between ancient and medieval representations of the months came in the 9th century, and was again closely associated with the Benedictines. For it was probably in their abbey at Fleury-sur-Loire (now known as St Benoît sur Loire) that the poem known as *Officia XII mensium* was written around 850. This poem, beginning with the enigmatic line 'Artatur niveus bruma Januarius arva' (meaning 'snowy January is shortened [for agricultural work] by winter cold'), goes on in eleven further lines to specify the duties and jobs relative to each month; a later poem known as *Martius hic falcem*, from the beginning of its third line referring to March, repeats the same scheme with a strong correspondence with the tasks assigned to the months. Allowing for the local variations in a non-hierarchical structure such as that of the Benedictines (with considerable local autonomy, evidenced by the four scenes devoted to vineyard labours in the wine-making abbey at Fleury), there is a strong similarity to the images of the Bominaco calendar: of the first six months January (cold), March (trimming the vines), and May (war), correspond perfectly to those of the *Officia XII mensium*. At the same time monthly duties were associated with the signs of the zodiac, and the month became the basic unit of the calendar. The liturgical calendar was based upon Easter, which fell – and falls – on the first Sunday after the Paschal full moon, that is to say the full moon occurring on or after 21 March. Once this date was established, the calendar of fasts and penitences could be worked out, especially that of Lent and the equally important ten-day fast from

Ascension to Pentecost, which began on the 40th day after Easter. The regular rest day established on Sunday by the new calendar, together with frequent holidays for religious feasts, provided an important impetus to the medieval economy by increasing the efficiency of manpower and the organization of work.

With the year divided according to Christian liturgy in the same century as St Benedict's life, and the concept of a working week introduced later, it remained to define the basic unit of the calendar: the day. This task had fallen to St Benedict himself, and his solution was gradually adopted throughout Christendom.

The scansion of the monastic day was in fact regulated by the *Rule* of St Benedict. The new way of life instituted at Montecassino represented a definitive renunciation of Imperial Rome, emphasizing the values of agricultural labour, the holding of property in common, and the importance of a self-enclosed spiritual world detached from the disintegrating empire and social life around it. The *Rule* was a template for everyday life, an alternative to the past, governing both body and soul throughout earthly life. Above all, it organized the monastic day, an innovation as seminal to the shift from Roman to Medieval Italy as the legal and social revolution brought about by the Ostrogoth and Lombard kingdoms. It was a remarkable imposition on the whole of Christendom of a purely abstract division of time based on the scriptures, for the canonical day corresponds neither to the Roman day, nor to the working day of early medieval man; nor does its division into seven offices bear any relation to previous customs. St Benedict himself explains that this number derives from the statement made by David in Psalm 119 that 'seven times a day I praise thee'. Another phrase in the same psalm, when the Prophet asserts that 'at midnight I rise to praise thee', illustrates the abstract nature of the canonical division of the day. For it was the interpretation of this assertion which conferred spiritual importance on the wholly unpractical office of Vigils, originally to be celebrated between midnight and one o'clock.

Again quoting Psalm 119, St Benedict goes on in Chapter 16 of his *Rule* to explain the nature and time of the other divine offices, adding that 'we shall praise our Creator at these times "because of thy righteous ordinances"'. The canonical hours are well known: the day continued with Lauds or Matins, celebrated at the first glimpse of morning light. Then, confusingly, came Prime. This was because the pagan-born Benedict followed Roman usage in dividing the 24-hour day equally into two parts: thus Prime corresponds to the Roman *prima hora*, even though it was not the first hour for his own community of monks. This was followed by Tierce, at mid-morning, Sext, at midday, Nones, in mid-afternoon, and Vespers at sunset. The next two chapters of the *Rule*

Figures representing the labours of each month from a ninth-century miniature in Vienna

establish how many psalms should be used during these offices, and in which order. The canonical day concluded with the celebration of Compline before the monks were allowed to go to rest for the night.

Initially this conception of spiritual time, and the scansion of the monastic day, only involved the world around the monastery to the extent to which people could hear the bell summoning monks to divine office. Otherwise, the day was simply divided into hours of darkness and hours of light; people outside had little need of such precision. A later view is offered by the 13th century English grammarian and poet John Garland (c.1195–c.1272), who included in his *Dictionary* a curious etymology of the word campana (bell). This was based on the superficial likeness between two medieval Latin words: *campana* itself, which derives from the expression 'vasa campana' meaning 'bronze vases of Campania'; and *campania*, which derives from Latin 'campus' or field, and became modern Italian 'campagna' meaning 'countryside'. It was on the basis of this shaky similarity that Garland wrote that 'bells are so called because of the peasants who live in the country and wouldn't be able to calculate the time if it weren't for the bells'. His statement provides an intriguing link between monastic and agricultural time, even though the etymology is false. For in fact the colonizing function of monasteries, and their central role in political and social life, placed them at the centre of medieval life. This was especially true in Italy, where as we shall see absentee kings and weak rulers by default often left effective autonomy over vast tracts of land to monasteries like Montecassino. This was very different from the situation in France, where the Capetian kings exercised control over bishops and abbots to such an extent that a leading historian speaks of an 'ecclesiastical feudal class' dependent on the king, and where from 897 to 1180 there were as many as 79 royal monasteries.

Garland's statement also shows how the solid figures, simple dress and quiet certainty of the Bominaco figures represent a concept of time and social order which was brought to the Italian peninsula by St Benedict – with ramifications throughout the western world – and survived to the apogee of the medieval church, which may be said to have come with the Jubilee of Pope Boniface VIII in 1300. They show the three orders of medieval society – those who pray (*oratores*), those who fight (*bellatores*), and those who work (*laboratores*) – but place the emphasis on manual labour. Such an emphasis is strictly Benedictine, since St Benedict himself stressed the importance of manual labour as penitence – because it was the consequence of the expulsion of man from Eden, and thus of original sin. In later centuries of the medieval period, work came to represent access to eternal life, while sloth and ease opened the doors of the soul to the devil. Hence the importance of work and the canonical division of the day.

The narthex or portico of the church of Sant'Angelo in Formis (Capua)

Sant'Angelo in Formis: detail of angels, showing the fluid wave-like movement through the composition

Sant'Angelo in Formis: the
Christ Pantocrator

Sant'Angelo in Formis: Abbot
Desiderius offering his church

This static, secular world view may be complemented by a reading of the vivid depiction and interpretation of the scriptures in the basilica of Sant'Angelo in Formis, rebuilt and expanded by Abbot Desiderius of Montecassino in 1073 a few miles east of Capua, together with the abbey which was suppressed in 1417. Now sadly dilapidated, with the ruined walls and gate of the abbey built on to by a hodgepodge of unattractive houses, Sant'Angelo is a wooden-roofed basilica with a narthex and a nave, and two aisles each terminated by an apse; the frescoes have been severely damaged by centuries of humidity and the church has in fact been in almost continuous restoration for the last decade. Many of the frescoes are only visible through scaffolding. Yet, with a little imagination, it is still a remarkable building and of immense interest since the frescoes were painted either by the same Byzantine masters summoned from Constantinople by Desiderius to decorate his new basilica or by their locally trained pupils. The Byzantine qualities of magnificence, splendour and superb craftsmanship mark this church as they must have marked its model at Montecassino, and the iconography of the fresco cycle is typically Byzantine. Precise Byzantine influence is apparent both in the fluid movement of drapery, hands and facial features – for instance in the extraordinary rhythm of the angels to the left of Christ in the *Last Judgement*, echoing both the form of his almond-shaped panel and of the angels' wings – and in the general iconographical scheme. The Abbot himself appears with a model of the basilica beneath the figure of *Christ in Majesty* on a jewelled throne in the central apse, with a square halo to indicate that he was still alive when the frescoes were made, together with the three Archangels Gabriel, Michael and Raphael, and of course St Benedict.

Christ and his evangelists look out on to a complex cycle of biblical stories: those from the Old Testament on the walls of the side aisles, and those of the New Testament in the main nave. The New Testament is accorded more importance, with 60 panels on three levels on the upper walls of the nave above the supporting columns. From the viewpoint of the *Christ in Majesty*, the series begins with the *Annunciation* high up on the left, on the top level. It runs along the top level to the west wall, back along the other side of the nave, and then drops to the next level; thus in three circuits of the nave it reaches its climax in a depiction of the *Ascension*. It is a superb, didactic – but never tedious – interpretation of the principal scenes of the life of Christ. The final scene, on the inside of the west wall and thus opposite the apse and main altar, consists of the *Last Judgement* with harrowing scenes of the torments of Hell. These are painted in a conveniently low position – at little over head height on the right of the door – to act as a forceful reminder to those leaving the basilica after mass.

[62]

On the left, in stark and beautiful contrast, is a depiction of the serenity of the thronging crowd in Heaven; above them a group of monks with St. Benedict in their midst reflects the certainty of Benedictine faith. This fresco cycle was based on a similar one at Montecassino whose scenes, as we shall see, are recounted in a poem written at the time of the dedication of Abbot Desiderius' basilica. Together they fixed the Benedictine interpretation of the scriptures in visual form, and this cycle is the finest surviving example of art under the Montecassino influence during the late 11th century. As at San Pellegrino many of the frescoes are destroyed beyond the possibility of restoration. But the best preserved – and restored – in the apse give some idea of the brilliant qualities of colour and dramatic use of light and shade; the intense reds, oranges, and greens on a blue background in the main apse were perhaps heightened in colour to suit the taste for brilliant chromatic effects which was formed by mosaics. The Sant'Angelo cycle provides the most complete impression existing of a frescoed Romanesque basilica, a striking representation of the spiritual ideas its iconography was designed to sustain.

For the Bominaco calendar and Sant'Angelo frescoes are more than mere pictures. Apart from their obvious decorative qualities they function as what Sicardo, a 12th century bishop of Cremona, called *litterae laicorum*: in his words, 'they serve to recall things of the past (stories and visions), and to provide indications on things present (virtues and vices) and future (punishments and rewards)'. Thus they represented both a moral and political vision and a socio-economic reality which provided a cohering factor in an age which saw first the disintegration of the late Roman Empire and then the disgregation of the Carolingian Empire which had sought to replace it. Monasteries were centres of territorial power as much as the late Roman cities through land ownership, financial capabilities, legal jurisdiction, and obviously spiritual life; at their peak monastic centres such as S. Vincenzo al Volturno, Montecassino and Farfa in the south, Bobbio and Nonantola in the north – and Montecassino's sister abbey at Cluny – assumed the role of cities. In the case of Bominaco, the zone of influence was more limited, but the heavy characters of its fresco cycle none the less mirror the central role and solidity of the Benedictine world view which conditioned much of southern Europe through the centuries from the 7th to the 11th century. The focal point of this world view was the parent abbey of the Benedictines at Montecassino.

Legend relates that Benedict was led to the site of Montecassino by three tame ravens in the year 529. His journey had begun about a hundred miles further north at Norcia, in Umbria, where he was born into a wealthy patrician family about 480. There it seems that he had been disgusted by the licentiousness of pagan youth and left Norcia to seek the ascetic life in a cave at Subiaco, east of Rome, a spectacular site which can still be visited in the so-called *sacro speco* today. According to Gregory the Great, the second chapter of whose *Dialogi* was a 'paen to St Benedict', this period of hermitage began when Benedict was about 15 years old and lasted for three years. That it was not a period without temptation is shown by the symbol of the blackbird often used to indicate the saint in paintings, for the blackbird's luxuriant song represents the comforts and sensual delights of his previous life. St Gregory in fact relates that the devil once sought to tempt the young hermit by appearing in the form of a blackbird; but to no avail. Word of Benedict's holiness soon spread and attracted followers; he was invited by the monks of the nearby monastery of Vicovaro to become their abbot. But his severity and humility were clearly at odds with the prevailing spirit at Vicovaro, for shortly afterwards some of them planned to murder Benedict by poisoning him. The attempt naturally failed: as he blessed the glass containing the poison it disintegrated, the source of St Benedict's second pictorial symbol of a broken glass – or a glass containing a serpent. He forgave the conspirators, but returned to Subiaco and founded 12 monasteries for his numerous followers. Soon, however, as the legend has it, increasing popularity again created problems, and it was as a result of the envy of a local priest that he left the area and moved southwards in search of a new refuge. The ravens led him to Montecassino, where he lived for 14 years until his death on 21 March 543.

The abbey sits on a rocky spur dominating the valley of the River Liri to the north and that of the Garigliano to the west. The site has always been of strategic importance, dominating what was probably the earliest of all Roman roads, the Via Latina, which passed through the ancient town of Casinum on the flat plain below on its way from Rome to Capua. The rock itself has such a dramatic form that from the valley it seems much higher than its 519 metres. Although the monastery may be said to have been 'founded' in 529, in that year it seems that little more than the tiny oratory of St Martin was actually built – probably on the site of a Roman temple dedicated to Apollo – together with some rudimentary structures for habitation. Moreover, whatever did exist lasted no more than 50 years, since the few monks who lived there were forced to abandon Montecassino after its destruction by the Lombards in 581; for over a century the monks of Montecassino were housed in the Lateran palace in Rome. In fact one of the many curious things about Montecassino is how two of the ruling powers who at one time destroyed the monastery, the Lombards and the Normans, later became closely associated with its re-building and political prestige (this pattern was repeated in a sense when the Allies responsible for the greatest devastation of all in 1944 later attempted to

The Abbey of Montecassino as it was before the 1944 bombardment

make amends by rebuilding the entire structure 'as it was').

The long climb to ecclesiastical dominion began with the so-called second foundation by Petronax of Brescia, who was abbot from 729 to 741. But the church and abbey as rebuilt by him were devastated and burned by Saracen raiders a century and a half later, when Abbot Bertharius was murdered and his monks forced to leave their monastery – this time literally fleeing for their lives. It was with the Emperor Charlemagne (c.742–814), who personally visited the abbey on his second journey to Italy in 787, that Benedictinism – while not yet an order – became a dominant force in Christendom. Already the prestige of both St Benedict himself and Montecassino were notable as the result of Gregory the Great's account of his life. The approval of such an important man, who as Gregory I was pope from 590 to 604 and was considered as second only to St Peter himself, greatly enhanced the role of Montecassino. In the early centuries, and after the early destruction, it was closely linked with the Lombard Principality of Benevento. When the northern Lombard king Ratchis – himself a usurper – needed a place of refuge after being replaced in a *coup d'état* by his brother in 749, it was to Montecassino that he fled. The abbey became a favourite refuge of Lombard kings and dukes at times of internecine strife.

The end of Lombard rule in 774 and absorption of the kingdom of Italy

[65]

into the Carolingian Empire did not diminish the importance of Montecassino. Partly, perhaps, because there were already family links between the abbey and the Carolingians; as we have seen, Pippin the Short's brother Carloman, uncle to Charlemagne, had become a monk there after resigning his position as mayor of Neustria. Certainly the hospitality given to Carloman, and consequent affection for the abbey and its founder in the mind of Charlemagne, were well rewarded. For when in 788 the Frankish king declared the *Regula Benedicti* to be the primary rule in all his domains, Montecassino became second only to Rome as a focus of Christianity. Thirty years later his son Louis the Pious made obedience to the *Rule* obligatory in the Frankish Kingdom.

Ironically, it was with the decline of the same Carolingian dynasty which supported Benedictinism that the abbey grew in importance. For the end of the first great period of influence of Montecassino, from the refoundation by Petronax of Brescia in 729 to the destruction by Saracen invaders in 883, coincided with the break-up of the Holy Roman Empire under Charlemagne's successors. Six years before the Saracen destruction, as we shall see, the Byzantine general Gregorius had captured Bari and the Eastern Emperors began to extend the Byzantine province of *Langobardia* further north; from this moment Byzantine influence supplanted that of the Carolingians. The abbey received privileges and tax exemptions from the Eastern Emperors, beginning with Leo VI (870–86), just as it had from Rome and would do from the later Norman kings. Links between West and East included the later Abbot John of Montecassino, who before his elevation to that role spent some time on both Mount Sinai and Mount Athos.

It was with the so-called 'third foundation' by Abbot Aligern, who had been a monk at S. Paolo fuori le Mura in Rome, that Montecassino began its rise to real magnificence and fame. Aligern, who was abbot from 948 to 986, repaired the abbey buildings with the financial support of the Byzantine *Catapan* or governor, developed a policy of attracting peasant-farmers into the lands of St Benedict – the *terra sancti Benedicti* – and then built a series of towers and castles to protect land, peasants and monastery. In 949, when he began, the monastery was virtually a ruin with few lands; little more than a century later new bronze doors were cast on which the possessions were listed as 47 *castella* (including castles, towers and other fortifications) and 560 churches.

Centuries earlier the Roman geographer Strabo had called the site of Casinum 'the last of the Latins', beyond which was Campania and the south. Now the strategic importance of Montecassino, and its site on the frontier between the Papal State and the southern kingdoms, meant that its existence was conditioned by the continuous struggle for control of southern Italy. At its most *stable* this vast area was contested by the Lombards, Normans and the Eastern Empire; but it also included the semi-autonomous republics of Naples, Sorrento, Amalfi and Gaeta. The Lombard cities of Capua and Benevento and the republic of Gaeta were Montecassino's nearest neighbours – and rivals. In 774 Montecassino was part of the southern kingdom of the Lombards, while in the 10th century Emperor Otto I (963–73) claimed it for the Saxons; in the 11th century it was claimed by the Normans, and at the same time by the Byzantine emperor Basil II (936–1025). Links with Rome were always close, though often complex and litigious, and Montecassino played a vital but delicate role in the conflict between Rome and Byzantium. It was at the instigation of Pope Benedict VIII (1012–24), who was concerned that Byzantine power in southern Italy extended almost to Rome, that the Saxon Emperor Henry II (who had been crowned by Benedict in 1014), returned to Italy to counter this encroachment. Henry himself, who seems to have felt a genuine veneration for St Benedict, supervised the election of a new abbot in 1022 and made generous gifts to the abbey.

Montecassino became an imperial abbey, and it became imperial practice to make a visit after coronation by the pope in Rome. In 999 the Emperor Otto III had already made a pilgrimage to Montecassino. Now in 1022 Henry II came, to be followed by Conrad II in 1028, Henry III in 1047, and Henry IV in 1082. Yet these visits do not imply constant power and stability, and the huge increase in lands and power during this period were not achieved without difficulty. For once again Montecassino found itself at the heart of a campaign for conquest: in the midst of the unresolved struggle between the Byzantine and German emperors for southern Italy a new power emerged, which managed in a remarkably short time to occupy the vacuum and create a united kingdom of the south.

As we shall see in the chapters on Cefalù and Bari, it was in the second decade of the 11th century that the first Normans appeared in southern Italy. Soon Norman knights were established at Aversa and Capua, and raiding bands were operating throughout the area; in 1031 one of them sacked and destroyed the abbey of Montecassino. Their stranglehold on the area was such that when Richer, a Bavarian monk and protégé of the Emperor Conrad II (1024–37), was made Abbot of Montecassino in 1038 he was unable to enter his own monastery and take possession. By the end of his abbacy in 1055, however, he had not only managed to free the *terra sancti Benedicti* from the Normans but increased the extent of the territory. He had also added new castles and other fortifications.

When Abbot Desiderius, the most celebrated of all abbots of Montecassino, was elected in 1058 he came to an abbey which had been under the control of Lombards, Carolingians, Byzantines and the Holy

Roman Empire, and was then subject to the Normans. But this constant pressure seems to have instilled in successive abbots the diplomatic qualities necessary to maintain a delicate equilibrium between these powers and nearby Rome. By dint of its antiquity and the prestige of its founder, the abbey had taken on a life of its own: frontiers changed, rulers came and went, capitals shifted, but Montecassino was always there. The idea of government as a theological, divinely ordered necessity had faded in the centuries since the fall of the Roman Empire, but nothing had yet been conceived to replace it. Montecassino as an encapsulation of the Benedictine ideal offered a moral and spiritual alternative in lieu of the future society, even though politically it was never able to exert more than a mediating influence. The Roman Church itself was not in a position to offer such an alternative; in the absence of the theocratic certainty which popes such as Innocent III and Boniface VIII brought to the papacy in the 13th century, Rome could not assert itself in the temporal sphere. Thus Benedictinism came to represent a fixed point in this shifting morass. That explains the symbolic importance of the frescoes we have discussed: they illustrate certainty in the midst of uncertainty, and as such reflect the constant role of Montecassino – as if the limestone spur on which the abbey stands lent physical substance to St Benedict's ideal.

This role was elevated to its acme by Abbot Desiderius. He was born of a branch of the Lombard princes of Benevento in 1027, and we may assume that his birth and upbringing contributed to the acumen which enabled him to succeed. The political strength and security of Montecassino during his abbacy were at least partly derived from his alliance with the Norman rulers of Capua and Apulia, Prince Richard of Capua and the notorious Robert Guiscard – who in the same period was not beyond sacking Rome. Desiderius' own father had been killed by the Normans a decade before his election, an event which may have led him to reflect that it was better to be an ally than an enemy of such a ruthless power. Once the alliance was secure, he was able to build up the possessions of his abbey, using all his diplomatic skill in bargaining, negotiating, and exchanging tracts of land with local lords. He managed to establish a delicate equilibrium between Pope Nicholas II in Rome and the Norman rulers in the south; at the same time he achieved the miracle of maintaining good relations with the Emperor Romanus IV at Constantinople – whose possessions on the Italian peninsula had been diminished by the arrival of the Normans. Without this diplomatic legerdemain Desiderius would have been unable to commission works of art from Constantinople with imperial blessing. In doing so, he contributed to the revival in Italy of the ancient art of mosaic and assisted the creation of the distinctive 'Benedictine' style of Romanesque art.

[68]

During his 30-year rule the *terra sancti Benedicti* encompassed about 200,000 acres, with 200 monks inside Montecassino and more than 600 churches directly dependent on the abbey. Outside the *terra* Montecassino possessed lands in Southern Italy, in Apulia, Calabria and Amalfi, but also beyond the traditional sphere of influence in Rome, Tuscany, Sardinia and even Hungary. Subsidiary monasteries were kept under careful control by means of monks known as *monaci prepositi* sent out from the mother house. To facilitate transport from these far-off destinations a castle was built at Torre a Mare on the mouth of the River Garigliano, in the Gulf of Gaeta. Thus merchandise from Rome and elsewhere could travel by sea, enter the Garigliano and sail up river as far as the dependent monastery of Suio – some ten miles inland – whence it travelled the remaining short distance overland to Montecassino. But the greatest achievement of Desiderius was the re-building of Montecassino.

At first Desiderius' building projects seem to have been modest: he completed a *palatium* which had been started by Richer, and added a library to it; then he re-built the abbot's quarters and the monks' dormitories. Next he built a new capitular room and commissioned the bronze doors mentioned above: on a visit to Amalfi the abbot had been impressed by the doors which a wealthy merchant of the trading community at Constantinople, Pantaleone, had bought for the cathedral of his home town. The Montecassino doors, of which only two original panels remain, were financed by Pantaleone's father in Amalfi. Then, in 1068, he had the old basilica completely demolished, and the discovery of the tomb of St Benedict underneath seems to have acted as a spur to even more ambitious projects. In the words of the monk and chronicler Leo of Ostia, Desiderius then bought 'huge quantities of columns, bases, epistyles, and marble of different colours' from Rome. They were transported to Suio by sea and river, then carried overland and up the steep slope to Montecassino. Leo provides a fascinating glimpse of Abbot Desiderius in Rome 'prudently distributing large sums of money' and collecting these fragments: he also tells us how the abbot summoned artists from Constantinople and Alexandria for the mosaics, thus bringing the two classical traditions together. It is intriguing to compare this antiquarian activity with Vasari's famous description of Donatello and Brunelleschi 400 years later as 'treasure-hunters' in Rome.

Gold and silver were purchased to decorate the interior, and construct a golden altar: materials evidently intended to create an impression of immense power and wealth. Archaeological evidence from research after the 1944 bombing of the later church has revealed Desiderius' building to be a basilica of about the same proportions as Sant'Angelo in Formis, and also the cathedral at Salerno which was rebuilt by Robert Guiscard at the same time under the inspiration of Desiderius' friend Bishop Alphanus. An imagined reconstruction shows it as a three-aisled basilica with the central nave larger than the two side aisles, and a simple transept. The quality of the mosaic flooring may be judged from fragments surviving in the museum at Montecassino: some pieces as large as an outstretched palm, others the size of a large thumb-nail, all richly coloured. It is not difficult to recreate in the imagination the floor which Leo of Ostia described when it was newly made: 'The mosaicists were to decorate the apse, the arch, and the vestibule of the main basilica; the others, to lay the pavement of the whole church with various kinds of stones. The degree of perfection which was attained in these arts by the masters who Desiderius had hired can be seen in their works. One would believe that the figures in the mosaics were alive and that in the marble of the pavement flowers of every colour bloomed in wonderful variety.' What has been described as a 'simplified imitation' of the Montecassino pavement may be seen in the church of S. Menna, also built by Robert Guiscard, in the curiously named village of S. Agata de' Goti (where a defeated Goth colony sought refuge from Belisarius during the Gothic Wars) south-west of Benevento. Plain white walls and the present unfurnished state of the recently restored church enhance the simple beauty of the mosaic floor, and of mosaics set both into the iconostasis and into the vertical part of steps leading up to the altar.

Unfortunately we possess little evidence of the details of the frescoes painted at Montecassino under Abbot Desiderius' patronage. But fragments of frescoed plaster in the museum of the abbey suffice to give some idea, and since the same painters probably worked at Sant'Angelo in Formis we can make reasonable conjectures. The colours of the fragments are similar to those of Sant'Angelo: bold blues, ochres, yellows and greens painted in large surface areas, together with fragmented strips of Byzantine border which derive from the garments of saints or onlookers in the major scenes. It is this immediacy and simplicity of the pleasure of colour so characteristic of early medieval aesthetic taste, preserved with more accuracy in the glazed mosaic tesserae than in the frescoes, which must have constituted the dominant chromatic note of the basilica at Montecassino as much as in S. Menna. No graded areas of colour merging into new colour, or subtle plays of colour and shadow influenced by available light – or even painted light, in the 17th century – but flat, ungraded and in this case large areas of bright primary colour juxtaposed to *create* the effects of light. This was done with precise purpose, for there was a direct correlation between light and God: in the mosaics of the church of SS. Cosma e Damiano inside the Forum in Rome there is an inscription dating from the 6th century which explains this eloquently:

[70]

The floor mosaic in St Menna (Sant'Agata de' Goti, near Benevento)

'The house of God shrines with the brilliancy of the purest metals and the light of the faith glows there the more preciously'; in a similar inscription in the beautiful Roman church of St Agnes fuori le Mura – built by a native of Campania, Pope Honorius I (625–38) – the colours are compared to the rainbow and the peacock. As in the case of the Bominaco calendar, perhaps the best point of reference is provided by the vivid illuminations of medieval manuscripts, with the drama of the stories brought out by brilliant colours – blues and reds again – rather than by formal subtlety. To a modern eye such a taste for the translucent and colouristic can easily descend to the level of kitsch – as in the mosaics of the reconstructed crypt under the modern basilica at Montecassino. But to the medieval eye, with a taste for the drama and immediacy of such violent chromatic impact, Desiderius' basilica seemed fit to add to the list of wonders of the world.

Even finer than the frescoes, we may judge from the surviving pieces, were the portals which surrounded the new bronze doors: elegant marble pilasters inlaid with large mosaic tesserae, creating a notable contrast in textures and colour even in the fragmentary state in which they remain in the abbey museum. Visually, on entering the basilica, these led the eye to the original Roman columns bought in Rome which formed the double row of columns supporting the arches of the main nave, and then on to the high altar and apse. After which the interior must have appeared a riot of light and colour: the elaborate furnishings brought from Constantinople included icons, an antependiam and an immense iconostasis with 50 candles and 36 lamps which lighted the basilica. The total effect must have been of overwhelming richness, and in fact the consecration of the basilica was one of the major events of the century. Pope Alexander II travelled from Rome for the ceremony, and Leo of Ostia compiled a list of other important participants: they included three cardinal bishops, ten archbishops, 42 bishops – from Taranto in the south to Perugia in the north – innumerable priests and deacons, and such secular rulers as Prince Richard of Capua, Count Rainulf of Caiazzo, Prince Gisulf II of Salerno, Prince Landulf of Benevento, Duke Sergius V of Naples, Duke Sergius of Sorrento, together with many sons and brothers and minor noblemen. Alphanus, poet and later bishop of Salerno, wrote two celebratory poems, one for the basilica and one for its builder.

But Desiderius' building activity did not cease with this celebration. As if inspired by the success of the consecration he went on to reconstruct the entire abbey in the remarkably short period between 1071 and 1074. This included rebuilding and expanding the cloister, refectory, dormitories, sacristy and infirmary, and even such minor buildings as the kitchens and cellars. It also entailed the construction of a hostel for pilgrims who visited the abbey, and new walls enclosing the entire site. For three years the

[72]

whole hill-top must have resembled nothing more than a huge building site. Furthermore, in this period of fervent activity new treasures and relics were donated to match the elegance of the new buildings, in particular by Robert Guiscard – now Duke of Apulia. One small example will illustrate this better than a list of jewels and precious stones: a new free-standing oven was of such elegance that it was mistaken by visitors for a chapel.

One of the most eminent visitors was Abbot Hugh of Cluny, who travelled to Montecassino in 1083. The abbot had a profound understanding of architecture, and is thought as a result of this visit to have introduced the new features of eastern origin into the great church that he began building at Cluny five years later. These features included the oriental pointed arch, the oriental pinched vault and the groin vault, which a leading historian of Romanesque architecture claims were 'rationalized' at Cluny and led to a distinct step forward in Romanesque engineering. It is also possible to speculate, as Professor Conant did, that this process of rationalization at Cluny of elements Abbot Hugh had appreciated at Montecassino 'started the process which eventually created the new Gothic type of engineering.' If it were possible to substantiate such a hypothesis beyond doubt, Desiderius' basilica – and his use of eastern architects and painters – would come to have an even greater role in the history of western art. This role is already of the first importance, for while Montecassino itself – as we shall see – was profoundly conservative in all aspects, the dynamic features of the new architecture were taken up and propagated by Cluny with far-reaching effects on European architecture.

Today, only fragments of Desiderius' masterpiece survive. Yet it is necessary to emphasize that the bombardment of 1944 was not entirely responsible. Desiderius' own abbey was destroyed by an earthquake in 1349. It was re-built soon afterwards, expanded in the early 16th century, and then re-built again in the 17th century. It was also sacked by Napoleon's army – which removed many important works of art from Italy. The basilica which Allied bombs destroyed in the still controversial raid was the re-built version of 1649 with a portal that was added half a century later; the crypt was that of 1545 but with decorations from the beginning of the present century, the wooden choir from 1696–1708, the organ from 1656 and the library from the late 17th century. The oldest surviving part was the Great Refectory, which had been re-built around 1568–70. The paintings hanging in the abbey varied in date from 1600 to 1923. Nothing medieval remained.

But the name 'Montecassino' represents much more than the fabric of the abbey, something that bombs could not destroy. Its symbolic role in the religious and social life of central and southern Italy has been compared to that in France of the house of the Benedictines at Cluny. In addition, the abbey was in the 11th century the most prominent centre of intellectual study in western Christendom. This authority reached into every part of medieval life.

The essence of Benedictinism – and of the abbey's authority – was contained in the *Rule* of St Benedict, which became the basis of western monastic life and moral conduct. It was written, St Benedict states in the final chapter, to provide a model for novices to the ascetic life. The aspects of this life stressed in the *Rule* are prayer, silence, manual labour, obedience and humility. Practical aspects, specific advice, daily life and the system of penitence are founded on these five features. In fact of its 73 chapters nearly two-thirds, the central part, are devoted to the internal organization of the monastery – concerning discipline, penitences, recruitment, and practical rules on everything from dress and organiza-tion of the dormitories to food and drink. Thus two hot meals a day were considered just, with a third if fruit and legumes could easily be found, the quantity of bread was specified, but if the monks had performed harder work than usual the abbot could increase the amount – as long as greed was not involved; similarly, a quarter of a litre of wine – mixed with water – was recommended as sufficient for each day, but if 'local conditions or special work or summer heat' necessitated extra quantities the abbot was free to provide it.

Such apparent licence was coherent with Benedict's monastic ideals, for the object of the *Rule* was to promote prayer; discipline and obedience were the means to this end rather than the end itself. St Benedict explained the aim of the monastic life as the salvation from eternal suffering through insistent prayer to Christ, and thus as a return to God – from whom man had been distanced by the 'indolence of disobedience'. Prayer sustained each action or event of the Benedictine day: meals, visits by guests, work, extra prayers during Lent, and the departure or return of a brother monk. Silence was to be maintained so that others, should they wish, could enter the chapel between formal offices to pray alone – preferably with the 'tears and passion' the author mentions. Such prayer was a private matter, best carried out in solitude and with due humility, since St Benedict stressed that the monk at prayer would be heard for the purity of his heart rather than for the number of words he uses. Prayer must therefore be brief and pure, unless it were to be prolonged by the ardour and inspiration of divine grace. The other characteristics of monastic life were subservient to prayer.

The value of silence, for example, lay in the fact that it was conducive to prayer. Excessive speech increased the possibility of error and sin: it was the master who should speak, and the disciple who should listen. On these grounds idle words and trivialities were to be condemned. Once again, in the sixth chapter, recourse is made to the authority of David, specifically to the words of Psalm 39: 'I will guard my ways, that I may not sin with my tongue'. Silence was specifically to be observed at meal times, during the afternoon rest after Sext, and on leaving divine office; but it was recommended at all times, and especially at night. When the use of the human voice was contemplated, St Benedict specifies time and place: for instance on a day when two meals have been eaten the monks were to sit together after supper and listen to a reading from the 'Collations' or the 'Lives of the Fathers', whereas during a period of fasting this should be done after Vespers. Then, after Compline – or after Vespers in a period of fasting – total silence must be observed. Transgression was punished severely.

In the present context one of the most fascinating chapters is that devoted to manual labour, since it informs the conception of the Benedictine year and hence indicates the importance of work to the medieval mind. Manual work was lauded by the author because 'indolence is the enemy of the soul'. The monastic working year was divided into three parts, based as other calendars we have seen on the movable feast of Easter. In the first period, which ran from Easter to the beginning of October, the hours between Prime and the fourth hour of the day (around 10 a.m.) and those from Nones to Vespers – with Nones being celebrated a little earlier – were to be devoted to manual work. St Benedict provides an insight into his conception of monasticism when he states almost as an aside that in monasteries where the monks are required to work on the harvest they should be pleased to do so since then they will be 'true monks when they live with the work of their hands' *like the Apostles*. Then in the second period, from the beginning of October to Lent when the requirements of agricultural life are minimal, the hours from Terce to Nones were to be devoted to work. The third period coincided with Lent: in this period of fasting the hours until the end of the third hour were to be dedicated to reading, after which the monks engaged in manual work until the tenth hour. The remainder of the day was dedicated to reading, and at the beginning of Lent each brother was provided with a book to read. Furthermore, with the thoroughness which helped to make his manual the general model, St Benedict observes that monks working so far from their abbey that they cannot easily return for the divine offices may kneel wherever they happen to be and perform them there. Similarly, he displays an understanding of human weakness: at the end of the brief chapter on manual labour he suggests that the abbot charge one or two senior monks to go through the monastery and check that the brothers are diligently engaged in reading. In fact the later Benedictine motto, *Ora et labora*, encapsulated this aspect of the spirit of the *Rule* with remarkable succinctness.

Obedience to the *Rule* was at the core of Benedictinism. Of the 74 commandments listed in the fourth chapter, that concerning obedience to the abbot is by far the longest. The next chapter is totally devoted to obedience, opening with the unequivocal assertion that 'the principal sign of humility is unhesitating obedience'. Yet it is important to understand that obedience was perceived as a 'joyous virtue', since it was a vital part of the life of faith and humility which a monk chose to live. Moreover, since the abbot was explicitly considered as being in the stead of Christ, such obedience was to Christ himself: an order from the abbot had to be obeyed instantly 'as if it were a divine command'.

Obedience was itself subservient to humility, to be praised as a virtue inasmuch as it was a sign of humility. For humility represented the heart of the Benedictine ideal and is the subject of the longest chapter in the *Rule*, the seventh, which is based on the scriptural assertion of Luke: 'For every one who exalts himself will be humbled, and he who humbles himself will be exalted'. The process of exaltation is represented picturesquely through the metaphor of Jacob's ladder. Humility – intended as self-abnegation – consists of 12 degrees each corresponding to a step on the ladder. These include the following degrees of abnegation: thinking of nothing but God and allowing His will to replace that of the monk; total submission to the abbot as representative of Christ; suffering in silence and accepting the minimum of material comforts; being patient and enjoying all humiliations; doing only as the *Rule* says; dressing simply and finding pleasure in the performance of simple tasks; practising silence and avoiding the use of a loud voice; using modest words and being humble in all exterior actions. Successful progress through these 12 degrees leads to what St John, in his First Letter, refers to as that 'perfect love [that] casts out fear', which marks the acme of Benedictinism.

The *Rule* is severe, but at the same time humane. St Benedict recognized human weakness and understood the difficulties involved in following such an ascetic life. One of the most telling insights into his personality and the spirit of his *Rule* is provided in the 64th chapter, where he refers to discretion as the 'mother of virtues'. Another example is the brief but pragmatic and delightfully entitled 68th chapter: 'If a brother is ordered to do something impossible'. At least in part as the result of this blend of spiritual excellence and flexibility, his *Rule* became the norm for the monastic life for at least 600 years, and new orders such as the Cistercians – as we shall see in the chapter on S. Maria del Monte – later sought to renew its force. It is still influential: as recently as 1969 the Cistercians of the

Strict Observance, known as Trappists, declared that 'Following the first Fathers of our Order, we find in the Holy Rule of St Benedict the practical interpretation of the Gospel for us' and observed that the *Rule* is pervaded by 'a sense of the Divine Transcendence and of the Lordship of Christ'. Thus it remains the paradigm for the purest form of the monastic life even today.

In medieval Italy this paradigm went far beyond a few small monastic communities (there are at present fewer than 4,000 Trappists in the world), and it was as a result of the specific provisions and universal acceptance of the *Rule* that Montecassino exercised a strong spiritual and moral influence on the monasteries and churches of southern Italy.

This influence acted as a regenerating force in the 11th century revival of the cult of local patron saints, whose importance lay in their providing a local, readily identifiable exemplar of faith and moral rectitude. The monks in the scriptorium at Montecassino elaborated biographies of these local saints for churches, monasteries and cathedrals throughout central and southern Italy: to give just a few major examples, at Chieti, Gaeta, Troia (near Foggia), Salerno and Benevento. The worship of these saints generated the local festivals and pious legends which are still today a characteristic feature of Italian social life – the very essence of 'campanilismo'. Moreover, the revival also led to the frenetic and often illegal acquisition of holy relics which was such a feature of the period from, say, 800 to 1300 – for instance the theft of the body of St Mark by the mariners of Venice, or that of St Nicholas by those of Bari. The Second Council of Nicaea in 787 had asserted that no church should be consecrated without holy relics, and subsequent councils reinforced this stance – to the extent of ordering that altars without relics should be destroyed. In a picturesque turn of phrase the Burgundian chronicler Raoul Glaber referred to the intense church-building activity which followed the year 1000 as replacing the vestments of the world with a 'white mantle of churches'. In the next three centuries as many as 80 new cathedrals and 500 cathedral-sized churches were built throughout Europe in addition to thousands of local parish churches. Each of them required relics and patron saints, and a scholarly biography to substantiate claims made for them.

The Benedictine ideal was also propagated through art, as we have seen in the case of Sant'Angelo in Formis and Bominaco. Traces of artistic influence may be found throughout southern and central Italy, and wherever the Benedictines established themselves. A map preserved in the abbey at Montecassino shows the sphere of influence as reaching as far north as a line between Bologna and Genoa, but the Benedictines also participated in the spiritual conquest of peoples far beyond Italy: in

Britain, Germany, Holland and Scandinavia. Decades of polemic concerning the phrases 'Benedictine School' and 'Benedictine Art' first propagated by Émile Bertaux in his 1903 book on art in southern Italy have made these expressions unacceptable to specialists. Yet in spite of chronological and stylistic problems the special combination of classical, eastern and northern artistic impulses created a particular Romanesque style in church architecture, mosaics and frescoes in southern Italy which the non-specialist viewer immediately recognizes and associates with the Benedictines.

However Montecassino exercised much more than patristic or artistic influence. It provided a model of social, intellectual and artistic life for the inhabitants of the Italian peninsula at the most difficult moment of their history – when other firm points of reference did not exist. The insistence on reading, which we have seen in the *Rule* of St Benedict, was of seminal importance: even in the 6th century we may assume – in the words of Herbert Bloch – that 'literacy of the monks and the existence of a library must be taken for granted'. The library was a focus of learning from the very beginning. One by-product of this was in the collection, preservation and copying of manuscripts, following – as we shall see – a tradition established by Greek monasteries in Calabria and Sicily. At least 70 codices were made during the rule of Abbot Desiderius, many of them of course concerning such Christian matters as patristics, hagiography, sermons, liturgy, Church history, dogma and at least eight works on canon law. Another by-product derived from the need to create young scholars from the monks who came to Montecassino. Paul the Deacon, famous as the historian of the Lombards, had been a tutor at the royal courts of Pavia and Benevento and brought his didactic experience to the abbey. He wrote a Latin textbook for his students based on older texts; one of his students, Hilderic, later produced a treatise entitled *Ars grammatica* which quoted classical authors for examples of good Latin – including, for instance, Cicero. The greatest teacher of grammar during the abbacy of Desiderius, Alberic of Montecassino, wrote works on grammar and rhetoric, and a treatise on the art of epistolary composition, the *ars dictaminis*, which was influential for centuries. He also composed several hagiographic works, including a life of St Benedict's sister Scholastica and a work together with Desiderius on the miracles of St Benedict himself. More surprising in the 11th century, especially in view of later notions of *recovering* the Roman past lost during the 'dark ages', was the collection and copying of classical pagan works such as those of Cicero, Terence, Ovid, Seneca and Virgil. Some classical texts which we possess today quite literally owe their survival to the library of Montecassino, without which they would probably have perished. These include such important works as Tacitus'

*Histories*, Seneca's *Dialogues*, Varro's *De Lingua Latina*, and the unique and entertaining *Golden Ass* of Apuleius. Works of many other Roman and Christian writers in Latin were collected in anthologies or 'florilegia' used for teaching. The influence of this practical and theoretical learning reached its peak with the pontificates of Desiderius as Victor III (1086–7) and John of Gaeta – a monk at Montecassino and head of the papal chancellery under Pope Victor – as Gelasius II (1118–9).

New works of a secular nature were also produced at Montecassino. Poetry flourished, as in the case of Abbot Desiderius' friend Alphanus – who is often judged to be the greatest poet of 11th century Italy. He was a learned man who had studied medicine at the school of Salerno and had travelled to both Constantinople and Jerusalem. His influence on the abbot seems to have been immense, and Herbert Bloch has speculated that his admiration for the former city may even have inspired Desiderius' interest in Byzantine art. Alphanus' greatest poetic compliment was to compare the basilica at Montecassino to Hagia Sophia in Constantinople in the words 'the church built by Justinian would prefer to change places with you'. Other poets writing in Latin produced fine secular poetry, keeping ancient traditions and techniques alive. Historical writing also achieved a new quality. Beyond the production of official chronicles of the abbey the 11th century saw the growth of a strong historiographical tradition. Some of the works produced at Montecassino were of vital importance in preserving the point of view of the Benedictines concerning contemporary events, for example Amatus of Montecassino's *History of the Normans*. Other works came to have even greater value: Paul the Deacon's *History of the Lombards* is still today a unique source of information on the Lombard kingdom in Italy.

Perhaps the most surprising aspect of life in 11th century Montecassino is the translation and composition of medical and scientific works. Here again Alphanus seems to have been instrumental, since as Archbishop of Salerno and an ex-student at the medical school there he was a vital link between the two centres of learning. He himself had translated from the Greek and written treatises on medicine, as had other monks at the abbey, and Abbot Desiderius' sympathy towards the remnants of the Roman Empire stimulated an interest in oriental authors almost unique in western Europe at the time. The most intriguing figure was Constantine the African: this Muslim-born convert was a native of North Africa, probably Tunis, and had travelled extensively through Ethiopia and Egypt, and even as far as Baghdad and India. Eventually he came to settle in Salerno, where he was converted to Christianity. Once established at Montecassino, on the recommendation of Alphanus, he composed and translated works on medicine. In his work on great men (*De viris illustribus*), Peter

[79]

the Deacon attributes to Constantine an astonishing range of erudition, from grammar, arithmetic and astronomy to necromany, sexology (one of his works was entitled *De coitu*), music, and languages such as Chaldean, Persian and Arabic. He is known to have composed at least 26 works, but his most notable achievement was the translation of a practical handbook on medicine and surgery from the Persian of Ali ibn Abbas, in ten books. This translation has been said to have introduced Islamic medicine to Europe. Constantine's influence on the medieval schools of medicine at Salerno and Chartres was notable, and his works were widely circulated and still influential in early printed editions at the beginning of the 16th century. Thus quite unexpectedly we find the Benedictine abbey of Montecassino at the forefront of the introduction of Arab science and medicine into Europe.

Yet while the letters and sciences as practised at Montecassino may be seen as innovatory, within the Church the influence of the abbey was conservative. As we have seen, one of the main characteristics of St Benedict's *Rule* was its extreme rigidity. This provided stability, but at the same time militated against innovation. In fact there was little real innovation forthcoming from Montecassino, and few signs of an exceptional spiritual life. Energy was devoted to maintaining the status quo, both in political and religious terms: this entailed maintaining the values of St Benedict as a model, a worthy successor to the Fathers of the Desert, and as the author – or improver – of the *Rule* which formed the basis of post-classical monasticism. Rome remained the *caput mundi* for this world view and traces of Roman social structure survive in St Benedict's manual, for instance when he asserts in the second chapter that the abbot should observe no bias in favour of a free man against a slave, since there is no 'rational basis' for such a distinction. The search for mosaic workers in Constantinople paralleled in a material sense the recovery of texts of Roman law, and the copies made of pagan authors in the scriptorium at Montecassino. They reflected the conservative stance, constantly looking back to Rome as a point of reference.

The prestige of Benedictinism in fact derived from the fact that it was the most ancient of the western religious orders. The great antiquity of Montecassino and indirect association with the mores of classical Rome lent weight to its claim to function as a model in various spheres of life: time and work, spiritual life, morality, letters, science and medicine, and classical studies. The lasting contribution of Abbot Desiderius, whose energy and success were the basis of Montecassino's power and influence in its golden age, was his role in stimulating the papal reforms of the 11th century associated with Pope Gregory the Great. But it is worth noting that these reforms were based on a return to the values of early Christianity, and that it was for this reason that the Church found a bulwark in Desiderius and his monks. In fact the literature and policies of Montecassino in the 11th century constantly reiterate the ancient virtues of chastity, martyrdom and the hermit life. Thus, paradoxically, a force which was essentially conservative and backward-looking stimulated ideas which appeared innovatory and reforming. It was the preservation of the values of St Benedict and his time which made the monastery the most important centre of thought of western Christianity – and the main ecclesiastical institution of Italy south of Rome. When real innovation came it was through the preaching orders such as the Franciscans and Dominicans, or the vigorous renewal of Benedictine values by the Cistercians – as we shall see in the chapter on Santa Maria del Monte.

But this is to look ahead. In morals, spiritual life, letters, script, architecture, painting and the practical matters of everyday life, Montecassino fixed the standards which endured on much of the Italian peninsula from the time of St Benedict himself to the beginning of the 13th century. These are the standards which are reflected in frescoes contemporary with Desiderius such as those in Sant'Angelo in Formis, and perpetuated in later cycles such as that of Bominaco. The reconstructed abbey, built 'exactly as it was' before the 1944 bombardment, stands as a modern symbol of the profound conservatism of the Order.

# MUSLIM PALERMO

EW traces of pure Islamic architecture can be found in Palermo today. But the urban structure, the name of the city, and its role as the Sicilian capital are legacies of the new importance acquired during Muslim rule of the island. Much of the topography of modern Palermo bears a medieval Arab stamp; subsequent occupation by Normans and Spaniards did not eradicate the fundamentally Arabic plan of the city which two centuries of rule imposed. Moreover, from its foundation by Phoenician colonists in the 7th century BC to the Arab conquest in the 9th century AD the city had not expanded beyond its original walls, so that medieval growth was entirely due to the Muslims. In the 3rd century BC the original settlement was known as Palepolis in order to distinguish it from a new Greek addition called Neapolis, built between Palepolis and the sea; together they were known as Panormus – a name which had already been used by Thucydides. In 254 BC Panormus was conquered by the Romans, who ruled over the town until the fall of the Western Empire; the Byzantine general Belisarius conquered it for the Eastern Empire during the Gothic Wars (in 536) and Panormus became part of the Byzantine *theme* of Sicily, the capital of which was at Syracuse – as we shall see in the chapter on Bari. Then, almost exactly three centuries later, it fell to the Aghlabid rulers of Tunisia. During their occupation it grew to become one of the finest cities of Europe, with a population of some 100,000 people – larger than all other European cities of the time. It was only with the Spanish urban development of the 16th century that Palermo grew beyond the dimensions of its Muslim prime; and even then without altering its medieval characteristics.

The Arab geographer Ibn-Haukal wrote a detailed description of Palermo after a visit to the city in 972. According to this unique witness, the city was then divided into five quarters (Fig.3). The first quarter, which he calls the 'main city', was the *Qāsr* or fortress within the ancient walls. This was the upper part of the city, away from the natural harbour

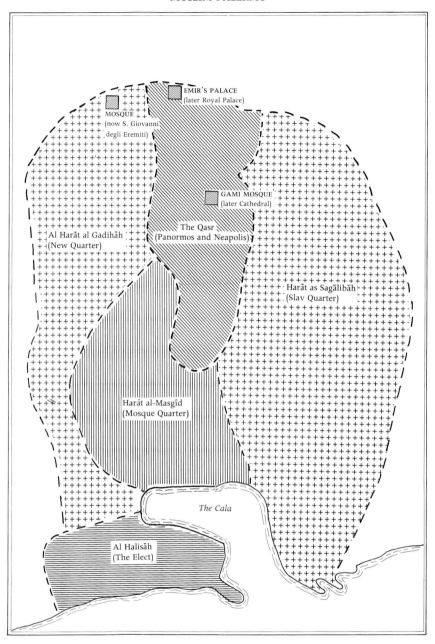

Fig. 3. Sketch map of Palermo in the tenth century, based on information in Ibn Haukal's contemporary description

[83]

on a safe and defensible site comprising the area of Phoenician Palepolis and Greek Neapolis. In the upper part of this area were the emir's gardens and palace, later to be enlarged by the Norman kings of Sicily and elaborated by the Spanish. More interesting are Ibn Haukal's comments on the principal mosque, which was almost at the centre of the *Qāsr*. After explaining that it had been rebuilt or converted from a church of the *Rum* or Christians, presumably Byzantine, he reports a local belief that Aristotle was buried there. Ibn Haukal went to see his wooden coffin, which was suspended in mid-air so that people could pray to this 'sacred' relic. One of the most intriguing aspects of this story is that the people of Palermo seem to have perceived the philosopher as a magus, since their prayers were made for such purposes as increasing rainfall. This mosque was later re-converted to its original Christian function, for the Normans built their massive cathedral on the same site. The area around it is still today known as the Cassaro, from *Qāsr*.

The other quarters of the city had been built outside the ancient walls by the Muslims, and began with the most important addition: *Al Halisāh*, or the 'Elect'. This was the first planned extension of Palermo for 1,000 years, a well-organized governmental and military quarter with administrative offices, a residence for the emir, two public baths and several mosques. It was built on flat land to the left of the harbour, following the Muslim practice of adding a well-planned addition to an older evolved city – for example in Abbāsid Baghdad; shortly after Ibn Haukal's visit the Fatimid Caliph al-Aziz began to construct a similar new residential and official quarter beside the ancient city of Fustat, to be known as al-Qahîra – which later gave the entire city its modern name of Cairo. Al Halisāh was protected by a stone wall, although it was not intended to be a fortress like the Qāsr. The official and residential nature of this quarter meant that there were neither markets nor warehouses. But besides the baths and mosques, it contained the emir's prison, the maritime arsenal (from the Arabic *dār âs-sīna*, meaning 'place of work' or 'factory'), and the *divān* or public offices and customs (whence the French 'douane' and Italian 'dogana'). The name of this Arab quarter has also survived in the modern name Kalsa.

The third Muslim-built quarter was known as the *Harāt as Saqālibāh* or 'Slav quarter', and contained the main harbour, numerous fountains, and several streams and rivers. It included an area larger than the Qāsr and Al Halisāh together and comprised the northern part of the city. The presence of the port suggests that the 'Slavs' in question were merchants, and a comparison with the Jewish quarters of ports like Bari, but they may also have been mercenary warriors. Its separation from the main part of the city and the absence of mosques illustrates that this 'Slav' quarter, however vital to the life of the city, was relegated to a secondary position.

Quite different in character and importance was Ibn Haukal's fourth quarter, the *Harāt al Masgîd* or 'mosque quarter'. This was sited between the lower extremity of the Qāsr and the official area of the Al Halisāh, around the Friday mosque named Ibn Sîqlāb – whose social function made it the principal meeting place of the city. Ibn Haukal provides a hint of the size of this mosque when he informs us that on one occasion he counted 7,000 people at Friday prayers. The temptation to dismiss his estimate as the exaggeration of a zealous pilgrim is tempered by his method of computation, for he tells us that this congregation was kneeling in over 36 rows each with more than 200 faithful. Ibn Haukal, always observant of resources precious in Arab culture, remarks that the people in the Hārat al Masgîd were forced to use wells since there was no available running water. In the upper part of this quarter, near the Friday mosque as in most Muslim cities, was the bazaar or commercial area of medieval Palermo. Here Ibn Haukal reports alleys devoted to druggists, tailors, armourers, grain dealers, oil sellers, copper workers and, above all, the enormous figure of 150 butchers. Beyond this commercial area was the fifth quarter of the city, the *Al Harāt al gadîhāh* or 'new quarter', which was presumably a natural growth of the Harāt al Masgîd and Qāsr as the population of the city grew to its medieval peak.

The area of 18th century Palermo, enclosed by walls erected by the Spanish rulers some two centuries earlier, was much the same as that of the Arab city (Fig.4). Moreover, although the city has now expanded miles beyond those walls, carpeting the fertile land which supplied medieval Palermo with cement and asphalt, the basic features of the Muslim city are still discernible today. For instance the irregular form of ancient Panormus – like a knobbly thumb pointing towards the harbour – stands out amidst the later grid-planned additions to the city; the slightly raised and irregularly shaped hill on which it stood – some 500 × 1,000 metres – was a natural defensive point for the natural harbour beneath. The harbour itself was then larger than the present *cala*: it included the area now known as Piazza Marina to the left of the keyhole-shaped inner harbour on the map, and was probably the site of the Muslim arsenal. This large piazza, the trapezoidal form of which can still be read in terms of an extension of the *cala*, was filled in during the 12th century by the Normans – thus increasing the land area of the new residential quarter.

The Al-Halisāh continued its function as an area of residence of the rulers of the city throughout the Spanish domination of Sicily: the number of noble palaces in the area – such as Palazzo Chiaramonte – bear witness to this tradition. While streets in the Qāsr followed the ancient custom of a width which perhaps allowed two horsemen to pass together, it is likely

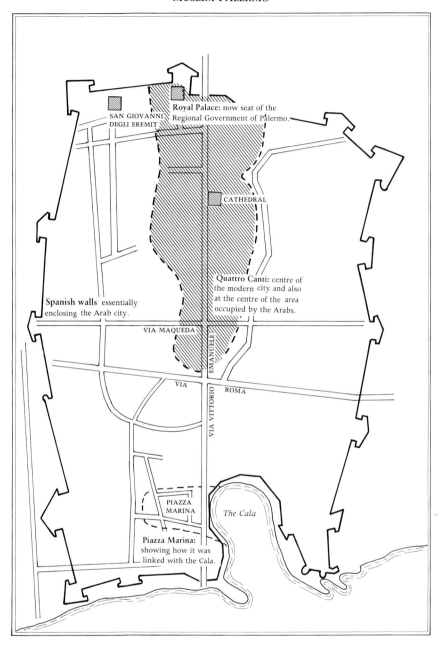

**Royal Palace:** now seat of the
Regional Government of Palermo.

SAN GIOVANNI
DEGLI EREMIT

CATHEDRAL

**Quattro Canti:** centre of
the modern city and also
at the centre of the area
occupied by the Arabs.

**Spanish walls** essentially
enclosing the Arab city.

VIA MAQUEDA

VIA VITTORIO EMANUELE

VIA    ROMA

PIAZZA
MARINA

The Cala

**Piazza Marina:**
showing how it was
linked with the Cala.

Fig. 4. Sketch map of Palermo in the eighteenth century and nucleus of the
present city centre

that the Al-Halisāh followed broader 10th century dimensions: the main street of al-Qahîra, for instance, varied in width to allow from seven to ten mounted men to pass together. In similar fashion it was required that the ramparts of al-Qahîra should be broad enough to bear two horsemen riding abreast, which may give a clue to the later walls of Palermo. We can postulate a distinct difference in the urban character of the Al-Halisāh and the other quarters: the former had well-planned streets with private single-storey houses which faced in from the streets in Muslim fashion and were provided with running water; the latter narrower streets and alleys characterized by shops and workshops, with public water supply from fountains and streams.

At the centre of the *Qāsr* stood the first mosque on what is now the site of the cathedral. The street on which it stands, Via Vittorio Emanuele, bisects the area of ancient Panormus, and probably follows the course of a Phoenician road which led from the seaward gate of the fortress down to the port. Originally it would have ended at the arsenal, but now continues across the infilled land. Already in the 10th century it was paved and lined with shops, almost certainly on the model of the central market at al-Qayrāwān (modern Kairouan, in Tunisia); in fact that desert city, where the Aghlabids expanded an earlier military outpost and built one of the greatest mosques in Islam, is probably the best place to gain some idea of Muslim Palermo. The ancient street system of Panormus, comparable to a fish bone with streets leading off to both sides of this main thoroughfare, was maintained by the Arabs – whose constructive energies were employed in the new quarters. Some 500 yards down the main street from the cathedral towards the *cala* an intersecting road was built at right angles in the 16th century, and given the name of the Spanish Viceroy during whose rule it was begun: Maqueda. Today the key feature for orientation in central Palermo is still the so-called *Quattro Canti*, built in 1611 at the crossroads of Via Vittorio Emanuele (then Via Toledo) and Via Maqueda. A short distance further down, across the site of the seaward gate mentioned by Ibn Haukal, runs the modern Via Roma. The *Quattro Canti* represents the heart, both literal and emotional, of old Palermo; but it is interesting to observe that it also stands at exactly the central point of the city as expanded by the Arabs. Around and behind the city was the great tilted plain of about 100 square kilometres, which the Arabs irrigated and made into a fertile garden. In the 16th century this garden was given the picturesque name 'Conca d'Oro' or 'Golden Conch', from its appearance as a shell gently tilted towards the sea.

This fertile land was the key to Palermo's growth. Water, as the observations of Ibn Haukal stress, was vital to the Muslim concept of the city, and the number of rivers and mills referred to by medieval visitors

[87]

suggests that both irrigation and sanitation were accorded the same high priority as in al-Qahîra and other Islamic cities. Even the new gates of the Qāsr appear to have been sited at least in part with regard to the availability of springs nearby. The role of water in Arab culture – in baths, the cultivation of products new to Europe such as papyrus and sugar-cane, or fruit such as melons – is reflected in the emphasis on the development of agriculture in the Conca d'Oro. Amongst the characteristic features of Palermo, remarked upon by all travellers until the 16th century, were the gardens and irrigation canals – which had been created by the Arabs centuries before.

The urban development of Palermo may in fact be seen in three phases: from the 6th to 2nd centuries BC; from the 9th to the 11th centuries AD; from the 16th century to the present. But the third, modern phase was conditioned by those two centuries of Muslim rule. The new walls and bastions built to resist modern artillery by the Spanish Viceroy Ferrante Gonzaga in the 16th century followed almost exactly the line of the Arab walls; the Spanish city fitted within the limits established over 500 years earlier. The Spanish walls survived until the middle of the 18th century, when expansion of the city began to erode these medieval limits until they completely disappeared. Yet still today the structure of the historic nucleus of Palermo may be considered as basically Islamic.

Toponymy has also preserved the Muslim influence. We have seen that two modern quarters, the Cassaro and the Kalsa, bear names of Arabic origin, and a reading of Ibn Haukal reveals that the modern markets known as Lattarini and Ballaro derive respectively from 'attārîn, the market of the spice and drug merchants, and the balhāra, a market named after the Arabic village near Monreale whose merchants traded there. Similar influences can be discerned throughout Sicily. The 19th-century Sicilian scholar of the Arab domination of his island Michele Amari, whose five-volume *Storia dei Musulmani di Sicilia* remains the classic work of reference, made a computation of place-names deriving from Arabic. It was based on the geography of al-Idrisi written – as we shall see in the chapter on Cefalù – for King Roger II, together with maps and other documents current in 1858. Excluding the many names of rivers, mountains, valleys and other natural features, he found 328 new place-names deriving from the period of Arab domination, from large towns like Marsala, Alcamo and Sciacca to tiny villages and hamlets. The most common Arabic words used in forming compound names were 'ayn (spring), *gâr* (cave), *ra's* (cape), *manzil* (halt), *rahl* (station), *gal'ah* (rock), and *burg* (tower). The word *rahl* occurred in as many as 107 place-names, *gal'ah* in 20, and *manzil* in 18.

The stamp of Muslim culture on both Sicily and Palermo was faint but indelible. The capital which the Arabs left as a legacy to their Norman successors was dramatically different from the provincial fortress overlooking a good but unimportant natural harbour which they had captured two centuries earlier. Palermo was a wealthy, flourishing and cosmopolitan city, first among those of Europe and second only to Cairo and Constantinople in the Mediterranean; the Arab historian al-Muqāddāsî stated that it was even bigger than the capital of the caliphate at Cairo.

Yet until the 9th century the chief city of Sicily had always been Syracuse, facing across the open Mediterranean towards the east. For the rulers and dominant influences of Sicily traditionally came from the east: the ancient Greeks, Byzantium, and the Greek Orthodox Church. The arrival of the Muslims forced a total change of focus, since conquest was made over the shortest sea-crossing from the Aghlabid lands in what is today Tunisia. Sicily suddenly faced west. The most prominent towns were now in the west of the island, across the Sicilian Channel from al-Qayrāwān and Tunis (ancient Carthage): Mazara, Marsala, Trapani and Palermo. It is fascinating to notice that this shift, although apparently new and dramatic, actually reflected the origins of Phoenician Panormus: the Athenian historian Thucydides tells us in his description of Sicily in *The Peloponnesian War* (Bk.VI, ch.1) that when the Greeks began to arrive on the island in great numbers the Phoenicians who occupied numerous headlands and islands 'abandoned most of their settlements and concentrated on the towns of Motya [ie.Marsala?], Soloeis [ie.Solunto], and Panormus . . . partly because from here the voyage from Sicily to Carthage is shortest'. The Muslim conquest represented a shift which was never reversed, with the economic and cultural interests of Sicily permanently moved from East to West. In another way the Arabs followed their ancient predecessors: the Phoenician name Panormos was written with the consonants representing the sounds b.l.r.m., so that they called their capital Balarm or Balarmuh.

The gradual conquest of Sicily was carried out by the Aghlabid rulers of al-Qayrāwān, a dynasty which had established a powerful autonomous state in northern Africa. Incursions and isolated raids on Sicily had been made by other rulers as early as 704. But it was the third Aghlabid emir Ziyādāt-Allāh I (817–38) who in 827 sent an expedition consisting of 70 ships, 10,000 men and 700 horses against Mazara across a strait which at its narrowest point is no more than 100 miles wide. Over the next 75 years a series of Aghlabid emirs continued the process of conquest, which was finally completed with the destruction of Syracuse and Taormina by Ibrahim II in 902. But within seven years of that date the Aghlabids themselves were overthrown and Sicily became part of the newly

The city of Palermo in mourning for the death of King William II, showing the chained port, the quarter called 'Kalza' (ie. Al-Halisah), the name 'Cassarum' (ie. Qasr), and turbaned figures of remaining Muslim population

[90]

established Fatimid empire. Then, in 948, the third Fatimid Caliph al-Mansur appointed as Governor of Sicily a-Hasān ibn-'Alî ibn-ābi-al-Husayn al-Kālbi (d.965). This ruler is normally referred to by his personal name a-Hasān, but his last name al-Kālbi gave rise to the dynastic name Kalbites for his descendants – who ruled Sicily for the remainder of the Muslim domination.

Thus Muslim rule of Sicily may be said to fall into three main phases: Aghlabid conquest and rule from 827–909; a turbulent interim under the Fatimids from 909–948; and Kalbite rule from 948–1091. Palermo itself fell to the Muslims in 831: according to the Syrian chronicler Ibn Athīr, in the previous year a combined army of Muslims from Spain and Tunisia sailed in a fleet of 300 ships to dominate the Christian resistance which had been fomented by the Byzantines on the southwest coast between Girgenti (modern Agrigento) and Mazara. Once this task was completed the army marched on Palermo and besieged the city until its Christian ruler requested safe conduct for himself and his family, after which 'he went by sea into the countries of Rum'. When the victorious Arabs entered Palermo in the month of *Ragāb* (14 August–12 September 831) they found 'no more than a handful of men': less than 3,000 compared with the 7,000 Ibn Athir claims defended the city when they had arrived. The 3,000 survivors were enslaved; thousands of others died. This bloody and dramatic subjugation of Palermo was in a sense the real beginning of the occupation and domination of Sicily.

The site of Palermo was attractive to the conquerors: it was easily defensible, possessed a good natural harbour, and was not distant from the north African coast. While previous Muslim raids seem to have been made with no precise strategy, and amidst constant disputes between North African Arabs, Spanish Arabs and freelance bandits, the occupation of Palermo marked the beginning of a concerted process of colonization. Although appointed by the Aghlabid emir Zîyadāt-Allāh I and his successors in al-Qayrāwān, the provincial emirs of Palermo were to all intents and purposes independent rulers – just as Zîyadāt-Allāh was himself independent of Fustat. The emir's duties however were specific, and conditioned this autonomy: he was to organize and administrate the army, to administer justice by electing the *gādi* (civil, penal and religious judges) and *hakîm* (lesser legal officials), to collect taxes, to defend Islam, to preside over public prayers (either in person or by a delegate), and to provide encouragement and aid for pilgrims on their way to Mecca.

That legal and bureaucratic organization was both rapid and close to the Aghlabid capital is suggested by the fact that within five years a *gādi* from Sicily is reported as dying in al-Qayrāwān. Similarly, we learn that in 835 the emir Muhammad ibn 'Abd Allah, who was cousin to Zîyadāt Allāh, coined a silver *dîrham* with the inscription: 'In the name of God this *dîrham* was coined in Sicily [Isqîlîyāh] in the year 220'. Within 40 years the rulers of Palermo exacted tribute throughout western Sicily – in the modern provinces of Palermo, Trapani and Agrigento – and occupied around 30 castles and cities including the powerful central fortress of Castrogiovanni (modern Enna). This tribute was a purely financial obligation, entailing no limitation on property ownership or religious practices. As such, it represents an early instance of the religious tolerance which was such a marked feature of Sicily under both Arab and Norman rule. Amari comments that to many of the inhabitants there was little practical difference between paying an emir in Palermo or an emperor in Constantinople.

Little is known of the city of Palermo during the period of Aghlabid rule. But in the turbulent half-century which followed it there is evidence that the city had been fortified and was well defended. An anonymous chronicler of the period mentions a siege in the year 916–917 which lasted for six months: he notes that it was so successful that 'the price of salt increased to two *carrube* per ounce'. It was ended only when the besieger Abu Saîd offered an amnesty to the people within the walls, who then opened the gates to him. This episode, apart from the fascinating detail of one of the practical consequences of a lengthy siege, provides some idea of the strength of Palermo's fortifications. That they were at least maintained and probably further strengthened is suggested by the fact that in the initial Norman attempt to take Palermo, in 1064, such expert besiegers as Robert Guiscard and his brother Roger the 'Great Count' laid siege to the city for three months without success. They were forced to derive satisfaction from sacking the surrounding countryside.

But while the Aghlabids may have conquered Sicily, the period of the chief Muslim glory of Palermo began with the arrival of the Kalbite governor a-Hasān in 948. His ruthlessness may not have augured well. The anonymous chronicler provides terse evidence of his military skill: 'He restored the country, put it in order, and put it on the right lines'. Even more laconic is the description of a plot on his life which a-Hasān discovered. The chronicler reports the governor's treatment of the rebel leaders as follows: 'He had their hands and feet cut off, and tied their corpses to poles. After that, things in Sicily went well.' Such ruthlessness – and the consequent political stability – paved the way for a burst of cultural activity: native Arab scholars produced important work in theology, mathematics, astronomy, medicine, and books on grammar and jurisprudence; others came from all over the Muslim world in a kind of medieval brain-drain to study in Sicily. Then, as the importance of the court at Palermo grew, the same native scholars often went to Spain in search of employment, and travelled east to go on pilgrimage to Mecca or otherwise enrich their knowledge. Examples of Sicilian authors and scholars abound in al-Qaywārān, Fustat and Baghdad, while some even travelled as far as Yemen, Khorassan and Persia. While the letters and verse were not of sufficient merit to claim a place in the mainstream of Arabic poetry, the flowering of poetry in Palermo and Syracuse was, as we shall see in the context of the Emperor Frederick II, to have far-reaching consequences.

It was under the rule of a-Hasān's descendant abu-al-Futāh Yusuf ibn-Abdullah (989–98) that Muslim Palermo reached its height, with a purely Arabic culture flourishing amidst the trappings of luxurious palaces and an enlightened court. Such abundance was based on the solid economic base of the agricultural wealth of the Conca d'Oro. The markets described earlier by Ibn Haukal between the *Harāt al-Masgîd* and *Al Harāt al Gadîhāh*, together with the expanded port, traded in the main products of Muslim Sicily: ammonia salts (exported to Spain), mineral products used by the Arabs such as antimony, alum, vitriol, sulphur, pumice, coral and jasper, and metals such as silver, iron, lead, mercury and copper. Non-mineral products included the native grain, wool, saffron, wine and linen, and also crops such as sugar-cane, date-palms, cotton, silk, hemp, oranges, limes and mulberries which were introduced to Sicily by the Arabs. It is curious to note that while to modern Italians the island of Sicily is most closely associated with sweets, oranges, olives and wine, the first three were only introduced by the Arabs and even the last profited from Arab skills in husbandry. Two centuries after Ibn Haukal's visit an Arab traveller to Norman Palermo, Ibn Jubayr, noted that vines there were grown in symmetrical rows unlike other areas. The 11th century Spanish writer Ibn al-'Awwām refers to the well-organized cultivation of onions and melons in Spain as being grown 'in the Sicilian fashion', that is, using Arab irrigation techniques. The gardens of the Sultans (and later of the Norman kings), which the new irrigation furnished with constant water, occupied land which had previously been arid. Agricultural production which was made possible included imports such as Persian sugar-cane, gourds and pumpkins, and the papyrus which Ibn Haukal claims was as good as that of Egypt. Today, much of the landscape of central Sicily is characterized by vast expanses of orange groves which are testimony to the Arab domination. At that time, however, the most characteristic agricultural product appears to have been the less grand onion. With a tone approaching contempt Ibn Haukal notes than all inhabitants of the city eat onions in great quantities: '. . . there is no man of any class who does not eat them every day, offering them in his house both morning and night'.

[93]

Palermo: the church of San Giovanni degli Eremiti

But the most interesting descriptions in Ibn Haukal's account are those concerning the two related categories of mosques and schoolteachers, each of which numbered about 300. In the case of the mosques he observes that 'most of them' were proper constructions with roof, walls and doors. Unfortunately none has survived to this day, but remains of a mosque were discovered at the end of the last century within the complex of San Giovanni degli Eremiti and it is likely that many other churches in Palermo stand on the sites of earlier mosques – like the cathedral. Local people explained the enormous number of mosques to Ibn Haukal as a result of the immense pride of the Arab inhabitants of Palermo: apparently each family of sufficient means wanted to possess its own mosque as a status symbol. Ibn Haukal provides a fascinating example of a street in which 'within the range of an arrow-shot I noted ten mosques, sometimes one opposite the other with nothing but the street between'. In similar fashion, not only did Ibn Haukal's own host during his stay in the city possess a mosque near his home, but he built another for his son 'about twenty paces away' so that the younger man could teach jurisprudence in it.

For one of the principal functions of the mosque was didactic, a fact which probably accounts for the similarity between the number of

[94]

mosques and the number of teachers. Ibn Haukal's total contempt for schoolteachers is notorious, almost as much as that he shows for the ignorance, lack of friendliness towards strangers, and barbaric habits of the people who lived outside the civilized city of Palermo. These qualities he attributes to the fact that Muslim inhabitants of the countryside and distant fortresses tended often to marry Christians, thus providing bastard offspring who were unable to maintain the values of Arab culture. Yet his real venom is reserved for the schoolteachers: he describes the army of 300 teachers as mainly worthless and ignorant. The majority of them are said to be spineless characters who chose their profession in order to avoid going to the more perilous holy wars and military expeditions. Since school-teachers were allowed exemption from such duties 'all the imbeciles took refuge in the teaching profession'. He also adds that this is all the more deprecable since it is one of the least-paid of the professions.

Unfortunately, Ibn Haukal was no Pevsner. He left no account of the architecture he saw. But there is a fascinating glimpse in a briefer account of the Palestine-born geographer al-Muqāddāsî, who visited most of the Muslim lands in 20 years of travel and wrote an account of his travels in 985–6. He says that the city was bigger than Fustat and contains many mills; above all he observes that since the houses were made partly of brick and partly of stone Palermo appeared to him a predominantly red and white city. It was left to Ibn Jubayr two centuries later to describe the magnificence of the Islamic buildings used by the Norman conquerors. It was he who described Palermo as 'a wonderful place, built in the Cordovan style', 'proudly set between its open spaces and plains filled with gardens', a city which 'dazzles the eyes with its perfection'. He resorted to a metaphor beloved by Arab poets when he compared the disposition of the Norman king's palaces around the higher parts of the city as 'like pearls encircling a woman's throat'. Ibn Jubayr's account of a visit to the sovereign is breathless with its litany of gardens, courtyards, squares, ante-chambers, colonnades and belvederes. Such a description brings to mind the elegance and seemingly never-ending courtyards of the Alhambra palace at Granada, whose atmosphere is perhaps not too distant from that of the royal quarters at Palermo. It is probably at Granada and Cordova itself, together with al-Qayrāwān, that Muslim Palermo may be best imagined; it must have been a truly astonishing capital.

Palermo was of course much more than an ornamental capital. During the two centuries of Muslim rule it served as a vital logistical base and colonial outpost for a series of daring raids on the Italian peninsula. The emir Muhammad ibn 'Abd Allāh, who had first coined money on Sicily, directed the earliest sallies. We learn from Ibn Athîr that although he never left Palermo up to his death in 850–1 after 19 years of rule, this emir sent out 'armies and squadrons' from his base to 'complete the conquests and bring back the prey'. At one time, indeed, it must have seemed to the indigenous inhabitants that Islam was about to conquer the entire peninsula.

The first incursion culminated in an attack on Brindisi around 838, which resulted in the destruction of the city by fire. Two years later, after the occupation of Taranto, a Muslim fleet demonstrated the potential of Aghlabid power in the Adriatic when it managed to resist an attack made by 60 Venetian ships. Not content with this success, the fleet then humiliated Venice by pursuing and harassing the survivors as far as Istria and the mouth of the River Po. Many Venetian ships were captured, and houses burned in the northern port of Ancona. This episode demonstrated that the Muslims were a real threat to trade between Venice and Constantinople, capable of dividing the two halves of Christendom. The qualities of Muslim fighting men were soon recognized, and in the hurly-burly of shifting alliances which characterized the politics of the time they were used as mercenaries by Christian rulers – just as Christian soldiers were later employed by the Muslim rulers of Morocco. It was as the result of the Lombard Prince Radelchis I of Benevento's employment of Muslim mercenaries from about 841 that they came to possess Bari two years later, as we shall see. The permanence of the intentions of these mercenaries is shown by the actions of the leader, a certain al-Mufārrāg ibn Salim, as related by Ibn Athîr: having taken and held 24 castles, and founded a mosque in Bari, al-Mufārrāg wrote to the Wāli in Egypt requesting official benediction as military governor of this new province. Although he was later murdered by a revolt of his own men, the resulting emirate of Bari survived until the combined powers of the Lombards, Franks and Byzantines besieged and took the city in 871. In the decade 840–50, the raiders moved both northwards and inland from Bari to Licosa (near Salerno), Gaeta, Benevento and Rome. In August 846 a Muslim raiding force sailed up the Tiber and sacked the basilicas of St Peter and St Paul – which stood outside the protection of the city walls; later the same year raiders burned churches and monasteries near Montecassino and arrived within sight of the rock of Montecassino itself. This first push northwards was halted when the combined fleets of Naples and Rome defeated the Muslims off Ostia: after that battle the corpses of killed Muslims were used to decorate the churches of Rome.

In the same period an extraordinary figure emerges from the chronicles in the person of the Muslim condottiere Sawdan. He was, according to the Syrian historian Al-Balādhūri (d.892), the third ruler of the emirate of Bari, and in fact operated in southern Italy independently of the Aghlabid emirs of Sicily. Adopting tactics similar to the later *condottieri* of the

Renaissance, Sawdan and his men ranged far and wide in rapid campaigns through the regions of Apulia and Campania. He raided the important cities of Benevento, Capua and Pozzuoli, and eventually occupied strategic castles throughout the area – for instance in Telese, Alife, Sepino, Boiano, Isernia, Canosa and Castel di Venafro. Devoid of the religious sentiment which restrained Christian bandits, he also sacked the great Benedictine abbey at San Vincenzo al Volturno and the sanctuary of San Michele on the Gargano peninsula. Yet he seems to have been no ignorant brigand, and within the aura of legend which surrounds this fascinating Robin-Hood-like character there are incidents illustrating the superiority of Arabic culture at the time. An example may be found in the 20th chapter of the book on practical statecraft written by Constantine VII Porphyrogenitus (944–59) and addressed to his son, the *De administrando imperio*. The Byzantine Emperor asserts that when Sawdan was eventually captured by the princes of Benevento and Salerno, they paid homage to his learning by visiting him in prison and listening 'in awe' to his ideas concerning both human and veterinary medicine. It was only with the arrival of the emperor Louis II (855–75), who came south in 867 and managed to coagulate the disparate Christian forces of the southern cities, that Sawdan and other Muslim raiders were finally forced to retreat from Campania. But even Louis failed in completely eradicating the Arab presence, as we shall see in the chapter on Bari, and even in his own more immediate project of uniting the southern part of the Italian peninsula to his northern lands.

From an emotional and psychological point of view, however, the most damaging attacks were those against the very heart of western Christendom, Rome itself. Yet it is important to observe that they were made possible by the collusion of a Christian power, for in one of the unexpected alliances which pepper Italian history the Muslims reached an agreement with Naples which provided a safe haven for raids along the coast of the papal state. Although this agreement was at least in part the result of enmity between Naples and Rome – and fear of the encroaching papal state – there were also commercial considerations. For the advantages to Naples of providing a port of entry for foodstuffs and other imports from the Arab world were potentially enormous; the contemporary rise to wealth and power of nearby Amalfi was almost certainly derived from alliances with the Muslims after its separation from Naples in the 840s. In fact the Arab presence in the port and streets of Naples was soon so great that in a letter attributed to the Emperor Louis II the city is said to 'appear like Palermo or Africa'.

The climax of the raids against Rome was reached during the pontificate of Pope John VIII (872–82), who was a Roman by birth and thus particularly concerned about the fate of the city. In a remarkable series of letters to the Imperial Vicar Bosone, to King Charles the Bald (875–8), and to the Byzantine *strategus* Gregorius – who in the same period occupied Bari for the Byzantines – the pope paints a vivid picture of the Muslim threat to his city and pleads for their assistance. In one of these letters he portrays the arrival of Muslim forces beneath the walls of Rome in dramatic terms: 'They cover the earth like locusts, and to describe their pillage would require more tongues than our trees have leaves. The countryside is deserted, suitable for savages; churches are ruined, the priests killed or imprisoned; nuns punished in captivity; villas and castles abandoned . . . and I neither sleep nor eat in my solicitude.' In another letter he expresses fear of an imminent attack, and states that the Muslims are building 'a hundred ships and fifteen ferries to transport horses across the river'. Yet the flowery language and inflated numbers were probably a matter of expediency, and it is clear that political concerns influenced Pope John's judgement – and fired his rhetoric. In a letter to Gregory, who the pope knew would certainly have more detailed knowledge of the local situation than his other correspondents, the language is tempered: Pope John simply requests the supply of ten warships to guard the mouth of the Tiber at Ostia. This difference suggests that in reality he merely *feared* Muslim attack, and exploited similar fears in other rulers with the aim of enlisting support. With their help, the pope would have been able to extend the papal state towards the south.

Such a plan, if it existed in his mind, did not however allow for the tenacity of the Muslims. They were not easily to be repulsed. In the long run the safety of Rome was guaranteed only after the death of Pope John VIII, by means of an agreement which allowed them their freedom as long as they settled outside the papal state. Thus a Muslim colony which lasted for some 30 years was established near Traietto on the River Garigliano – within a day's ride of Montecassino and 70 miles as the crow flies from Rome. Another such base was also established further south at Agropoli, on a rocky promontory in the south of the Gulf of Salerno. In the case of the Garigliano a semi-permanent force of infidel robbers and traders was thus legitimized by the Church; one of the results of this was the Muslim attack on Montecassino in 883, which resulted in the sacking and burning of the monastery. The Muslim settlement on the Garigliano, though small and short-lived, is one of the most extraordinary of the many colonies established in Italy by invaders during the period from the fall of Rome to the Renaissance.

Muslim raids were not confined to southern Italy; neither were they merely naval attacks. At this time of maximum Arab expansion into Spain and France there was also an overland threat from the north. The chronicler Liutprand of Cremona tells us of Saracens from Fraxinetum (La

Garde-Freinet near St Tropez), who after 'ruining' Provence launched an attack against Acqui – only 40 miles from Pavia: 'The whole country accordingly was in a panic,' he relates, 'and no one waited for the Saracens to approach unless he had a perfectly sure refuge.' The northern ports also came under attack: Genoa in 935, as we shall see, and Pisa in 1004 and 1011. It is again Liutprand who informs us that 'the Africans with a huge fleet arrived [in Genoa] and taking the people by surprise burst into the city, massacred every one except the children and women, and putting on board ship all the treasures belonging to the city and to God's churches sailed back to Africa.' The entire peninsula was under threat.

In fact the increased Byzantine presence in southern Italy, which led to the establishment of the catapanate in Bari and dominion over the three *themes* of Langobardia, Calabria and Lucania, was a direct consequence of this threat. For it was the Lombard rulers of Benevento and Capua, together with the papacy, who sued for an increased Byzantine presence in order to create a buffer state between the Muslims and their own lands. The turning point was in 915, when a combined fleet of western Christian and Byzantine ships defeated the Arabs of the Garigliano – where, again in Liutprand's words, they 'kept in security their wives, children and captives, and all their goods and chattels'. This anarchic period, when Pavia and other cities were attacked by the Magyars as well as threatened by the Arabs, was followed by a period of relative stability in the north under the militarily powerful Saxon Emperor Otto I (963–73) and his successors Otto II and Otto III. In the south, around 975, the Byzantines created an equally powerful and well-organized state governed by the Catapan at Bari. From that moment the Arabs were forced to content themselves with their possessions in Sicily, until both they and the Byzantines were in turn defeated by the Normans a century later.

On a broad historical perspective the Arab presence on the Italian mainland was no more than a temporary irritant; little evidence of the Muslim achievement remains even in Sicily. Roger I, the 'Great Count' and Norman conqueror of the island, occupied the castle now known as Maredolce or the 'Favara' in the countryside near Palermo when he arrived in the area in 1071. That once magnificent castle, built by the Kalbite emir Ga'fār (997–1019), with its baths, park and artificial lake, must have made a great impression on the Norman who had travelled south from the quite different climate and surroundings of the Cotentin peninsula. Now it is little more than a ruin, with its original Arab walls built over by later Norman additions, but its magnificent baths, streams of water, orange and lemon groves made it a paradise which Arab poets praised. The Benedictine chronicler Amatus of Montecassino wrote in his history of the Normans that it was a 'palace with delightful gardens and

Palermo: the 'poetic' cloister of San Giovanni degli Eremiti

full of fruit'; the Jewish traveller Benjamin of Tudela tells us that it was the place favoured by William II, and the Emperor Henry VI received ambassadors from Palermo there. It is today one of the saddest ruins in Sicily. Other vestiges of Islamic architecture soon disappeared or underwent drastic rebuilding; the emir's palace, for instance, was expanded first by the Normans and then by the Spanish, and is now the seat of the regional government of Sicily. But paradoxically the remaining Norman buildings suffice, for, in the words of an Italian scholar of Sicilian architecture, 'we can gather an idea of Palermo's splendour during the centuries of Moslem rule from many of the buildings erected by the Norman rulers after they had destroyed the Arab originals.' The mysterious domed church of San Giovanni degli Eremiti with its poetic cloister could be transported to the Alhambra without appearing out of place.

By 1091 the Normans had conquered the whole island of Sicily. The Kalbite creators of Palermo's splendour were definitively banished, and their artefacts subjected to plunder and pillage. The Syracuse-born Arab poet Abd-al-Jabbār ibn Hāmdās (c.1055–1132), could – from his undesired exile in captivity in northern Africa – apostrophize the Mediterranean

[100]

from the opposite shore in the following terms: 'O Sea, beyond you I have a paradise, in which I knew happiness rather than misfortune.' But the paradise remained, as we shall see, in the irrigated valleys of the Conca d'Oro and the royal park of the Norman kings; it was captured for all time in the beautiful mosaics of hunting scenes in the so-called 'sala' of King Roger in the royal palace at Palermo. Traces of it remain to this day.

## 4

# *BYZANTINE BARI*

T HE natural function of Bari's harbour from ancient times until today
has been that of agent for commercial exchange between West and
East. The basilica of San Nicola, which symbolizes Bari's past as no other
church, looks due east from the promontory on which medieval Bari
stands across the Adriatic, towards Greek Epirus and Macedonia and then
on to Constantinople. Both site and fabric of the basilica in fact bear
witness to the city's Byzantine past; for it stands on the site of the
*praitorion* or palace of the Catapan, the imperial officer who governed
southern Italy for the Eastern Emperor. The present church is a relatively
late construction, begun in 1087 when the relics of St Nicholas of Myra
were brought to Bari from Asia Minor by local mariners. But fragments of
beautifully decorated Byzantine plutei and capitals were re-used in the
Norman fabric, both in the façade and in the crypt.

In his study of the basilica Franco Schettini has identified parts of the
lower wall with the older palace. His hypothetical reconstruction of the
*praitorion* is fascinating, and provides some idea of the immense wealth
and power of the Catapan in the 10th and 11th centuries. At the heart of
the complex, on the site of the present nave, was a civil basilica raised
above ground level with three naves and open arcades accessible from
steps on the sides – like the Basilica Julia and Basilica Aemilia in the Roman
Forum; the central nave was probably open to the sky, like an atrium. The
formal quarters of the Catapan were set at the eastern end of this basilica,
parallel to the sea in the manner of a transept: at its centre was a concave
space like an apse for the throne which was used on important occasions.
At the opposite end of the atrium was a large enclosed square whose
external walls probably housed guards, stables and other outbuildings.
The whole area, which was probably the site of earlier official buildings
used by the series of *strategi* who preceded the catapanate, was rebuilt and
strengthened by the Catapan Basilius Mesardonites in 1011.

In size, function and magnificence, the *praitorion* was comparable to the

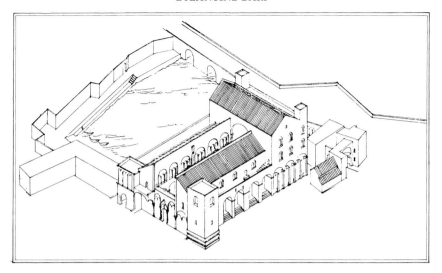

Fig. 5. Hypothetical reconstruction of the Catapan's palace on the site of San Nicola at Bari (after F. Schettini)

*palatium* at Pavia. It included halls for formal occasions, offices of all sizes for imperial officials from the military governor to notaries, clerks and scribes, an open courtyard for large assemblies, and barracks for the garrison of guards. There was even a private port facility with an easily guarded arched entrance. The entire architectural complex would have been decorated with balconies and fine sculpted detail, and the interiors enriched with tapestries, gilding and painting. We may imagine their splendour from the Byzantine predilection for the translucent and bright colours, but also from contemporary works such as the Madonna, dated 1020, in the crypt of SS. Marina e Christina at Carpignano (northwest of Otranto within the *theme* of Langobardia), or the mosaic fragments at Montecassino and the floor of S. Menna at Sant'Agata de' Goti. There was probably also a prison, some cultivated land within the walls, and the churches or chapels of St Sophie, St Basil, St Eustratios, and St Demetrius. We may imagine an imposing and towered palace-castle like that of the imperial *palatium* at Ravenna, whose portico and arcades can be seen in the mosaics of San Apollinare Nuovo, like Diocletian's palace at Split, or an imperial villa such as that of Hadrian at Tivoli with its *canopus*. When permission was given by Duke Roger to the Archbishop of Bari to destroy the *praitorion* and build a church to house the relics of St Nicholas, the task of demolition took two months.

The process of creating the Byzantine presence in Italy had taken several centuries, falling into two distinct geographical areas and

The façade of the church of San Nicola, Bari

historical phases: first, what we might term the 'northern period', with Ravenna as Seat of the Exarchs from 553 to 751, when, as we have seen, Italy was roughly divided into Byzantine and Lombard spheres of influence; and second the 'southern period', beginning with the theme of Sicily, founded about 692–5, the duchies of Calabria, Otranto and Naples which flourished in the 9th century, and finally the Catapanate at Bari, which lasted from its foundation around 960–70 until its capture by the Normans in 1067. In his *De administrando imperio* the Emperor Constantine VII Porphyrogenetus (913–19) rather grandly – and incorrectly, as far as Pavia was concerned – explained to his son the extent of Byzantine possessions in the following words: 'You must know that in ancient times the whole dominion of Italy, Naples, Capua, Benevento, Salerno, Amalfi, Gaeta, the whole of Lombardy, was at the mercy of the Romans, that is when Rome was the capital of the Empire. After the transfer of the imperial seat to Constantinople these territories were divided into two administrations, and two patricians were sent by the Emperor: one governed Sicily, Calabria, Naples and Amalfi, and the other, who resided at Benevento, governed Pavia, Capua and the remaining territories.'

Greek presence in Bari (or 'Barion') was however much more ancient than this, as the magnificent ceramics in the Archaeological Museum testify. As early as the middle of the second millennium BC the promontory and its well-protected natural harbour – now infilled as gardens and Corso Antonio de Tullio – were settled over an area of some five hectares. Around the 11th century BC a new settlement of fishermen occupied the same site (reminding us of Horace's later epithet for the Roman city, 'fish-famous Barium', and the role of fish in the modern economy and gastronomy of Bari). Then in the 8th century Hellenic influence appeared as the Greeks began to colonize throughout the Mediterranean, and came into contact with the tribes known as the Iapyges who inhabited the plains of Apulia near Bari. The first Greeks to sail up the Adriatic, according to Herodotus in his *Histories*, were the sailors of Phocaea; but they were soon followed by others from Rhodes, Corinth and later the Athenians. The agricultural wealth of the plains behind Bari, altogether some 2,600 square kilometres of fertile land, attracted merchants from these cities who exchanged their more sophisticated wares for wheat. In the 6th and 5th centuries important Greek tombs appear in Bari, and in the next century the city was surrounded by a stone wall. During this entire period Bari was subjected to a twin Greek influence: a direct link via the Adriatic with the Aegean cities; an overland link with Magna Grecia in the south of Italy, and other Greek settlements in Campania. Even in Roman times, when Barion became the Roman *municipium* Barium, minted bronze coins – one of which, the half-ounce, bears a ship's prow on the reverse – and functioned as a port continuously from the 3rd century BC to the 2nd century AD, the language of the citizens continued to be Greek. Moreover, since Bari was engaged in East-West commerce throughout antiquity it is likely that even Christianity was introduced by traders and pilgrims travelling to and from the East, perhaps as early as the end of the 2nd century, rather than from Rome. For just as Genoa always looked West, as we shall see, so Bari has always looked East towards Greece.

Throughout the Roman Empire and the later Byzantine Empire there were two main routes of communication between Rome and Constantinople: the earliest road was the Via Appia, which began at Brindisi, ran west overland to Taranto, then on northwards through Matera, Venosa, Benevento, Capua and Terracina to Rome; the later road was the Via Traiana, which started further south at Otranto, followed the Adriatic coast north from Otranto through Brindisi to Bari, and then turned inland to Benevento where it joined the Via Appia (we know that this was completed in 114 AD from the inscription on the beautifully-preserved triumphal arch which the Emperor Trajan erected in Benevento to celebrate the junction of the two roads). Thus Bari was both on a vital

South porch of the Cathedral of Bari, with re-used Byzantine columns and
lozenge decoration on the bases

overland route and one of the key Adriatic ports used by ships from the East, constantly open to the dissemination of Byzantine culture. Early Byzantine influence is for instance visible in architectural fragments such as columns, capitals and plutei used in the medieval churches of Bari. The first cathedral was itself a Greek basilica built in the late 5th or early 6th century: possibly by the first documented bishop of the city, a certain Concordio who attended a council in Rome in 465. Since during the last years of the Roman Empire and the rule of Theoderic (493–526) Bari and the whole of northern Apulia enjoyed a period of peace and prosperity, with excellent markets for wheat and the produce of newly implanted olive groves, the conditions for undertaking a major building project existed. We know that the building of other similar churches at nearby Trani, Canosa and Siponto was initiated by bishops who had attended the same council in Rome. Stylistic features also suggest a similar date: in the south porch of the cathedral there are two columns placed on marble cubes which are decorated with a lozenge enclosing a stylized flower, a characteristic of work done at Constantinople in the same period. Similarly, the many Byzantine capitals re-used in the crypt of San Nicola – finely decorated with organic motifs like those in St Mark's at Venice – belong to the same period and place; the façade of the church is also decorated with fragments which enhance the simple blind arcading. It has been argued that these fragments were purchased later by the Normans in order to improve the status of their buildings. But, against this, it must be observed that the original cathedral was demolished in 1034 by the Byzantine Archbishop, who then oversaw the building or re-building of its replacement; thus its completion within 30 years was both anterior to the Norman arrival and carried out by an architect working under Byzantine supervision who would probably be inclined to re-use Byzantine fragments of such high quality – especially since they were contemporary with and thus perhaps integral to the original building. Moreover, it would seem unlikely that such long-standing Hellenic and Byzantine influence in Bari should be interrupted precisely at the moment in which the direct presence of Byzantium was strongest.

The fortunate position of Bari also had negative consequences, especially in times of war. During the Gothic Wars (535–53), for instance, the city found itself on the front line. Then, for a period of some 300 years, from the semi-mythical destruction of several cities on the Apulian plain by the last Ostrogoth King Totila in 542 to the fall of the Muslim emirate in 871, Bari went through a turbulent and inglorious period. Around 582 the Emperor Maurice, who acceded in that year, instituted the Exarchates of Italy and North Africa, with the capital of the former in Ravenna. This was an essentially military organization of Byzantine territory with semi-

Detail of San Nicola, Bari

autonomous duchies, and may well have included Bari; no evidence exists, however, and for about a century the city disappeared from view. Perhaps the bishopric was lost, and Bari seems to have suffered the loss of population and economic decline common to many Italian cities at the time. In 663 a military expedition led by the Emperor Constans II (641–68), designed primarily to consolidate Byzantine possessions in Italy but also to block the Muslim advance, is thought to have assaulted Bari. But within five years, around the time of the death of Constans, Romuald, the son of the Lombard King Grimoald, reconquered the lost territory and Bari became a Lombard town.

For the whole of the 8th century it survived as a minor port under the jurisdiction of the Lombard *gastaldo* of Canosa, its economy based upon fishing, some commerce and salt extraction. Only at the end of that century do an increased population and greater prosperity appear to have enabled Bari to become an independent territory. Then, in 849, the Lombard south was divided into the twin principalities of Benevento and Salerno. In the absence of a central power with effective control over the whole territory, a Muslim mercenary in the service of Prince Adelchis I of Benevento (839–51) was able to carve out for himself an autonomous emirate at Bari – as we have seen in the chapter on Palermo. This emirate lasted from 847–71, its permanence marked by the construction of a mosque on the site of the cathedral, and was only suppressed when the Byzantines returned to Apulia in force as part of the strategy of the Emperor Basil I (867–86). Yet even in the midst of these turmoils a certain ambiguity of point of view existed in Bari, as though the city could not bring itself to look exclusively landward. Links with the east were never severed. During the 8th century, when Bari was ruled by the *gastaldo* of Canosa, a family thought to have come from Constantinople built a church called S. Nicolo dei Greci which was presided over by Greek monks according to the Orthodox ritual. It was also during this period of Lombard rule that the emigration of refugees from the iconoclasm of Leo III (717–41) occurred, causing an influx of new Greek blood and ideas to southern Italy. Even though Lombards or Muslims ruled their city, the people and culture of Bari looked towards the East.

This may indeed by reflected in the unusual circumstances of the restoration of Byzantine rule – and thus of direct Greek influence. For the return was occasioned by an *invitation* to occupy the city issued in 876 to the Byzantine *strategus* of Otranto, Gregorius. The immediate scope of the invitation was to guarantee protection against the endemic insecurity of the time, which fostered constant harassment by Muslims, Lombards, and even Franks. But the fact that the elders of Bari looked East for their ultimate security is interesting. When Gregorius granted their request, the *gastaldo* and some of the elders were sent to Constantinople as hostages; Bari became the capital of the theme of Langobardia, which then included all the Byzantine possessions in Italy. Apart from a hiccup 12 years later, when Lombard rule returned briefly in what the Byzantine chroniclers perceived as a 'rebellion', Byzantine domination was this time to last continuously until the Norman conquest in 1071. Moreover it was carried out with the intention, made explicit by Basil's son Leo VI (Emperor 886–912) in his collection of military observations known as the *Tactica*, of Hellenizing the conquered peoples. But in a sense this policy, though warlike and imposed from Constantinople, may be viewed as a return to the norm; certainly it was a policy which renewed and strengthened the commercial and social life of Bari rather than disrupting it.

For in many ways Constantinople was as 'western' as Bari, and in this sense Bari itself represents the same ambiguities and paradoxes of Byzantium. This is why Bari could desire Byzantine rule, even though it later rebelled against it. Constantinople was founded as heir to Rome, and even the later emperors of Greek origin called themselves Romans and referred to their capital as the new Rome. Moreover, they acted as a bulwark against the East and North-East in being the persistent enemies of Persians, Turks, Arabs, Slavs and Russians; at the same time of course, and this is the paradox, their culture acted as a filter for Persian, Arabic, Syrian and Armenian influences into the West. Their perception of their role was one of *preservation* of ancient values. Thus the legal and administrative structures of the late Roman Empire achieved a continuity in Byzantium, and in this the fundamental mentality of the eastern emperors remained western. From the time of the Emperor Justinian I (527–65), whose attempt to reconquer the west provoked the Gothic Wars, the rulers of Byzantium saw the recovery of Italy – and ideally of the entire western empire – as one of their first duties.

In Bari the process of re-colonization was neither simple nor quick. For the Byzantines had lost ground in Italy since the fall of Ravenna and the exarchate; their power-broking role in northern and central Italy had been assumed – as we have seen in the case of Pavia – first by the enlarged Lombard kingdom and almost immediately afterwards by Pippin the Short, Charlemagne and their Carolingian successors. Apart from its immediate success in gaining the promise of land for a papal state, the visit made by Pope Stephen II to Pippin in 753–4 marked a definitive shift of papal vision from East to North. Less than half a century later, the Treaty of Aquisgrana of 802 assigned northern Italy and Istria to the Franks, and Venice, Sicily, Calabria and Naples to the Byzantines. As a result of this division Bari found itself in an ambiguous situation: within the Byzantine theme, but within easy striking distance of the southern Lombard capital.

The principal route from the East to Rome via Bari passed *through* the Lombard principality of Benevento. It was for this reason that in the brief period between the fall of the Muslim emirate to the definitive re-establishment of Byzantine rule, from 871 to 888, Bari changed hands with dizzying frequency. This small and relatively unimportant city became a microcosm of the 'theatre' in Gibbon's observation that in the period from 840 to 1017 'the three great nations of the world, the Greeks, the Saracens, and the Franks, encountered each other on the theatre of Italy'.

In those 17 years Bari was attacked by Constantinople's most celebrated admiral, Niceta Orifa, who was sent by Emperor Basil I; besieged by the Carolingian Emperor Louis II (840–75); became a pawn in marriage negotiations between Basil and Louis concerning the former's son and the latter's daughter; was taken by the combined Frankish-Lombard troops led by Prince Adelchis and the Emperor Louis in person – arousing the ire of Basil; was involved in a curious episode when Louis was taken captive by Adelchis (the first time an emperor had been held prisoner, creating a European scandal); was attacked by new Muslim forces; returned to Lombard rule and was governed by a *gastaldo*; and then, finally, reconquered by the Byzantines. The turmoil was not quite over: Prince Aio of Benevento, Adelchis' successor, briefly reconquered Bari for the Lombards, but he was soon expelled by an army sent by Emperor Leo VI 'The Philosopher' (886–912) to curb what the powers in the East perceived as a rebellion. At last in 888 Bari began a period of relative peace which was to last until 1071. The Byzantines had reconquered what the historian Michael Psellus (1018–96) was later to refer to in his *Chronographia* as 'the noblest part of our empire'.

Now Bari became the capital of Byzantine Italy. Up to that time Byzantine rule in southern Italy was exercised over what was known as the *theme* – or province – of Sicily, founded between 692 and 695 with its capital at Syracuse. This original theme had been subdivided for administrative purposes into the duchies of Calabria, Otranto, Naples, and Campania. This system had been introduced by the Emperor Heraclius I (610–41), who divided his empire into 29 themes, and it constituted an important shift from previous practice based on Roman administration. Whereas the empire had previously been governed by a twin system of military and civilian governors, the parallel districts were now merged into a single theme ruled over by a *strategus* with both military and civilian powers. The *strategus* was nominated directly as a personal imperial representative, and answered exclusively to the Emperor. To avoid the possibility of corruption the *strategus* was forbidden to own property within his theme, to engage in any commercial activity, and to loan money for interest. Similar considerations were perhaps behind the short duration of these commands, and of those of the later catapans: according to one count there were 33 *strategi* in the theme of Langobardia from 875 to 975, and 28 Catapans in the century of the catapanate from 975 to 1071. In the 9th and 10th centuries the *strategus* was generally accorded the honorary title of 'patrician', and presided over an *officium* with two distinct branches, the civilian and the military. The civilian branch had as its chief administrative officers a judge, protonotary, and keeper of the cartulary; beneath these were the soldier-peasants, who were assigned land in exchange for military duties and were therefore the real colonists. For military administration the theme was subdivided into *turme*, each ruled over by officers known as *turmachi*; the *turme* was further subdivided into *drungoi*, each commanded by a *drongaro*.

The theme of Sicily had been the base of Byzantine power in southern Italy for nearly 200 years. But the Muslim conquests in Sicily, including the subjugation of Syracuse itself in 878 and then the last Byzantine possession on the island at Taormina in 902, necessitated a drastic reorganization. The position of Bari, further north on the Adriatic coast with a good harbour, closer to the Greek world and safely distanced from the centre of Muslim power in Palermo, recommended itself. Furthermore, the Byzantines were at that time engaged in an advance into the Slav lands across the Adriatic: control of both coastlines and a strong military base on the Italian coast were clearly desirable. It was for this reason that the new theme of Langobardia was established, initially with its capital at Benevento (from 892 to 894) and then in Bari when the *Strategus* Barsakios chose to set his headquarters in a less hostile environment. The move was fortuitous, for shortly afterwards the residual Lombard population rebelled and the Byzantine garrison left behind was completely destroyed.

A clue to the strategic importance of the new theme of Langobardia in the minds of successive emperors may be found in the status of the men sent to govern it. The Gregorius who had been summoned by the elders of Bari had been tutor to the sons of the Emperor Basil, and was therefore a man of considerable status. But the arrival of Nicephorus Phocas as the personal representative of the Emperor Basil marks an escalation, for he was the scion of one of the most powerful families in Constantinople – one of whose descendants was to become emperor, as Nicephorus II Phocas (963–9). The later Catapan Basilius Mesardonites (1010–17), as we shall see, was a member of the imperial family of Argyros. The employment of such men was rendered necessary by the theoretical scope of the immense new theme, for in the eyes of the emperor Langobardia included the Lombard principalities of Benevento, Salerno and Capua, and the duchies of Naples, Amalfi and Gaeta. This meant a territory which reached as far as Montecassino, and almost to Rome. In practice, however, neither the

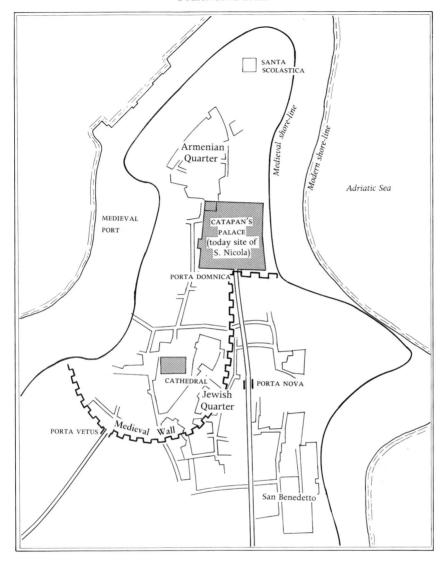

Fig. 6. Sketch map of Bari during Byzantine rule (*c.*1000)

earlier *strategi* nor the catapans exercised effective control over the northern part of the theme.

During the first period of Bari as Byzantine capital, under a series of *strategi* from 894 to 969, we may imagine the city as more of a fortress than a viceregal residence. In fact it was never a large city even in late medieval terms. The promontory itself projects northwards from the mainland for some 750 metres, varying in width from a maximum of about 500 metres to

[113]

a minimum – between the medieval port and the Catapan's residence – of only 200 metres. The medieval walls began well into this promontory, with just two gates: the Porta Nova, which lay on the principal road of the city running due south from the Catapan's residence and on past the monastery of San Benedetto south from the city; and Porta Vetus (sometimes known as Porta Occidentalis) at the south-west corner, leading directly from the cathedral and port area northwards towards Bitonto and Canosa. The urban development fell into two distinct areas, separated by a north-south line just to the west of Porta Nova: to the east the court of the Catapan, with its official residences and presumably other private buildings belonging to court officials, the court, and the monastic complexes of San Benedetto and Santa Scolastica; to the west the medieval port surrounded by a ring of small churches, the cathedral, commercial quarters and the two communities of Jews and Armenians. All this was contained in a small area, for the distance as the crow flies from the site of Porta Nova to the furthest point of the promontory is no more than 500 metres. The city was protected by the sea on three sides, and only a relatively short wall was needed to landward to complete its defences; in fact the site is reminiscent of that of the impregnable Templar fortress of 'Atlit, or Castle Pilgrim, on a similar promontory between Jaffa and Haifa. Bari was equally impregnable to an enemy without a fleet, while the Byzantine fleet would be strong enough to guarantee supplies and fresh troops to the fortress in the case of a siege laid by a land army. At the same time, however, even a strong fleet would need an army to attack the city successfully. In the *Life* of the Emperor Basil I, who was responsible for the successful policy of annexing Apulia in the 9th century, this fact is emphasized: the author observes that during the attack on Bari ordered by Basil 'there were not sufficient forces to combat the large number of barbarians, especially because it was necessary to engage in battle on the plains and move inland from the sea, which seemed both dangerous and impossible for a maritime army.' There were few rulers or invaders in southern Italy who possessed both a powerful fleet and an army strong enough to besiege such a fortress, so Bari was a precious site. Later the Normans were to demonstrate brilliant use of such a double weapon when they took the promontory by completely encircling it by sea and land; the nearest ships were linked to the land by wooden bridges, enforcing their grip on the city. But such power and strategic skill was not to be employed against Bari for several centuries yet.

In the three decades of peace which followed the establishment of the capital at Bari there is little evidence of changes to the physical fabric of Bari. It is likely that the *strategus* at this time erected an official residence on the future site of the Catapan's *asty*, perhaps even on the site of an earlier structure built by the Muslim emirs. New churches of the Greek rite were constructed, such as S. Eustrazio, S. Sofia, S. Basilio and S. Gregorio, around the courtyards which later became those of the *asty*. The last-named still exists today, though little of the Byzantine structure survives intact; it was probably on the Greek cross plan, with a cupola like the church inside Santa Scolastica. Remains of another church, probably dedicated to S. Apollinare like the more famous basilica in Ravenna, were discovered during archaeological excavations in the castle, and it seems likely that the church later known as S. Maria del Buon Consiglio was also built in this period. This latter building, now in ruins, has during recent excavations been seen to possess in its main nave a fine early 11th century pavement in small blocks of limestone and marble arranged in decorated forms such as check patterns, scales and flowers – similar to other nearby Byzantine churches of the period; beneath this floor is another, earlier, marble and terracotta floor with geometrical designs, probably dating from the first period of Byzantine domination. Private housing was also on the eastern model. Domestic buildings were grouped around small courtyards some four metres square, with a well and stairs leading up to the habitations above.

The social structure of the city underwent more dramatic change: Byzantine practices such as dating the start of the year from 1 September, as in Constantinople, were introduced. The presence of so many Greek churches, even though the Latin rite was also practised in other city churches, must have exercised considerable fascination over the non-Greek inhabitants – whose integration, moreover, was encouraged by the colonizing policy of the *strategus*. This policy, similar to that of Rome in earlier centuries, led to the employment of local people in the Byzantine administration, and the consequent formation of a local ruling class. One of the means to this end was a generous use of honorific courtly titles, used to attract the local nobility into government and to obtain their loyalty. Thus large landowners from the plains behind Bari, Lombard notables, and wealthy merchants all came to be part of the Byzantine system. Even in the legal sphere a certain flexibility was allowed, and elements of Lombard law co-existed with the newly-introduced Byzantine law. Lombard customs such as the *morgengabe*, when a satisfied bridegroom donated a quarter of his wealth to his bride on the morning after their marriage, existed side by side with Eastern customs. Soldiers were recruited into the army amongst the local people, and the names of some of the military leaders of the middle rank – such as the *turmachi* – show clearly that they were of Lombard origin. Yet the flexibility and adaptability of the Byzantines in Bari also contained the seeds of discontent. While in the case of economic, cultural and religious matters the *strategus* was willing to

[115]

share his power and collaborate with indigenous forces, when it came to the sharing of *political* power it was a different matter. The apparent stability was constantly under threat.

At first the threat was external, with sporadic attempts by the Lombard princes to reconquer Bari, but also raids by such diverse groups as Muslims, Hungarians and Slav pirates – none of which caused any great difficulty. Then, in the years between 928 to 936, there was a general popular uprising in Apulia, sponsored and fuelled by Prince Landulf I of Capua and Prince Guaimarius II of Salerno. The immediate result was the dispatch of Byzantine forces from Constantinople to placate the rebellion. It is likely that these events were the cause of the re-organization of Byzantine administration in this period, when the theme of Calabria was created to absorb the remaining fragments of the old theme of Sicily. If so, then success was short-lived, for ten years later there was a new series of popular protests within the city of Bari. Clearly stronger measures were called for. The next move on the part of the Emperor, at this time Constantine VII Porphyrogenetus (944–59), once more emphasizes the role of Italy in their expansionist policy. For in 955 the general Marian Argyrus arrived with an army large enough to bring the two themes fully under control. He succeeded in placating the revolt in Apulia and led a campaign into Campania and Sicily. The direct imperial nature of his mandate may be seen in the fact that he assumed in his person the double role of *strategus* for both Langobardia and Calabria, a role which he maintained from 955–963; his success, with what ferocious repression we may only guess, was such that there is virtually no information at all from Byzantine Italy during his presence there.

Then in the last year of Marian's mandate, new and much more powerful forces entered the field. On 2 February 963 the Saxon king Otto I was crowned Emperor in Rome, and at once declared his aim to be the recovery of the entire Italian peninsula for his Empire. Otto justified his claim on the basis that his second wife Adelaide was the daughter of the Burgundian King of Italy Rudolf II and Berta of Tuscany: she was therefore both sister-in-law to the present King of Burgundy and an ex-Queen of Italy. This claim created a direct conflict between the Western Emperor, Otto himself, and the Eastern Emperor Nicephorus II Phocas (963–9). Once again, Bari found itself on the frontier, and in 968 – and perhaps again the following year – Otto besieged the city; but like many other potential invaders, his plans were thwarted by his lack of a fleet. His belligerence was tempered by an unexpected event when Nicephorus died, and Otto was able to negotiate peace with his successor John I Tzimisces (969–76). This peace was sealed by the marriage of his son Otto (later Otto II) to the Byzantine princess Theophanu, which took place at Rome in April of 972.

[116]

These events had made it evident to the powers in Constantinople that a more powerful military and administrative organization was necessary. Thus, probably in 969, a new theme was created under the name Lucania, and shortly afterwards the office of Catapan was created to provide the necessary authority over the three themes. The catapanate, equivalent to a viceroyalty, was probably conceived by Nicephorus Phocas but implemented by his successor John I Tzimisces in or around 975. Thenceforth the three *strategi* commanding the three military districts in Italy reported to the Catapan, who was responsible to the Emperor. The headquarters of the theme of Langobardia was at Bari itself; that of *Lucania* at Tursikon, today little more than a village known as Tursi overlooking the valley of the River Agri just inland from the Gulf of Taranto; and that of *Calabria* at Reggio. The new catapanate was soon in vigorous expansion, especially towards the north. In 987, under the Catapan Calociro Delfina it reached as far north as the port of Termoli, now in the Molise Region, and in 1018 the Catapan Basilius Boioannes organized a chain of fortifications across northern Apulia. These included Melfi, Troia, Dragonara, Civitate, Castel Fiorentino, and incorporated an area whose name has preserved Basilius's action; for, in the curious way that word changes often bedevil etymology, from 'catapanato' the Normans seem to have derived the still existing name of 'Capitanata'.

It was in this second period as Byzantine capital, which lasted from 969 to the Norman conquest in 1071, that the physical fabric of Bari was improved to become the worthy seat of an official as important as the Catapan. At the same time the city grew in commercial importance, with increased imports from the East and increased exportation of surplus agricultural produce, in particular of cereals, wine, almonds and figs. Large numbers of rural settlements, known as *choria*, were founded to expand agricultural production. One of the most interesting consequences of this development was the beginning of the large-scale production of olive oil, which remains to this day one of the staples of the local economy. Together with colonization and agricultural improvement the greater security on maritime routes provided by Byzantine domination increased trade both with the East and with ports on the Adriatic. The earliest extant shipping documents concern the transport of oil to the East; others testify to the volume of this trade. One such document of 992 provides a fascinating insight into the element of contingency planning incorporated in Byzantine strategy: in that year the Venetians obtained tax exemptions in the port of Bari in exchange for a promise to ship a Byzantine army from Constantinople in case of need. Given the skill of Venetian negotiators and their power in international commerce, this suggests that the exemptions must have been considerable; it also shows rigid control over the fiscal

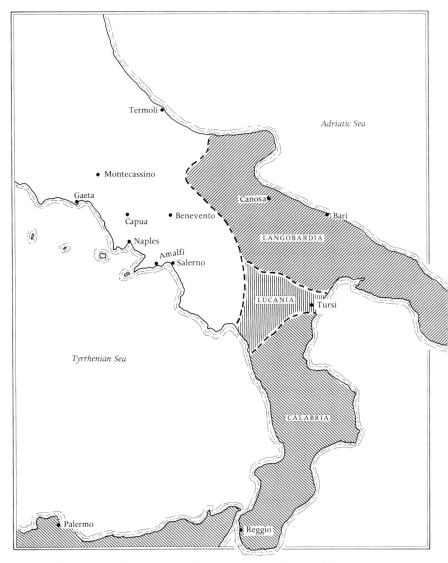

Fig. 7. Sketch map of southern Italy showing the *themes* of the Byzantine catapanate

activities of the port, since goods destined to merchants from Bari are specifically excluded from the agreement. The degree of commercial activity implied by the few surviving documents is sufficient to explain an accelerated population growth towards the end of the 10th century, with distinct communities of Byzantine Greek, Jewish and Armenian merchants occupying quarters near the medieval port.

[118]

The development of the urban fabric also reached its peak in this period. In 1002 a Muslim siege lasting for several months was eventually lifted when a Venetian fleet under the personal command of the Doge Pietro II Orseolo appeared off Bari. In commemoration of this event a church dedicated to the Venetian patron saint St Mark was constructed in the city; a stone statue of a lion, symbolizing Venice, was also erected at this time and is still visible today in Piazza Mercantile. Although the then Catapan Gregory Tarcaniota received the Doge in what is described as a *palatium* after that event, indicating that the official residence was already a building worthy of such a dignity, it was a decade later that this building was re-built and expanded. As we have seen, the *praitorion* or *asty* was the most significant construction of the Byzantine period. A Greek inscription discovered in 1932 and now in the museum of San Nicola allows us to date the rebuilding with some precision, for it states that the Catapan Basilius Mesardonites (1010–17) rebuilt or completed it. In his analysis of the text André Guillou has dated it to 1011. The inscription, engraved in stone and written in iambic verse, reads as follows:

At the cost of great sorrow and with much wisdom the all-powerful Basilius Mesardonites, first among notables, of the imperial race, has built the *asty* with consummate technique restoring it like new, with bricks as hard as stone . . .

He had also built a vestibule to 'free the soldiers of the camp from their fear' – a phrase which provides an insight into the military uncertainty of the period – and a church dedicated to St Demetrios. The fact of the 'bricks as hard as stone' suggests a permanency of purpose which events betrayed, and the use of the word 'restoring' is also interesting as evidence of a pre-existing structure – presumably the residence of earlier *strategi*. Excavations in 1982 and 1984 beneath the area in front of San Nicola in fact showed that older official and also residential buildings – the latter revealed by the presence of objects used for domestic purposes such as pans, vases and fragments of glassware – existed on the site before 1011. Basilius' building plan should be thought of as an expansion of the existing palace, to become the complex of buildings we have seen in the hypothesis at the beginning of this chapter. It was clearly intended to represent the status of the new Catapan, for Basilius was a member of the imperial family of the Argyrus, and perhaps even a brother of the Emperor Romanus III Argyrus (1028–34). It was during this period that population further increased as the result of mass migration from the surrounding country-side. At some time in the first half of the 11th century new city walls were built, certainly by the date of their first mention in 1143. The other ambitious project of the time, illustrating the grandiose ideas of the catapans, was the demolition and reconstruction of the cathedral. Ironically, even this project was to be overshadowed by the Norman construction of San Nicola – which many Italians assume to be the cathedral of Bari even today.

The presence of eastern-made architectonic elements in Bari suggests a degree of prefabrication in Byzantine building there. The direct maritime link between the imperial marble quarries at Proconnesus and colonial outposts such as Bari and Venice, and of course Montecassino, meant that it was relatively easy to transport even such heavy materials as columns. Documents show that marble was in fact transported either in a raw state to be completed by local sculptors, or in a finished state already prepared in Byzantium. The surprising thing is that while some marble slabs were imported incomplete and finished *in situ*, there seems to have been no school of Byzantine artefacts in southern Italy producing work of sufficient quality for official or ecclesiastical buildings of the first rank. Bari, Montecassino and Venice each imported directly from Constantinople. This fact helps to explain the precise affinities between carved slabs in San Nicola and in the Treasury of St Mark's in Venice. Decorative elements for the interiors of the churches and the ceremonial robes of both lay and ecclesiastical authorities, such as cloth, miniatures, icons, ivory, enamelled objects, gold and silver jewellery, were also imported – contemporary examples may be seen in the museum at Montecassino. The marble slabs were employed in porches, doorposts, sarcophagi, and typically Byzantine architectonic features such as the iconostasis, a raised screen rather like a rood-screen on which the icons were placed. An example of imported stone-work was the pulpit for the cathedral commissioned by Bishop Andrea II (1062–78), which can still be seen. Only fragments of paintings have survived, such as the heavily Byzantine wall paintings in an unidentified church excavated in Via Lamberti in Bari. Another painting has been found in the church of S. Martino, even though there is no documentary evidence of the existence of this church before 1104: a representation of Christ with the Virgin and the Archangel Michael shows the brilliant colours preferred by Byzantine fresco painters. Clearer evidence is available in the illumination of manuscripts, such as the fine scene of the Lombard *morgengabe* of 1027 between the blacksmith Mele and the noblewoman Alfarada, of a local family in the Byzantine service, preserved in the archive of the cathedral; or in the scenes of both imperial formal ceremonies and agricultural life in the roll known as *Exultet I* in the same archive.

The link with Montecassino was close, for apart from the Catapan's palace and the new cathedral, two of the most significant buildings in this period were the Benedictine foundations of San Benedetto and Santa Scolastica. In terms of area these monasteries were second only to the *praitorion* itself. The former was founded in 978, just outside the city walls in a position which suggests a desire to control the south-east gate and road south from the city. This hypothesis is strengthened by the fact that the monastery possessed a fortified tower and its own walls. Little is known of the medieval building, since it eventually fell into disuse and in 1745 was largely demolished; the church itself was re-built, and re-dedicated as San Michele. The monastery of San Benedetto stood outside the walls in 987, and a further index of the growth of the city is provided by the fact that by 1071 it was considered *inside* the city. In 1059 it is mentioned as a dependence of Montecassino, suggesting its strategic importance in the expansionist policies of Abbot Desiderius – who became Abbot the previous year. The church of the sister convent of Santa Scolastica, now in ruined condition but on a magnificent site with the sea on two sides, has been dated 1047 during recent archaeological excavations; the monastic complex may well be older. More interestingly, the same excavations have shown that walls and pilasters surviving to about one metre in height must have been part of a church planned on the Greek cross with a cupola surmounting the square base (although the surviving and contemporary church of S. Pietro in Taranto has a flattish, cylinder-like 'dome' on an identical structure). The size and importance of these two monastic complexes, which must have exercised a dominating effect on Bari in the 11th century, illustrate both the extent of urbanization and the influence of Byzantine models on Benedictinism.

Neither were they the only religious foundations of the period. In 1005 the Greek church of S. Giorgio is recorded as having been built by an Armenian cleric, and in 1011 Basilius Mesardonites founded the church of S. Demetrio near the other four which virtually encircled the *praitorion*. The prohibition against private building on the part of the Catapan clearly had an important effect on ecclesiastical patronage in Bari, and perhaps contributed to the apparent dearth of building in the earlier Byzantine period up to 969. This new foundation by Basilius was either an indication of his personal status, or of a relaxation of the prohibition. The latter hypothesis is strengthened by the fact that in 1031 the church of Santa Maria Nuova was built by an official of the court of the Catapan called Teudelmana. Two further monasteries were also built in the mid-11th century, that of S. Nicola *supra portam veterem* and another called S. Giacomo whose site is unknown. Taken together, this quantity of building and urban development – comparable to that of Pavia in the 9th century – is remarkable for such a short period, from 969 to 1071, and on such a restricted site.

But the successful policy of colonization and consequent increase in prosperity germinated the seeds of revolt. This time the threat was internal. The first sign came in May of 1009 when a certain Melo or Meles, a distinguished nobleman of Bari of Lombard origin, led a revolt against the Catapan together with his brother-in-law Datto. This rebellion was the tangible symptom of a growing malaise amongst the citizens of several towns of northern Apulia, who desired greater autonomy. But the ferocity of Melo's rebellion was new: it may be judged by the fact that the Catapan and his Byzantine garrison were forced to flee their newly strengthened fortress just eight years after its completion. Moreover, apart from Bari the rebels also held the nearby towns of Trani and Ascoli. Two years were to pass before Basilius Mesardonites was able to re-occupy his own fortress and Bari after a long siege. Melo and Datto fled into exile; later, Melo's wife Maralda and son were captured and sent to Constantinople as hostages (that the son was named Argiro suggests previous loyalty to Basilius on the part of Melo). But even that was not the end of the rebellion: throughout his six years of exile at Salerno, Capua and Rome, Melo is said to have meditated the means to 'liberate his fatherland' from Byzantine tyranny. He eventually returned at the head of forces provided by Prince Guaimar of Salerno and Pope Benedict VIII, and this time defeated Basilius' army in the field. Were it not for the innate divisiveness of the cities of Apulia, which were unable to present a common front, the history of the succeeding decades would have been quite different; as it was, Melo was himself soon defeated by the troops of the new Catapan Basilius Bioannes (1018–c.1028). At first Melo sought refuge at the court of the Emperor Henry II (1002–24), whose troops had been marauding southern Italy. But then a far more momentous – if semi-legendary – encounter occurred.

The chronicler William of Apulia describes the event in his book *The Deeds of Robert Guiscard*, in which he relates the story of a group of Norman knights returning from the Holy Land. This is the relevant passage, in the translation of Einar Joranson:

> Some of these [Normans] climbed the summit of Monte Gargano, to fulfill a vow they had made to thee, Archangel Michael. When they saw there a certain man dressed in the Greek fashion, whose name was Melo, they marvelled at the exile's strange garb and at the unfamiliar windings of a turban on his bandaged head. As they gazed upon him they inquired who he was and whence he came. He replied that he was a Lombard by birth and a freeborn citizen of Bari, but had been banished from his native soil by the ferocity of the Greeks. As the Gauls commiserated him in his exile he exclaimed: 'I could, if you please, very easily return, provided some of your people would come to our help!'

He averred that with such assistance the expulsion of the Greeks could be effected quickly and easily.

William of Apulia then adds in the next paragraph that:

. . . after they returned to their native land they began to urge their compatriots to go with them to Italy. Apulia was described to them as a land where the soil was fertile and the people were by nature listless . . . and it was promised that a prudent patron would be found under whose leadership victory over the Greeks would be easy.

Even allowing for the obvious political purpose of this story, and the hagiographic nature of William's work, it offers a contemporary view of the arrival of the Normans in Apulia. But the account of William of Apulia is often dismissed as legend, and each historian of Byzantine and Norman Italy in the last century has elaborated his own theory concerning the arrival of the Normans in Italy. The most likely version is that during the pontificate of Benedict VIII (1012–24) a group of Norman knights led by a certain Rodolfus rode to Rome. This knight had, in the words of the chronicler Raoul Glaber 'incurred the displeasure' of their ruler Duke Richard II (996–1026) and 'feared his wrath', and sought the intercession of the pope. Pope Benedict persuaded him that he and his fellow knights might most usefully be employed in the service of the loyal Lombard princes of Benevento, Capua and Salerno against the threat of the Greeks from Constantinople. From Rome these knights then travelled south along the Via Appia to Capua and the court of Pandolfo IV, where on the basis of the papal recommendation they were taken on as part of a military force which was to invade Apulia under the leadership of Melo. They then continued south along the Via Traiana to Bari under his command.

But through the dust-cloud of scholarly disquisition a single fact emerges clearly: a group of Normans arrived in southern Italy in or around 1017, and under the leadership of Melo went into action against the catapanate. Whether they met on the Gargano or at Capua, and whether they came from the Holy Land or Normandy, it is evident that the events in Bari from 1009 to 1017 – and the historical personage of Melo – were instrumental in bringing the Normans into play in Apulia. One of the ironies of the situation is that in accepting Norman aid Pandolfo signed his own death warrant, for the arrival of the Normans signalled the end of centuries of Lombard rule in southern Italy. As we shall see in the chapter on Cefalù, with the next wave of Normans who came to Italy and went into battle under Melo's leadership were the first members of the Hauteville family who were later to defeat the Byzantines and create the Norman Kingdom of Sicily.

[123]

Towards the middle of the 11th century the violent and devastating raids of the Normans, especially those led by the newly-arrived Robert Guiscard, increased in intensity. They pillaged and burned villages and towns throughout the theme of Lucania and the northern part of Calabria, but also closer to the seat of Byzantine power in Langobardia. Unpredictable natural factors also contributed to a general decline, and may even have rendered the cost of Byzantine domination greater than its benefits as perceived from Constantinople. In the spring and summer of the year 1058 a particularly bad drought, again mainly in Lucania and Calabria, almost completely destroyed the agricultural production of the catapanate. The drought was followed by a severe famine and outbreaks of dysentery, with a consequent decimation of both the human and animal populations during the next two years. Since much of the catapanate's importance derived from its agricultural production and the export of vital food supplies to both Constantinople and markets within Italy, we may imagine the effect of such a double catastrophe – something like that of the more famous famine of 1348 in Tuscany. Defeated, demoralized, the *raison d'être* of their colonization in southern Italy undermined by military and economic changes, the Byzantines gradually retreated. Thus, in 1071, with the departure of the last Catapan Stefano Paterano (1069–71) and the arrival in Bari of Robert Guiscard, two centuries of direct Byzantine rule and a millenium and a half of indirect Greek presence came to an end.

One of the most remarkable facts in the medieval history of Bari is that through this almost interminable series of sackings, raids, occupations, rebellions, changes of ruler as dramatic as anything in the north – Greeks, Romans, Lombards, Byzantines, Muslims, Franks – a cultural and civic homogeneity parallel to that in Pavia emerged. Perhaps the simple fact of mutual resistance to so many potential conquerors over such a long period inculcated a common pride or at least an intimate shared feeling which might be equated to the later sentiments of the *populus*, for instance in Cremona. In this context it is noteworthy how the concatenation of attacks over the centuries seems to have stunned the chroniclers into understatement: what would appear, even today, as a quite astonishing series of attacks by such diverse peoples as the Muslims and the Hungarians is for instance laconically dismissed by a chronicler in Benevento writing of the year 904: 'The Hungarians devastated and burned all the towns. And the Saracens in Calabria.' In Bari, the constant stunning and subjugation appear to have fostered a common identity between people forced by the conditions to turn in on themselves. This might explain the early use of the word *cives* or 'citizen' in Bari and other southern cities. A contemporary judge named Andrea, who had studied law at Bologna, made the interesting affirmation that whoever established his residence at Bari immediately became a citizen of the city (*statim barrensis efficitur*). While southern Italy is usually thought to have been well behind the north in this respect, the judge's comment was in fact coeval with the emergence of a similar concept in northern cities like Cremona; the revolt led by Melo against the Byzantines in 1009 and again in 1017 is exactly contemporary with that of the revolt against imperial rule symbolized by the destruction of the *palatium* at Pavia in 1024. Were it not for the establishment of the Norman kingdom, it is likely that Bari and other southern cities – like Naples – would have seen the development of *populus* and *comune* similar to their northern counterparts – and perhaps even earlier. But the Normans perpetuated the "Greatness" of the city.

The legacy of the Greek presence was immense and enduring. In fact its extent and influence in southern Italy as a whole is often overlooked, but Kenneth M. Setton has pointed out that from the pontificate of the Sicilian Greek Agatho (678–81) to that of the Calabrian Greek Zacharias (741–52) almost all of the popes belonged to a predominantly Greek culture (11 out of a total of 13). They included Sicilians, Syrians, a Thracian and one pope from Antioch. Furthermore, in the 7th and 8th centuries there was a triple movement of Greek emigration towards southern Italy: first, that of mainland Greeks during the invasions of Avars and Slavs at the time of Emperor Maurice (582–602) – when the Chronicle of Monemvasia states that the entire 'city of Patras emigrated to the territory of Rhegium in Calabria . . . [and] the Lacones too abandoned their native soil . . . some sailed to the island of Sicily'; second, that of Hellenized Syrians and Egyptians in the 7th century as a consequence of the rise of Islam; and third, of refugees from the iconoclastic oppression of the Byzantine Emperor Leo III and his son Constantine V Copronymus in the period from 725 and 775. This flood of immigrants has been estimated as high as 50,000 Greeks who brought with them the Basilian and Chrysostomine liturgies in addition to their Hellenistic culture. Among the refugees were the painters responsible for such frescoes as those in S. Maria Antiquas inside the Roman Forum, where representations of the eastern martyrs were painted to replace those being destroyed in Constantinople. By the year 800 there were at least a dozen Greek monasteries in Rome, while in the next three centuries something like 200 Greek monasteries were founded in the south of Italy and in the 10th century Greek was the popular idiom spoken in Calabria. The cultural influence of these monasteries was immense, as we have seen in the case of Montecassino, and sometimes unexpected: a Benedictine reformer like John of Gorze, and an early eremitical leader like Bruno of Chartreuse, founder of the Carthusians, were both influenced by experiences in southern Italy – especially the asceticism and manual labour of the Greek monks; from the *Life* of Stephen of Muret, founder of the abbey at Grandmont near Limoges in 1076 (which was soon ceded to the Cistercians), we learn that it was a visit to southern Italy and contact with Basilian monks which inspired him to seek papal permission to found a hermitage where he might imitate them (it also states, probably in error because the dates do not fit, that Stephen visited the shrine of St Nicholas at Bari).

A further indirect Byzantine influence was exercised through donations to the monasteries, both of cash and of other property and works of art. These included several recorded donations by wealthy citizens of Bari to Montecassino and S. Vincenzo al Volturno, and in one interesting case the confiscated goods of a rebel which the Catapan Basilius Mesardonites allocated to Montecassino. One of the most intriguing personalities in this Greek monastic movement was that of St Nilus, a Calabrian monk and ascetic by temperament who knew the works of the Greek fathers. He visited both Montecassino and Rome, exercised an important influence on the Emperor Otto III – whose mother was the Byzantine princess Theophanu given to Otto I's son in the earlier Saxon-Byzantine pact – and eventually founded a Basilian monastery which is still in existence as near to Rome as Grottaferrata. The last Greek episcopal see in southern Italy, at Bova within the medieval Byzantine jurisdiction of Tursi, was Latinized only in 1573.

Bari became a Norman city, referred to by Idisi in his geographical compilation for King Roger II of Sicily as 'a large and well-populated' place, a renowned city of 'Rum' in which ships were built. The principal architectural interest for a visitor today lies in such quintessentially Norman churches as San Nicola. Yet the Greekness shows through, both in the Byzantine fragments of the façade and crypt, and in the presence of St Nicholas himself. For although he is the patron saint of Russia, and the model for a northern invention such as Santa Claus, Nicholas of Myra was a Greek: he was probably born in the Ptolomeic province of Lycia in Asia Minor, and died at Myra (120 kilometres south-west of modern Antalya, in Turkey) in 342. The first church in his honour was in fact built at Constantinople by the Emperor Justinian around 430, and later he became the titular saint of three other churches in the Byzantine capital. It is more than likely that the reverence which led the sailors of Bari to steal his relics – or rescue them from the Muslims – derived from the emphasis placed on his sanctity by their Byzantine rulers. State and Church departed; but the culture remained. It is therefore fitting that San Nicola should stand on the site of the palace of the Catapan, that the area around the basilica should still today be known as the courtyards of the Catapan, and that its fabric should bear direct testimony to the Byzantine past of Bari.

5

# NORMAN CEFALÙ

The epitome of the oddity of Norman rule in Sicily is the representation of Christ Pantacrator (or 'All-Powerful') in the cathedral at Cefalù, once an Arab fishing village and now an Italian seaside resort. The splendour of this mosaic, one of the finest works of art in the whole of Christendom, together with the eccentricity of the cathedral's site symbolize the religious faith of the Norman rulers, the political ambition of their first king, Roger II, and by virtue of its unfinished state the failure to establish the kind of permanent hegemony which he envisaged. The Pantacrator dominates both the apse and the undecorated nave, its fine haloed head, with dramatic eyes and dark curly beard, and the brilliant blue cloak with a golden tunic revealed underneath as Christ raises his right hand in blessing, capture the eye to the detriment of all else as the visitor enters the cathedral (although as this is written a series of 32 brilliantly coloured modern stained-glass windows – equally eye-catching against the bare sandstone clerestory – has just been completed by Michele Canzoneri). Its very dominance has led to hypotheses about the genuineness of Roger's religious sentiment: that he was an unbeliever who wished to exploit the power of the church in establishing temporal dominion, or that he wished to create an overwhelming sense of his own power to hold Sicily in thrall. This most pure and oriental of Byzantine mosaics in Sicily in itself represents an irony, since the Normans were later to adopt a predominantly Arab style in their architecture in order to rival Byzantium.

Seen from the sharply-rising rock behind and above, the cathedral appears to stand over the sea; Lawrence Durrell described it aptly as 'a great whale basking in the blueness'. It is almost as though the Pantacrator were blessing the sea, which lies only 300 metres away on the axis of the nave – and a third of that to the north. For the site of this cathedral is intimately connected to the sea and its perils. In 1129 King Roger II of Sicily was caught in a violent storm while sailing from Naples to Palermo:

Cefalù cathedral: the Christ Pantocrator in the apse

as he prayed for safe delivery from the storm he made a solemn vow to God that he would build a magnificent church wherever he made a landfall. The ship was washed up on the beach under the fortress of Cefalù, in a Muslim fishing village.

The site was recorded by Pliny as *Ceph Loedis*, and to judge by fragments of ancient wall along its northern shore the strategic value of the rock had been recognized even earlier. For centuries it had been an outpost of the Byzantines of the theme of Sicily, who knew it as *Kefalidion*, and it was natural that the newly installed Aghlabid rulers of Palermo should immediately seek to gain such a vital stronghold on the north coast of Sicily. They besieged *G.f.ludi* or *S.f.ludi*, as they called it, in 838; but reinforcements summoned from Constantinople by the garrison forced them to retreat. Some idea of the strength of the fortress on the rock may be adduced from Ibn Athir's comment that 'the Muslims had been besieging Cefalù for some time'. But they did not desist, and the following year captured the fortress – which remained in their hands for the next two centuries. It was an ideal observation post, but improbable site for the construction of an important cathedral. Indeed, the very choice of site – and the nature of its choosing – by Roger II provides a charming insight into the intensely religious character of this exotic monarch, so often

Cefalù cathedral: general view before development of the coast

associated with harems and astrologers. Although he was known as the 'baptized sultan' he was in fact intensely Christian; it is as if he were dominated by this stunning image of Christ, with its huge omniscient eyes and the dramatic strength of personality which dominates the church. The construction of this improbable cathedral, almost literally 'in the desert' and left incomplete by his successors, is itself a token of the sincerity of his faith. If the artistic perfection of works directly commissioned can be an index of the sincerity of intention, then the portrait of King Roger in the church of the Martorana in Palermo enhances this view. There, in mosaics of astonishing beauty and quality, King Roger is shown accepting the divine right to rule: he is portrayed with a full black beard and moustache being crowned by a representation of the Saviour which clearly evokes the Cefalù Pantacrator.

The splendour of the Cefalù and Martorana mosaics is also a testimony to the aesthetic taste of King Roger, who even in the midst of war was capable of enjoying beauty. The chronicler Alexander of Telese relates how the king once quite literally paused during a desperate battle to admire the beauty of the city he was attacking, Alife, and its fine streams. Even allowing for an element of hagiography, the tale might be said to ring true in the light of his personal interest in art and architecture and the high

[129]

quality of the work he sponsored. It is appropriate that the Christ figure at Cefalù is the most purely Byzantine of the many Pantacrators of southern Italy – including that at S. Angelo in Formis. Appropriate, but odd. For the Normans in Sicily never sought to impress upon Sicily their own aesthetic character, as they did in England, but evolved a fascinating hybrid of Byzantine and Islamic styles. The most explicit statement of this blend and the aesthetic tolerance which facilitated it may be seen in the sarcophagus of King Roger II, now in the cathedral at Palermo but originally intended to stand in his own personal monument at Cefalù. Four magnificent telamons supporting this sarcophagus represent the four nations of the Norman Kingdom of Sicily: Latin, Norman, Greek and Arab; and traces of all four cultures can be seen in the cathedrals of Cefalù and Monreale – which from one angle may evoke Durham Cathedral, another St Étienne in Caen, another Haga Sophia at Istanbul, and yet another the al-Azhar mosque in Cairo. The same multiculturalism – to use a modern Canadian term – may be seen in the bible which the Cefalù Pantacrator holds open: for one page is written in Greek and one in Latin, representing the twin tradition of the medieval Church.

Cefalù is earlier than the more elaborate cathedral of Monreale founded by Roger's grandson William II, and more interesting from the point of view of evolution of the Norman cathedrals of southern Italy because it bears more pronounced northern characteristics – both Norman and northern Romanesque. But it was never completed. Building began in 1131 and continued until Roger's death in 1154, by which time the apses, chancel and part of the façade were finished and work had begun on completing the external walls. But when Roger's son William I inherited the kingdom, diminished financial resources imposed changes in the project. It is also likely that William lacked interest in this church so remote from his seat of power, and Cefalù was never to figure again with such importance in Norman times. King Roger had even built a royal residence in the town. Today a tower decorated with contemporary mullioned windows some 200 paces up the appropriately named Corso Ruggero from the cathedral is indicated as the remains of this residence. But one historian has argued more plausibly that this *domus regia*, cited in a document of 1159, was on the site of the present town hall exactly opposite the cathedral. He also noted that even before the cathedral was built Roger founded a church dedicated to St George in Cefalù.

Given William's probable lack of interest and certain lack of funds, it is hardly surprising that even the revised plan was not brought to completion in Norman times. By 1170 the nave and the upper part of the façade were finished, but then work dragged on for centuries: the three-arched atrium was added only in the 15th century. Thus, though

Cefalù cathedral: the original apse, clearly showing changes in the building plan due to diminished resources

spectacular in site and splendid for the apse mosaics (and in spite of the new stained-glass windows), the cathedral remains very much an unfinished masterpiece. Observed from the higher ground behind, the tall apse and transept appear absurdly disproportionate; the unfinished state of the top of the odd south transept – lacking the intersecting blind arcades and the frieze, which would certainly have been added – is in stark contrast to the interior splendour. Apse and transept appear squashed back, with a wholly inadequate nave – rather as St Peter's in Rome would have been had the nave not been stretched from the original Greek cross plan (Roger II founded the Greek church of St Saviour in Messina and followed his father in favouring the numerous Greek monasteries and churches in Sicily). Moreover, the entire nave was destined to be covered in mosaics, which would have changed not only its general character but might have rendered the Pantacrator less dramatic against the overall effect. Missing architectonic features also contribute to the bareness within: for instance in both arms of the transept there is a gallery which clearly should have continued around the choir; similarly, there is a lack of symmetry between the two halves of the transept, since the south arm has cross-vaulting which does not appear in the north arm.

[131]

It is curious to observe that the Arab traveller Ibn Jubayr, who visited Cefalù between December 1184 and January 1185, makes no mention of the cathedral in construction. He describes Cefalù as 'a coastal town, with ample produce from its vines, well-ordered markets' and informs us that a 'community of Muslims lives there'. He also notes the rock, and the fact that on its 'large circular summit is a fortress, than which I have never seen any more formidable'. But he says nothing about the immense building project beneath the rock, which already at that time must have dominated the town.

Although the site of this cathedral may have been dictated by the haphazard of Mediterranean winds and currents, its immense scale was dictated by political exigencies. Just as the stylistic mix reflects a pragmatic desire to include the three indigenous cultures which a new Sicilian ruler could not afford to ignore, so the ambition of the project and its truncated building history accurately reflect the history of Norman Sicily. For it was only one year before the founding of Cefalù that Roger II had been crowned at Palermo as King of Sicily, Calabria and Apulia. This coronation had been carried out by the representative of an 'antipope', Anacletus II, and against the wishes of the legitimate pope, Innocent II; moreover, it was the direct result of Roger's open support for the antipope, which had raised the ire of the supporters of the legitimate pope – including Innocent's ex-abbot and mentor St Bernard of Clairvaux. News of the event reverberated throughout Europe as a new claimant to royal status appeared amongst the long-established monarchies of England, France and Scotland, and the newer but well-established monarchies of Castile, Aragon, Navarre, Sweden, Denmark and Hungary.

Roger needed to imprint the fact of his kingship on the minds of his contemporaries. The magnificence, splendour and craftsmanship of Byzantine art made it the ideal vehicle for this medieval exercise in public relations; it was ready-made, mature, and could be imported with relative ease either in finished form or with the artists themselves. The immense scale of the foundation at Cefalù, which can be seen in the surviving apse and transept, was due to this desire on the part of King Roger to legitimate his role and make a grandiose architectural statement worthy of his newly acquired status.

Roger's family had been in southern Italy for less than a century, and an even shorter time in Sicily. As we have seen, tradition places the arrival of the first Norman knights in southern Italy in the early decades of the 11th century. Their success in obtaining military glory and lands seems to have stimulated a second wave of Norman knights to travel to southern Italy with the intention of permanent emigration. In one of the variants of the early history of the Normans in Italy, the monk and chronicler Amatus of

Montecassino relates how a group of 40 Norman knights returning from pilgrimage had aided the people of Salerno against a Muslim attack; their valour was such that the Salernitans wished to entice more such knights, and to this end sent messengers with gifts to Normandy. Knights in an overcrowded duchy in the cold north were easily convinced by the possibilities and the luxuries of the south. In the words of Amatus, they were enticed by gifts of 'citrus fruit, almonds, gilded nuts, cloth imperial and equestrian trappings adorned with purest gold'; an Old French version of the same legend shows how southern Italy was perceived from Normandy as a 'land that yielded milk and honey'. The second wave of Normans came in search of this land.

For it was as landless men that the Hautevilles arrived in Apulia. Tancred of Hauteville, Roger's grandfather, held a small fief in Hauteville-la-Guichard, on the gently rolling hills which lie south of Coutances and towards the sea on the Cotentin peninsular. The land was quite insufficient to provide a living for his 12 sons. In a 20-year series of emigrations made as the sons came of age and learned of the success of their elder brothers, Tancred's sons transferred to Italy. The first to leave were three sons from Tancred's first marriage, William, Dreux and Humphrey, who arrived in the Norman-held town of Aversa (just south of Capua) in the fourth decade of the 11th century and fought for the Norman knight Rainulf – who had by then held Aversa for 20 years. These brothers must have been remarkable soldiers and loyal men. In less than a decade their standing was such that William, who was known as 'Iron-Arm' after single-handedly defeating a famous Muslim warrior and who Amatus calls 'handsome, kind, and young', succeeded to Rainulf and became Count of Apulia; his brother Humphrey became Count of Lavello. In the next 15 years they consolidated their power, and divided up the conquered territory, Dreux and Humphrey succeeding in turn to William as Count of Apulia. They prepared the ground for the even greater success of the sons of Tancred's second marriage.

The first of these, Robert, later known as Guiscard, seems to have departed after the death of his half-brother William in 1046. He came, according to Amatus of Montecassino, to seek help from his brother Dreux but 'not only did he receive no help from his brother, he was not even given advice'. Forced to earn his own living, in the next 40 years Robert was to become the most feared and ferocious bandit of southern Italy, defeat the papal armies of Leo IX (1049–54) when he descended into Apulia to destroy the Norman robber-barons and took the pope himself prisoner, succeed to Humphrey (in 1057), marry the daughter of the Lombard prince of Salerno, attempt to take Constantinople and become emperor, save Rome and Pope Gregory VII (1073–85) from the Emperor Henry IV, allow his soldiers to burn the papal city – become, in Gibbon's words, at once 'the deliverer and scourge of Rome', fulfil the Norman destiny by eventually capturing Bari from the Byzantines, and finally die in his bed of a fever as Duke of Apulia – once again on his way to attack Constantinople at the age of 70. In 1059 Pope Nicholas II had invested him with the duchies of Apulia, Calabria and Sicily (the last as yet unconquered) after cancelling the excommunication imposed after the burning of Rome. This investiture had unexpected consequences: the pope's intention was not to concede real power over those territories to such a notorious brigand, but rather to extend his own control and unite 'indigenous' forces against the imperial threat of the German Emperor Henry IV (in the context of this book it is interesting to note that Robert swore in his investiture oath to pay the tribute to the pope of 12 *denari* for each pair of oxen on his land in '*money coined at Pavia*'). The fact that within the remaining 25 years of his life Robert came to exert real control over those duchies – together with his younger brother Roger – is a measure of his character.

The achievement of Robert Guiscard was never well regarded by northern historians. Otto of Freising, for example, perceiving the conquest from the point of view of the Swabian court, claimed that Robert 'by valour, deceit, and cleverness became victor over an unwarlike people and finally found himself in possession of Campania, Apulia, Calabria and Sicily'. It is also true that Robert left no tangible monument to his power in Italy: he was remembered above all as a brigand and tyrant, and as the man who burned Rome. Yet there was one monument to his patronage, interesting for two reasons: first, because it provides an exceptional instance of interreaction between the two apparently disparate directions of Norman conquest in the 11th century; second, because it suggests a source of inspiration for Roger II's cathedral at Cefalù.

The twin towers of Cefalù are often compared to those of the church of St Étienne in Caen, founded as part of the Abbaye aux Hommes by William the Conqueror, with two slender square towers of the same date as Cefalù; another frequent comparison is made with the towers of the now-ruined abbey of Jumièges, on the Seine downstream from Rouen (and consecrated in the presence of William), with similar towers rising to about 40 metres in height from a square base to an octagonal top. But a more pertinent comparison may be made with the cathedral of Coutances, within whose diocese Hauteville stood. It was founded by Geoffroy de Montbray, a prelate-knight who was later one of William the Conqueror's supporters, and its nave was consecrated in 1056. But De Montbray lacked sufficient funds for the completion of his church, and made an appeal to the sons of Tancred de Hauteville. Robert, who was made Duke of Apulia and Calabria three years after the consecration of the cathedral and thus

Cefalù cathedral: the façade

possessed the means to satisfy the request, financed the building of the chancel and transept and above all of the original twin octagonal towers. This generosity towards his home diocese may not however have been immediate in execution, and there is an intriguing possibility that the enormous spoils derived from the capture and sack of Muslim Palermo in 1072 financed the cathedral at Coutances. We know from the chroniclers that in that year he made many other such donations, including doors and columns for the cathedral at Troia, in Apulia, and gifts to Montecassino including 600 golden byzantines, 2,000 Arab *tari*, and a large oriental carpet.

It would be fascinating to know whether Robert Guiscard's generosity towards Coutances was inspired by his father Tancred, and to have more information about the relationship between Guiscard and a man like Geoffroy de Montbray. The twin towers financed by him were re-built in the 13th century in their present massive form, at the same time as the spectacular lantern, after a fire destroyed much of the town in 1218. But the fact of his patronage offers rare evidence of contact between the northern and southern ramifications of the Norman adventurers. It also suggests a more intriguing hypothesis concerning the twin towers of Cefalù: that although Roger II was considered a 'baptized sultan' and enjoyed the luxury of the Arab buildings and gardens he inherited with

[135]

his new kingdom, it was to the model of his home cathedral that his mind turned when the time came to fulfil his vow to God.

The king's father, Roger, later known as the great count, had probably left Normandy aged 25 in the year after the consecration of the cathedral at Coutances. In the same year Duke Humphrey died and was succeeded as Duke of Apulia by Robert Guiscard. This was of little immediate help to Roger, who as the youngest son of Tancred's second marriage was 16 years younger and barely knew his brother. But he soon demonstrated that he was made of similar stuff: sent ignominiously to the extreme south by Robert, he soon proved himself a warrior of such value and such a thorn in his elder brother's side that in order to avoid open rebellion Robert was forced to concede half of Calabria to him in 1062. This was the beginning of the conquests which led to the kingdom of Sicily, for with his ambition fuelled by success Roger at once embarked on the campaign to add Sicily to the Apulian lands. The campaign was long and conducted against what might appear at first sight incredible numerical odds, with 300 Norman knights pitched against the entire Arab population of Sicily. One historian has been led by these elements to describe the conquest of Sicily as 'a dress-rehearsal for the crusades'. Eventually internal jealousies and bitter rivalry between local Muslim rulers created a breach into which Roger was able to march, and enabled him to take the island in much less time than it had taken the Arabs themselves two centuries earlier. The bitterest rivalry of all, as the chronicler Ibn Athir relates, was between Ibn at-Tîmnâh, ruler of Catania and Syracuse, and his brother-in-law Ibn al-Hāwwās, ruler of Girgenti and Castrogiovanni (modern Agrigento and Enna). One day, in a drunken fury, Ibn at-Tîmnâh apparently ordered that the veins of his wife – who had argued with him – be cut and that she be left to die. Rescued by her son, she was taken to her brother Ibn al-Hāwwās at Castrogiovanni. Then the repentant Ibn at-Tîmnâh attempted to retrieve his wife by diplomatic means; but this attempt failed. Next he launched an attack against the fortress of his brother-in-law, but his army was defeated and chased back to Catania.

Ibn at-Tîmnâh's last desperate resort was to appeal to Count Roger, offering him the island in exchange for military support against his brother-in-law. In the chronicler's picturesque dialogue:

> Ibn Tîmnâh went to [Roger the Frank] and said to him: 'I will make you lord of the island.'
>
> 'Why, when there are such large forces on it that we cannot match them?' Roger asked.
>
> 'They are divided, and the majority obey my orders,' Ibn at-Tîmnâh replied, 'and they will do as I command them.'

Together these strangely-assorted allies besieged and took Castrogiovanni and other castles, and many Muslim residents of Sicily went into a voluntary exile which marked the beginning of the end for Arab domination. Thus a family squabble made the conquest of Sicily a relatively easy task, both by providing a breach in Muslim forces and in providing in the person of Ibn at-Tîmnāh a guide with expert knowledge of the island. Within a decade of the concession of Calabria, and only 15 years since his arrival in Italy, Roger took Palermo in 1072. He was granted the title of Count of Sicily by his brother, together with possession of the entire island with the exception of Palermo and half of Messina. Yet such possession was in name rather than in fact, and two decades were to pass before he finally achieved total control of Sicily. Then, in the decade between this success in 1091 and the end of the 11th century, Count Roger laid the basis for future Norman rule of Sicily. One of the most significant events was the birth of his son Roger in 1095 by his third wife Adelaide, after previous wives had given birth to a series of daughters (the fact that his first wife had come from Evreux, south of Rouen, and the second from Mortain, only 30 miles south-east of Tancred's lands, suggests ties with the homeland which make the Coutances-Cefalù hypothesis plausible).

Once he had established his capital at Palermo, Count Roger was the first of the family to use Muslim warriors for his army, to develop a policy of mutual toleration, and to indulge in such eastern practices as keeping astrologers and philosophers at his court. He wisely drew on the skills of local men, whatever their race or creed, demanding in exchange total loyalty to his person rather than to an abstract faith. This political tolerance – inspired more by common sense than by theory – led to the formation of an extraordinary cultural melting-pot. While during the following century the rulers, high officials, bishops and friars were mainly of Norman French origin, there were communities of indigenous Latins, Byzantine Greeks, Jews, and both Berber Muslims and other Muslims native to Sicily. Alongside these major national and cultural groups there were trading communities from Amalfi, Genoa, Florence, Pisa, and also a number of Lombards from southern Italy; these maintained the use of their own dialects, and their importance often led to *de facto* upgrading from the loose structure of merchant communities to the independent social and financial status of colonies. Thus, to take one instance from many, there was a Genoese colony in the inland city of Caltagirone, where still today street names betray the existence of the medieval presence and traces of Genoese remain in the local dialect. At the same time Count Roger operated a kind of re-conversion to Christianity, establishing bishoprics, encouraging new monastic settlements and building churches throughout the island. Most of Roger's life was in fact devoted to the conquest and

[137]

settlement of Sicily, yet at his death the Hauteville hold on the island was still not secure enough to guarantee its future.

The deaths of Robert Guiscard in 1085 and his brother Roger in 1101 left the Norman holdings in southern Italy divided into three states: the duchy of Apulia, the county of Sicily and Calabria, and the principality of Capua. The absence of such powerful personalities had as a consequence the disintegration of the network of alliances and submissions on which these states depended. The infant Roger was brought up under the regency of his mother Adelaide, during which the coherence of the states was constantly at risk. It was only on achieving his majority in 1113, when his mother left Sicily to marry King Baldwin of Jerusalem, that he could fully devote his attention to strengthening and enlarging the county. From the beginning his plans were ambitious, including a disastrous expedition against the Muslims at al-Māhdiyāh, (modern Mahdia, on the east coast of Tunisia between Sousse and Sfax). But the situation was perhaps worse than that his father had found, for cities and barons had managed to gain a certain autonomy during the disintegration of the Sicilian state and Apulia suffered the consequences of disputes between the heirs of Robert Guiscard. It must have seemed an impossible task. But then, when Duke William, the last male heir of Guiscard, died in 1127, Roger took what he claimed as his heritage in Apulia with the help of a powerful army. It was there that his decisive character came to light: contemporary chroniclers reveal him as a careful and thoughtful man who examined every possible aspect of a problem before making his move; but once his mind was made up, his actions were characterized by an astonishing ruthlessness and cruelty which made him a byword for tyranny. Yet his cruel disposition was matched with a desire for peace and just government – although such features as the use of his Muslim mercenaries against Christian forces in Apulia was hardly likely to increase esteem for him in his enemies. Opposed in his intention to unite the Norman lands by Pope Honorius II, who feared a great power in southern Italy and gained the support of the rebel barons of Apulia, Count Roger returned to Sicily; but in the spring of the following year he came back, defeated a papal army, forced the rebels into submission, and in the words of Alexander of Telese 'ordered the grandees of Apulia to present themselves to him' at Melfi and swear an oath of loyalty. From that moment the three states were destined to become a single kingdom. Thus salvation from shipwreck and possible drowning the next year must have appeared to Roger a sign of destiny while he prepared for the final step in the process of consolidation of the new kingdom, his coronation in 1130 (a hint of this sense of destiny can be seen in the mosaic portrait of King Roger receiving his crown from Christ in the church of the Martorana). It may also be assumed that the foundation of a huge cathedral like Cefalù, the first great Norman building in Sicily, had equal importance in the new king's mind. Coronation and foundation together represented the acme of Norman achievement after a century of presence in southern Italy, a new power which is symbolically represented by the solemn authority of the Pantacrator.

King Roger was described by the chronicler Archbishop Romuald of Salerno as tall, stout, with a leonine face and loud, harsh voice. Together with the dark beard and moustache of the Martorana portrait these details enable us to obtain a better physical description than that of many contemporaries. As far as his character was concerned, he seems to have been dominated by piety, sincerity and extraordinary energy. In a famous observation Idrîsi states that 'Roger accomplished more while asleep than other men in their waking hours'. He was also a great lover of hunting, like his grandson Frederick II, as we can see in a perfectly preserved room of his private quarters in the Palazzo Reale in Palermo. This small and charming room has a high vaulted ceiling decorated with fine mosaics of hunting scenes, with plants, birds and exotic animals. A contemporary chronicle provides an additional insight into his private character, telling us how he was deeply affected by the death of his wife Elvira, and saddened by the loss of three sons during his lifetime, traits which would appear to contradict the traditional image – perpetuated by such descriptions as Otto of Freising's of the king's 'tyrannical frenzy' – of outright tyrant and autocrat. In this context it must be remembered that he was the enlightened patron of letters, science, maths and geography, and enjoyed the presence of learned men – mainly Muslims.

He held the Muslims in great honour, and was always ready to defend them. Moreover, apart from his interest in the Arabic sciences he was ready to introduce features of Muslim rule into his own government. Although an Englishman named Robert of Selby was head of Roger's chancery for most of his reign, and Greeks also held important offices, there seems to have been a preponderance of Muslim practices and officials. Ibn Athir states explicitly that 'he followed Muslim customs', and instituted such offices as *gānib* (field adjutant), *hāgib* (chamberlain), *sîlahi* (equerry), *gandār* (bodyguard) and others which were not in use among the Franks. Even more interestingly, and 'modern' in terms of western government, he introduced a *Diwān 'al mazalîm* or prototype ombudsman's court where his subjects could present complaints concerning abuses of power by royal officials. Yet it is also true that the brothers Robert Guiscard and Roger 'the Great Count' had maintained Muslim usages from the beginning: we learn from the verse chronicle of William of Apulia that when Robert first subdued Palermo he left behind a knight who was to rule with the local title of 'ammiratus' or emir. This Muslim title continued to be used for the city governor throughout the period of Norman domination. Duke Robert's action was the first sign of a sensible attitude towards the local population and its customs which evolved into a policy of toleration and enabled Palermo to become one of the centres of contemporary Arab culture.

The most important of the Muslim scholars at King Roger's court was al-Idrîsi (1100–66), a Hispano-Arab born in Ceuta who had studied in Cordova and was considered the most distinguished geographer of the period. His treatise on world geography, the *Nuzhat al-Mushtāq fi Ikhtirāq al-Āfaq*, is usually known in more colloquial fashion as the *Kitāb Rujār* or 'Roger's Book' and stands as perhaps the greatest monument to the Norman king's reign. Its stimulus derived from Roger's desire to have a precise account of the lands within his realm – possibly inspired by the slightly earlier Domesday Book of William the Conqueror. But in the hands of al-Idrîsi the book became much more than that. The full title means 'the recreation of him who yearns to traverse the lands', and the book consists of an up-to-date compendium of geographical knowledge derived both from classical and Arab geographers and from data based upon the reports of observers sent throughout the known world to gather information. He brought Ptolemy's geographical work up to date and also used the writings of important predecessors then unknown in the west, such as the 10th century Arab geographer al-Mas'ūdi (who was known as the Herodotus of Arab geographers). Al-Idrîsi's work became one of the best-known of medieval geographical treatises: it was printed in summarized form in Rome in 1592, and in a complete Latin translation in Paris in 1615. It is still today a fascinating source of information about medieval Sicily and Italy. Al-Idrîsi also made for Roger a silver celestial sphere, and a disc-shaped map of the world.

Close links were also maintained with the Kingdom of Jerusalem during the early part of the reign. As we have seen, the infant Roger had 'ruled' under the regency of his mother Countess Adelaide until she married King Baldwin I of Jerusalem. This alliance – for it was a match of money and power – included the condition that Roger would inherit the crown of Jerusalem if no son was born to the childless Baldwin from his new marriage. The accounts of chroniclers of Jerusalem such as Albert of Aix and William of Tyre supply vivid descriptions of Adelaide's arrival at Acre: she reposed on a carpet of gold thread on a galley gilded with gold and silver, with seven further ships carrying her personal treasure. This suggests the enormous wealth of Sicily as Roger took power, but unfortunately for Adelaide her new husband used her money to pay his debts. Within four years, he annulled the marriage to her and sent her back to Sicily. In memory of his mother's humiliation, Roger II remained hostile to the crusader kingdoms for the rest of his life; while this hostility may have hindered the crusading cause, it allowed Roger to devote his entire energy to the Kingdom of Sicily, rather than dissipate it on hopeless crusades like many of his contemporaries.

The most tangible evidence of this may be seen in his architectural legacy. The Normans had been building in Sicily at least since the construction around 1091 of the abbey church of Catania (later the cathedral), that of the cathedral of Mazara del Vallo completed two years later, and the Basilian monastic churches endowed by Count Roger I at Santa Maria in Mili S. Pietro and San Pietro in Itala. Both these latter churches have small hemispherical cupolas on cube-shaped drums which point the way towards later incorporation of Islamic features. They also show the first Norman use of the intersecting blind arcading which was probably of Arabic origin, similar to that of the Puerto del Sol in Toledo, and soon became a regular feature of Norman architecture (as in the contemporary Norman cathedral at Durham). But the most significant Norman buildings in Sicily were commissioned by Roger II. In the same year as the foundation of Cefalù he began the construction of the Palatine Chapel in Palermo. The basis of this beautiful and eclectic building is a three-apsed early Christian nave, to which a strongly Byzantine chancel and cupola have been added; then, as if adding oriental icing to a western cake, the structure was decorated with pointed Arab arches, Byzantine mosaics, and the beautiful white grotto ceiling which compares with those of the Alhambra or the Safavid mosques of Persia. The figures and animal motives from the princely cycle of Islamic tradition find their apotheosis here in the sphinx, griffin, deer, lions and peacocks, or in the representation of a lion slaying a camel on Roger II's coronation mantle in the Kunsthistorisches Museum in Vienna. Together with these Byzantine and Arabic elements, however, are strong iconographic aspects which show how ties with France were never severed even in this exotic climate. For closer examination shows that the saints who are given the place of honour in the scenes from the life of Christ are French: St Martin of Tours and St Denis, figures which would be inconceivable in a pure Byzantine environment like that of Sant'Angelo in Formis. After the tentative start on the churches of the 1090s here is a full-blown Arabo-Norman style of breathtaking originality which stuns the visitor even today. At the same time the little church of San Giovanni degli Eremiti was built, probably, as we have seen, on the site of an earlier mosque whose remains were discovered at the end of the 19th century. This extraordinary building, with its cupolas, the wooden dividing screen to separate men and women during mass, and a cloister reminiscent of Muslim shrines, in fact suggests a converted mosque rather than a purpose-built church.

Contemporary mosaic of the coronation of Roger II by Christ, in the church known as La Martorana in Palermo

Private patronage produced equally exotic buildings. At the peak of his power the fleet of Roger II dominated the Mediterranean, and was commanded by the Greek-born *ammirātus ammirātorum* George of Antioch (in Arabic the title was *amîr al-umāra* – whence our word 'admiral'). He was successful and wealthy enough to found the church named for him as Santa Maria dell'Ammiraglio in 1143. The site he chose was near the later house of a wealthy patrician named Goffredo Martorana, whose wife founded a convent to which Santa Maria was granted in 1433 by King Alfonso V of Aragon; since that time the church has been known as 'La Martorana'. Ibn Jubayr's phrase 'the church of the Antiochan' may be a reflection of earlier usage: he describes it as having walls embellished with gold, slabs of coloured marble inlaid with gold mosaics, and windows with gilded glass which 'bewitch the soul'. The interior which Ibn Jubayr describes with such relish was decorated with mosaics including that of Roger II's coronation; the fragment containing this scene was originally at the west end of the nave, but was moved into the nave along with the other mosaics when the church was stretched onto a Latin cross plan. This lovely fragment emphasizes the sincerity of this strangely Byzantine king, with his slender hands, arched eyes and stylized long nose, and his totally eastern gown and crown. He stares out with quiet confidence, with his left hand palm open towards the benign figure of Christ, a more friendly version than that of the Pantacrator. The shared intimacy stresses the legitimacy of Roger's coronation, as though he is saying: this is how I received my crown, so it is valid in the eyes of God. Indeed, in a curious reversal of roles, it is Roger himself with his intense gaze and black beard who most closely resembles the Pantacrator at Cefalù. At the same time, however, Ernst Kitzinger has pointed out that this physical resemblance is distinctly *un-Byzantine*, for while he wears the clothes of a Byzantine emperor, Roger's image is assimilated to an even higher ideal: the portrait here is what he calls an abbreviated version of the mosaic decoration of the Palatine chapel 'with a western twist', a powerful political manifesto emphasizing the fact that Roger II owed his crown to God rather than earthly powers such as a pope or emperor. The church itself was another curious instance of the cultural blend achieved by the Normans, with its Greek cross, Byzantine mosaics, Islamic cupolas and its strikingly beautiful Norman campanile; today, in a way that is typical of this Sicilian architectural palimpsest, the whole is fronted by a convex Baroque façade added in the 17th century – rendered all the stranger by the neighbouring Islamic structure of San Cataldo, which was built as a synagogue and converted to a church in 1161 during the reign of Roger's son William I. The Islamic influence on the original church of Santa Maria dell'Ammiraglio was such that the much-travelled Ibn Jubayr was moved to call it 'the

The mosque-like church of San Cataldo, Palermo

most wonderful edifice in the world'. Such a degree of influence was only to be surpassed during the reign of Roger's grandson William 'the Good', when Islamic presence at the Norman court reached its peak – and when Ibn Jubayr made his visit to Palermo.

Roger II died in 1154 after more than 40 years on the throne. He was succeeded by his son William (b.1120), known as 'the Bad', who already three years before Roger's death had been 'associated' to the throne in a kind of apprenticeship to ensure a smooth handover. William was a weaker man than his father, supposedly more interested in magic and astrology than in his kingdom. Above all, he seems to have been incapable of maintaining the wealth and solidity of his kingdom against the external threats of two empires, Germany and Byzantium, and the internal threat of barons and emirs against the centralized administration set up by King Roger. His 12-year rule was marked by a series of desperate campaigns to maintain power beyond his kingdom – fighting at various times against Pope Hadrian IV, the German emperor Frederick Barbarossa, and the ruler of Byzantium Manuel I – and to dominate insurrections within Sicily.

This period, almost an interregnum, was followed by the rule of his son William – who succeeded him in 1166 at the age of 13. The young William

II, who soon became known as 'the Good' in contrast to his father, at first reigned under the regency of his mother Margaret of Navarre. He was not a leader in the military tradition of Robert Guiscard or Roger II, and rarely even appeared in public. It is thought that he made no more than two or three brief overland journeys during his reign, preferring the comforts of his palaces and gardens in Palermo. In fact, Ibn Jubayr remarks that 'no Christian king is more given up to the delights of the realm, or more comfort and luxury-loving' – an observation substantiated by the rich robes and crown of his portrait at Monreale. The marriage negotiations of William demonstrate the ease with which this oddball kingdom could vacillate between disparate cultures. After coming within a hair's breath of marrying a daughter of the Emperor Manuel I of Constantinople in 1072, five years later he married Joan, daughter of King Henry II of England and sister to Richard Coeur de Lion. This confirmed an earlier connection with England, since his tutor as a child was the Walter of Offamil who during his reign became Archbishop of Palermo and one of his most intimate counsellors. It was Walter who supervised the construction of the cathedral at Palermo, whose surviving original parts in the east of the building show a more markedly northern inspiration in the high transept, slender towers, blind arcades and intersecting arches – closer to Durham than to Cefalù or the Palatine Chapel. Although there is little evidence, it may be assumed that closer contacts with the Norman kingdom in the north were maintained during William's reign.

William 'the Good's' main achievement was the foundation of the cathedral of Monreale, in 1174, on the mountain slopes overlooking the Conca d'Oro and the royal park, where the monumental style of southern Norman architecture is perfectly blended with a complete series of Byzantine mosaics. Monreale serves as an index of the sincerity of his Christian faith, rather like Cefalù for Roger II. Indeed a further indication may be seen in the contemporary portrait of Thomas Becket – a Norman by birth – in the cathedral at Monreale, added to the mosaics-in-progress when news of the assassination reached Palermo from the pope's summer residence at Anagni (where a representation of the murder was made on an enamel box still in the sacristy which may have served as a model for the mosaic). It is evident that in this case spiritual concern outweighed the political fact that William was son-in-law to the king of England.

As might be expected of a man whose entire life was spent in close contact with Arab civilization, William the Good went even more native than his grandfather. He read and wrote Arabic, and adapted an Arab way of life: he kept Muslim concubines and black Muslim slaves, and a Muslim was supervisor of his kitchens. Ibn Jubayr observes that 'He pays much attention to his (Muslim) physicians and astrologers, and also takes great

[145]

care of them. He will even, when told that a physician or astrologer is passing through his land, order his detainment, and then provide him with means of living so that he will forget his native land.' The traveller concludes with typical fervour: 'May God in His favour preserve the Muslims from this seduction!' On the contrary, it appears that the Christians were seduced, since the Norman women wore coloured veils, used Arab jewellery and perfumes, and even painted their fingers with henna in Arab style. The entire city was imbued with this Islamic spirit, 'a wonderful place, built in the Cordovan style' with gardens, open spaces, rich and magnificent buildings, a city which 'dazzles the eyes with its perfection' according to Ibn Jubayr. Yet we must not be led into believing that William's adoption of local customs entailed conversion or near-conversion to Islam. Arab customs were adopted, but the faith eschewed. On another occasion Ibn Jubayr notes that King William's Muslim servants and eunuch pages 'all, or nearly all, conceal their faith, yet hold firm to the divine law'. Moreover, it appears that such deception was necessary, for in spite of his adoption of Arab ways King William's tolerance was not absolute. The same chronicler mentions in an aside that although there were lots of mosques and Muslims in the market at Palermo none of them met for Friday prayers because it was forbidden.

Reclusiveness did not mean exclusion from the world, since William possessed the means to draw the external world into his own private world. He encouraged scholars just as Roger II had done, and it was in his reign and under his patronage that the works of Euclid, the *Almagest* of Ptolemy, and works of Aristotle were translated from Greek into Latin. In this way the seed was sown for the vital and astonishing scientific achievements in Apulia during the reign of his cousin Frederick II. Fittingly for such a private man, on his death in 1189 William II was buried in his own cathedral in a simple white marble tomb. Thus the direct Norman line ended with the death of Roger II's childless grandson. The last Norman 'king' was the infant William III, grandson to William the Bad via his illegitimate son Tancred, who 'ruled' under the regency of his mother for a few weeks in 1194 until forced to concede the throne to Henry VI. He is thought to have died four years later as a prisoner in Germany, or possibly as a monk. Whatever the case, within half a century of Roger II's death in 1154 the Norman kingdom came to an end, to be replaced by that of the Hohenstaufen and ultimately Frederick II – as we shall see.

As far as Sicily was concerned the Norman legacy was greater than that of Frederick II, since their administrative divisions and economic choices created a Kingdom of Sicily which lasted in one form or another until the unification of Italy in the 19th century. The title 'king of Sicily' was perpetuated by the Anjou and Aragonese rulers of Naples, and the later

[146]

'Kingdom of Two Sicilies' was essentially a Norman survival. Furthermore, it has been argued that Norman administrative and agrarian policies were the prologue to the north-south divide in civil, economic and social development which plagues Italy to this very day. From enormous wealth, Sicily plunged in the 12th century to relative poverty. For during Norman rule the focus of European trade shifted dramatically from the Mediterranean northwards to the Po and the Rhine: while Amalfi and the Sicilian ports had previously monopolized trade in and around the island, during the period of Norman rule Venice and Genoa moved down and usurped the southern ports. At the same time, the invaders from the north imported the social and political framework in which the southern population later elaborated their own distinctive agrarian culture, at the same time transforming the south and fixing it indelibly on the Norman model. Similarly, the 'foreign policy' of Roger II foreshadowed that of later Italy: he annexed Malta to the Kingdom of Sicily, and then attempted to gain a permanent foothold in northern Africa by attacking Tripoli and other cities which then paid tribute to the Sicilian king.

Yet, paradoxically, these permanent effects were the legacy of a family which passed through the island rather like a comet. In fact the pleasure palaces and gold, mosaics and gilded glass which 'bewitch the soul', esplanades and fabulous gardens, all imply a strangeness in Roger II and his grandson William II which is difficult to imagine from the beautiful but austere and cold countryside near Hauteville-la-Guichard. If to the Hautevilles Sicily seemed exotic, to the Sicilians the exotic was represented by Roger II and his grandson William II. This is perhaps why the cultural and scientific achievements of the hybrid court which Roger created at Palermo remained isolated. The blending of Greek, Latin, Muslim and Norman cultural influences symbolized by Roger II's tomb had no permanent impact on Sicily: it was to the north, first in the Apulia of Frederick II and then in the Tuscany of the humanists, that these influences prospered. This same strangeness also provokes the ultimate question concerning the Normans in Sicily, in particular Roger II, and their fundamental identity. Roger was born in Palermo of a family which had left Normandy a century earlier, was raised in Sicily, wore Arab dress, maintained a chiefly Arab army, kept a seraglio, eunuchs and Muslim slaves, and wore a state-dress which consisted of the tiara, mantle and dalmatic of the Greek Basileus in Constantinople. Apart from lingering traces on the exterior of Cefalù there are few northern influences on the art-works he sponsored. This prompts the question: how Norman was King Roger? Or, to expand the terms of the question and re-phrase it, to what extent were the Norman rulers Norman?

The only objective answer can be, not to any great extent. Merging themselves into an alien environment like Sicily – which had already absorbed Phoenicians, classical Greeks, Romans, medieval Byzantine Greeks and Arabs – the Hauteville family engendered a culture that was substantially hybrid and new. But the very nature of this culture meant that it was twice-distanced, both from Normandy and from Sicily (like the expatriate military caste of the Indian sub-continent during the Raj), and therefore necessarily transient. It is for this reason that a cathedral like Cefalù, which reflects the oddity of their being in the uneasy juxtaposition of *raison d'être*, site, fabric, and Pantacrator, may stand as emblem for the century of 'Norman' power in Southern Italy.

# PART II

## Towards new power and wealth
## 1100–1250

# 6

# A MARITIME REPUBLIC: GENOA

G ENOA has suffered more than most medieval Italian cities by the disfiguring of modern urban development and the need to drive roads through a naturally inhospitable environment. Its very site, a narrow strip of flat land around the good natural harbour with a sudden and steep rise to the mountains which block it off from the Italian peninsula, militated against planned growth. There was no broad, flat plain to build a parallel modern city as at Bari, or expand easily on three sides as at Pavia or Cremona. In a profound sense the city has always been closer to the open sea than to the mainland behind the mountains. Genoa's suburbs were at Kaffa in the Crimea, Pera on the Golden Horn at Constantinople, Acre in the Holy Land, or Tunis, Malaga and Lisbon. But however far-flung, these places were always Genoa; the emotional link remained, as we can see in the instruction Columbus inserted into his will to ensure that his heirs would always maintain a home in their city of origin. According to an anonymous 13th century poem known as the *Exposicio de mondo navigandi* it was the *duty* of all Genoese to go to sea, to explore and to engage in trade. An example of the mental set of this land-blocked people may be seen in the poet's reference to inhabitants of the city generally as 'navigators' and the assumption that each individual is essentially a 'merchant, roaming throughout the world'. In the midst of much technical information on sailing and ship's equipment the metaphor of life as a voyage is developed in the poem to provide both moral and spiritual support for the merchant adventurer, to the extent that each individual is 'a mariner who never ceases to voyage' until the end of his life. This poetic assertion was encapsulated in the medieval proverb *Genuensis ergo mercator*, 'a Genoese and therefore a merchant'.

The gently curving arc of the medieval *Ripa Maris* or sea front, which survives in dilapidated form to this day, reflects this equation. Its main feature was the porticato or covered gallery, built in front of existing buildings according to the directions of the *consuls* of the city in 1133–4.

[151]

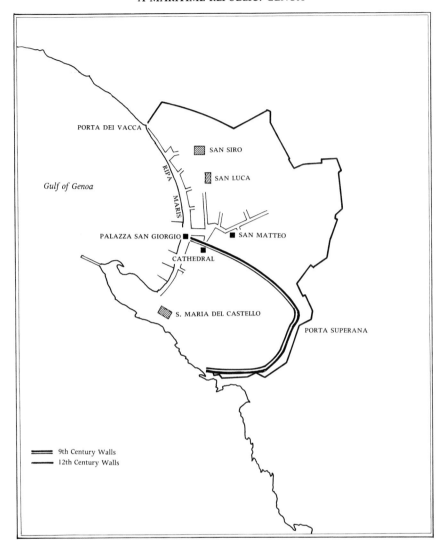

Fig. 8. Sketch map of medieval Genoa (c.1250)

The *ripa* united navigator and merchant in being at the same time a new sea-wall and a commercial infrastructure. The dimensions of the vault and even the materials to be used were specified by the consuls, and created a single gallery which was eventually 900 metres in length. Most interesting of all is the fact that it was a public space conceived from the beginning as a covered market. While private owners of land and buildings behind the ripa were able to build *over* the porticato, the space beneath remained public. Unfortunately, the site of the original moorings of the port is now buried beneath 19th century infilling and a 20th century flyover. But later building and re-building have respected the line of the porticato, which underwent dramatic restoration a century ago; the Genoese architect of the Beaubourg Centre in Paris, Renzo Piano, has recently made a proposal for the recovery of the *ripa maris* and creation of an archaeological museum on the site of the original port.

Behind the *ripa,* narrow streets and alleys – *carugi* in Genoese dialect – lead sharply up and away from the sea into the heart of the old city, intersected by others parallel to the seafront. This network of gloomy *carugi* is often reminiscent of the Arab *souk* which influenced the structure of medieval Genoa and other Mediterranean ports like Palermo and Malaga. Within the network were aristocratic enclaves grouped around a single church and piazza, like private islands amidst the maze of public streets – which were protected from private development by a communal ordinance of 1180. In the *carugi* fighting took place during the frequent tussles for power between these family enclaves, the wooden houses often burning down while the stone towers and palaces of the nobles survived; the rigid matrimonial customs of Genoa made them dangerous places for young noblewomen, since a stolen kiss or touch of the breasts in public meant instant betrothal (so that daughters of the great Genoese families only passed through them under heavy escort). They also constituted a serious fire risk, so that on windy days the *cintraco* or town-crier had to walk through the town warning people to watch their fires carefully; one documented case concerns a fire in 1213 which destroyed 54 buildings in a single day in the area near the money-changers' stalls. The *carugi* opened on to markets which were the lifeblood of the city, such as the market of San Giorgio which stood on the site of the Roman Forum. At the centre of the ripa, and formally completing it, stands the Palazzo San Giorgio, once the customs house and now the headquarters of the Port Authority. Behind it, standing a few paces forward from the porticato in an especially dilapidated section, is the heavily restored surviving structure of the Palazzo del Mare, which was built on this symbolic site by the *Capitano del Popolo* Guglielmo Boccanegra in 1260 as a worthy seat for the government of Genoa.

From the right of the Palazzo del Mare as seen from the sea, the façade of the cathedral of San Lorenzo can just be discerned some 200 paces uphill from the medieval moorings. The impressive façade of horizontal bands of black and white marble, and an unexpectedly large nave opening off the small cathedral square, provide an index of Genoese ambition and pride at the beginning of the 12th century. Near the cathedral is Piazza San Matteo, which stood at the heart of the enclave of the powerful Doria family. The

[153]

A surviving section of the
original *Ripa Maris*

The public passage, once
used as a market, under the
*Ripa Maris*

church, founded in 1125 but with a later façade, is a reduced version of the cathedral, raised above the level of the piazza on a terrace cut into the hillside; this tiny piazza gives a good sense of these family enclaves, hemmed in as it is between Doria palaces of various centuries. Piazza San Matteo stands almost at right angles to the central point of the ripa: to the right from the Palazzo del Mare lies the site of the original fortress of Genoa, marked by the church of S. Maria del Castello and the tower which indicates the enclave of the Embriaci family; to the left is the church and piazza of San Luca, centre of the enclave of the Spinola family, whose palace is now a picture gallery (just beyond San Luca is the totally rebuilt church of San Siro, once the cathedral of Genoa but abandoned as such in the 10th century because it was *outside* the city walls).

Palazzo del Mare, San Luca, San Matteo and S. Maria di Castello formed a trapezoid which encloses the medieval centre of Genoa, whose urban structure is intact while many of the buildings have been re-built or restored. But there is no discernible pattern in their distribution, no single point to which they all refer save the ripa. For medieval Genova possessed no great public piazza like other Italian cities: public life was carried out in diluted form along the ripa, and around the principal markets. There is no single space within the old city where its most important monuments are simultaneously visible – unlike, say, Cremona, where most of the historically important buildings are grouped around a single piazza. Apart from the public porticato-market open to the sea, the medieval centre consisted – and consists – of a network of narrow streets with occasional small squares opening off them. Even the piazza in front of the cathedral, which though relatively small may seem at first sight to meet the requirements of a public meeting-place, was until redevelopment in the 19th century about half its present size. It is a curious paradox that the town hall was only begun in 1291, when Genoa was about to cede its power as a maritime republic to Venice and enter into a period of decline after 200 years of immense power and wealth.

The history of medieval urban expansion in Genoa may be divided into two main periods: first, from the construction of the first set of walls in 864 to the building of the *Ripa Maris* around 1133; and second, from the building of the expanded walls between 1155–63 to the construction of the Palazzo del Mare in 1260. Each of these periods began with the physical expansion of the city to contain the newly growing population, and each concluded with the building of a feature which is characteristic both socially and architecturally of Genoa: the *Ripa Maris* provided an elegant seaward façade to the city which had grown to fill the first set of walls; the Palazzo del Mare was set by Guglielmo Boccanegra into the *Ripa Maris* like a jewel into its setting after the rapid 12th century increase in

The Palazzo San Giorgio, added to the *Ripa Maris* in 1260

the wealth of the city. The latter was an architectonic solution at the same time destructive and conclusive, since it broke the established harmony of a perfect semi-circle and completed the physical shape of the medieval city.

As Roman 'Genua', and later 'Janua', the city had a long history before this medieval growth. Recent archaeological surveys have found evidence of settlement on and near the fortress site dating from as early at the 6th century BC. But little is known of the ancient history beyond a series of dated sackings: around 200 BC Genoa was sacked by the Carthaginian Magone; in 537 AD it was conquered by the Byzantines of the Eastern Empire, who maintained a port there to counterbalance their capital of Ravenna on the opposite coast. Then in 643 Genoa and its coastline became part of the Lombard kingdom of Italy when King Rothari (635–52) added the coast from Luni to Ventimiglia to his realm; under Liutprand (712–44) a *palatium castri* was built on the site of the Roman fortress. Thus the *Maritima Italorum* of the Byzantines became an integral part of the Lombard and later Carolingian *Regnum Italiae*. Charlemagne himself had an ambassador bearing the gift of an elephant from the Caliph at Baghdad shipped from Tunis on Genoese ships – which gives some idea of their capacity. In an important sense, in fact, the history of the maritime power of Genoa began in the 9th century. For it was then that Genoa, under the rule of delegated *vicecomites* chosen from the old feudal aristocracy, became part of the newly formed Carolingian March of Tuscany destined to protect the *litus italicus* or 'Italian coast' from such raiders as the Muslims; from that moment the history of Genoa is better known. It was this new role, with a viscount responsible to the Marquis of Tuscany ruling the city, which led to the building of the first walls in 864. At this time the seat of the cathedral was moved from the 6th century church of San Siro, which found itself outside the city walls, to the recently-built church of San Lorenzo. The walls, in the form of a horseshoe open towards the sea and backing up to the castle hill, enclosed a largely uninhabited area of about 22 hectares and contained four gates. One of these, the Porta Superana, which opened on to the Roman road leading south along the coast, was re-built or replaced in 1155 by the gate known today as the Porta Soprana or Porta Sant'Andrea. This elegant gate bore an inscription which testifies to the immense pride and sense of power of the Genoese in the mid-12th century. Two lines of it read, with a pun on 'bring' and 'gate' which cannot be translated into English:

If you bring peace, you may enter this gate;
If you desire war, you will leave in sadness and defeat.

(*Si pacem portas, licet has tibi tangere portas;/Si bellum queres, tristis victusque recedes*). These lines are particularly appropriate because Genoa itself has often been thought of as a gate. One fanciful etymology derives the medieval Latin name from *ianua*, which means the outer door of a house and is here intended as a 'gateway'. Thus, by an obvious process of analogy, Genoa came in the later middle ages to be represented by the Roman god Janus: one of his faces looking inland, and the other out to sea. The fact that Janus was credited with the invention of money, and that the oldest Roman coins bore an effigy of Janus on one side and the prow of a boat on the other, must have seemed particularly apt in the case of Genoa. But this is not the only etymological explanation: one of the legends about the origin of Genoa concerns a certain Ianos, a Trojan who was credited with the original foundation of the city – clearly parallel to the story of Aeneas and Rome. Yet another etymology derives the name from Greek *xenos*, used in the sense of people who mix with foreigners, as appropriate to Genoa's natural disposition to maritime trade as the previous semi-legendary explanations of the name.

In fact, however, the emergence of Genoa as an important medieval maritime power seems to have derived from defensive considerations. For

[157]

it seems likely that the mariners and coastal peoples of Genoa banded together to defend the city from Arab raiders in the 9th and 10th centuries. In 950 King Berengar II re-organized the frontier marches of his kingdom, dividing ancient Liguria into three sections: the 'Arduinic March', the 'Aleramic March', and the 'Obertengian March', the names deriving from the families responsible for their defence (Roger II's mother Adelaide was a member of the Aleramic family). Genoa was in the last-named, governed by Oberto – later a recurrent name in Genoese history. But Oberto soon shifted his loyalty to the Saxon Emperor Otto I, and in 958 Berengar and his son and joint-ruler Adalbert issued an important diploma to the *cives* or citizens of Genoa which granted them privileges amounting to effective autonomy. Thus in the 10th century Genoa first became a county, and by 1056 was recognized as a semi-independent city ruled over by a bishop named Oberto. But it was still at that time a small city of little importance or power. It is interesting to observe that this origin as a defensive consortium stresses the characteristic quality of Genoese society in the succeeding centuries: the nature of a *collective enterprise between private individuals*.

This element of collective enterprise in turn lies behind the development of the *compagne*, or 'companies' which were the distinctive feature of Genoese politics at this time (and were parallel to the development of the *comune* in other cities like Cremona). Deriving from *cumpanis*, meaning literally 'with bread' and therefore suggesting an intimate relation which also implied free and egalitarian sharing, the compagne were identified with specific areas or quarters of the city. They are thought to have derived from the earlier tripartite division of the city into the *castrum* which was the original fortress, the Carolingian *civitas* within the 9th century city walls, and the area outside the walled city to the north known as the *burgus*. At first these compagne were probably temporary groupings of merchants and mariners who shared the expenses, risks and profits of mercantile commerce. But soon they included everybody whose living was in some way connected with the ships, and were transformed from a kind of aristocratic consortium into popular associations. At the time of the beginning of Caffaro's chronicle, around 1099 as we shall see, there were eight such compagne which together virtually ran the city as the *Compagna Communis*, which was a council of representatives of the compagne elected for a four-year period. The city was divided into eight quarters corresponding to the compagne, each with access to the seafront: within the area of the old city walls at the southern end of the port were the compagne of Castello, Piazzalunga, Maccagnana, San Lorenzo; next were three compagne comprising areas which had been outside the old walls but were enclosed in the 12th century, Porta, Soziglia and Borgo; last of all was

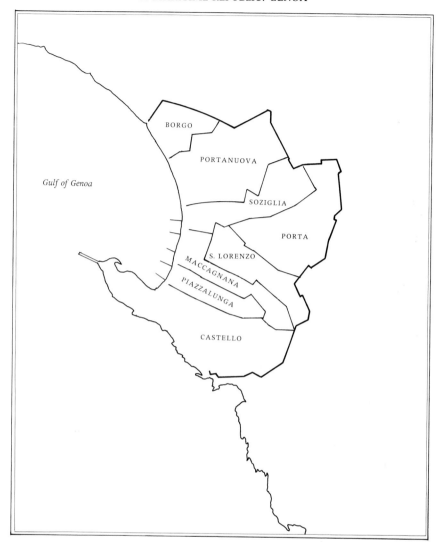

Fig. 9. Sketch map showing the areas of the *compagne* in twelfth-century Genoa

a new sub-division of Borgo called Portanuova, whose name is self-explanatory, at the northern limit of the city. The Borgo terminated at the newly-built – and still existing – *Porta dei Vacca* where the 12th century walls were to reach the seafront at the north-west of Genoa (see Fig.9).

Early medieval Genoa had been a small community gathered within the horseshoe-shaped walls around the castle, the cathedral and the market of San Giorgio, the *castrum* and *civitas* together. The stability provided by

[159]

the government of the *Compagna Communis*, together with the wealth pouring into the city from 1099 onwards as the result of conquest in the Holy Land, made the 9th century walls obsolete. But strong government meant that growth was controlled: the quays and seafront were made public property in two decrees of 1134 and 1139; the *Ripa Maris* was constructed with precise urban limitations on private ownership, as we have seen. Then, between 1155 and 1159 when the city feared the arrival of Frederick Barbarossa, new walls were built to enclose both the old city and three of the extra-mural compagne. Towers and moats were added later. Some idea of the size of these walls may be gained from the surviving sections, and above all from the two gates: the *Porta Soprana* already mentioned, with its heavily restored fine circular towers announcing and dominating the tall but narrow entrance to the city; and the *Porta dei Vacca* also built in 1155. A further index of this rapid growth may be seen in the number of churches built and re-built between the First Crusade in 1099 and the construction of the Palazzo del Mare in 1260. Beginning with the cathedral of San Lorenzo itself, consecrated in 1118, these included Santa Maria di Castello (re-built *c.*1120), Santa Maria delle Vigne (re-built 1103), San Matteo (1125), San Siro (re-built 1141), San Salvatore (1141), San Lazzaro (1150), San Marco (1173), San Luca (1188), and the hospital of San Giovanni di Pre (1180). These churches were built or re-built, decorated and furnished with the proceeds of Genoese successes in the Holy Land, and the same source financed a spate of private buildings. In 1180 the consuls issued an arbitration which forbade building along certain streets within the old city which threatened 'the public air'. This decree, which presumably reflects the fears of the consuls, provides a hint to the extent of private building activity. But the problem was not resolved. For the conflict between private and public interest was later to lead to the disintegration of the power of the *Compagna Communis*, and to internal disorders which undermined the corporate strength of Genoa.

These disorders were a direct consequence of Genoa's medieval expansion, since the feudal families whose power and lineage derived from the Carolingian *vicecomites* were clearly loath to relinquish the power they had attained. The enclaves of these great families had developed parallel to the more popular manifestations of the compagne, and were the result of a Genoese conviction that power and security derived from strong personal relationships: unlike the institutionalized framework of Byzantine practice or the centralized Lombard system, the personal bond of family and a city united by a network of personal relationships, were at the base of both political and commercial relations for the Genoese. The Guercio family, dominated by three brothers, controlled trade between Genoa and the Byzantine East in the second half of the 12th century as

[160]

Piazza San Matteo, heart of
the Doria enclave

Looking outward into the
narrow *carugi* from Piazza
San Matteo

[161]

though it were a private family business – together with the Embriaci, Guaracchi and Doria families. The same pattern followed as new trading posts and colonies were established throughout the Mediterranean. Each family operated in its chosen sphere, and repeated the cohesiveness of business practice in the urban development of the home city. For instance, the Doria family concentrated its ownership around their family church of San Matteo as we have seen, and the Spinola and Grimaldi families near the church of San Luca in the Borgo – although these very powerful families eventually came to own property in several parts of the city, and within different compagne. They built their own defensive towers – often with interconnecting wooden bridges – which guaranteed effective military control over the city in times of uprising. At one time there were as many as 60 such towers, but today only that of the Embriaci survives intact. Grouped around the kernel formed by the main family palace were shops, markets and warehouses, and baths for the use of the clan group and allied families. Kinship and patronage together led to the formation of an entire quarter on the basis of a single aristocratic enclave. Thus within the apparently egalitarian compagne strong islands of ancient feudal privilege survived. In the late 13th century these enclaves gradually substituted the compagne, and the city was divided into family-based areas each known as an *albergo*. In modern Italian this word means 'hotel', but in late medieval Genoa it was used to signify a strong neighbourhood association; members of an albergo were often so strongly associated with the family at its core that they assumed the aristocratic name as their surname.

In the 12th and early 13th century this double system of family enclave and compagne was complementary: family power and enterprise enriched an entire compagna, while the *Compagne Communis* restricted and regulated private building. Moreover, loyalty to the city itself remained paramount. Great families and merchants used their wealth to embellish the city as they embellished their own enclaves with churches and fine palaces, so that Genoa became one of the finest cities in Europe. Al-Idrîsi described it as 'a city of ancient construction, with fine surroundings and imposing buildings. It is rich in fruit, in sown fields, in villages, in farmhouses, and lies near a small river. The city teams with wealthy merchants who travel by land and by sea engaging in tasks both easy and difficult. The Genoese, who have a formidable navy, are experts in the perils of warfare and in the art of government: among all the Latin people they are the ones who enjoy the greatest prestige.'

The description by a Sicilian Arab is pertinent, since the recently acquired prestige of Genoa was directly related to the Arab conquest of Sicily. For the organized maritime power of Genoa was born from the necessity of combating Muslim pirates who periodically harassed the coast. These raids increased in frequency from the conquest of Palermo by the Aghlabids in 831 to the rule of the Almoravides in Spain in the 11th century. The Syrian historian Dhāhābi relates one such raid under his chronicle for the year 934–5, when a fleet of 30 ships was sent from al-Māhdiyah to attack the lands of the Franks. He says that they 'knocked down the walls of Genoa, conquered the city, and captured a thousand women' – who were taken back as booty to al-Māhdiyah. Contemporary Christian sources stress the fact that the *churches* of Genoa were sacked and robbed at this time. In fact, unwittingly, the Muslims were involved in two events which contributed to the wealth and power of Genoa.

The first of these events was the First Crusade. The significance of Genoese participation in the conquest of the Kingdom of Jerusalem cannot be exaggerated, as medieval chronicles of the city make clear. Among the most important of these was the chronicle written by the consul and chronicler Caffaro da Rustico (1080–1166). Caffaro's career began with his departure for the crusade with the Genoese fleet in 1099, and included several spells elected as consul, responsibility for negotiations for mooring rights with Count Raymond III of Barcelona in 1127, command of the fleet which attacked the Spanish moors and took Minorca in 1144, and service as Genoese envoy to both King Alfonso VII of Castille and Frederick Barbarossa. With the direct knowledge acquired from these military, political and diplomatic activities, Caffaro set about compiling and dictating his *Annales Ianvenses* for the years 1099–1163. He also wrote a short volume entitled *De Liberatione Civitatum Orientis* on the liberation of Jerusalem, written with the obvious intent of glorifying the part played by the Genoese. His annals began with the taking of Jerusalem, and the emphasis he places on this event reflects its central role in Genoa's rise to the status of an international military and commercial power.

Like its rivals Pisa and Venice, Genoa initially looked on preparations for the crusade with diffidence. But this faded as commercial opportunity presented itself. Hamstrung by the lack of a strong fleet, the crusaders were forced to seek help from the maritime powers. Ships were provided by the maritime cities in exchange for privileges, commercial concessions, and the promise of entire quarters in the towns of the Holy Land. Thus the first Genoese expedition, a privately financed fleet, departed in the summer of 1097 and participated in the conquest of Antioch – the first foothold. It was rewarded with a quarter consisting of 30 houses, a piazza and a church. Other expeditions soon followed, and the Italian merchant fleets became allies indispensable for the crusading forces (a few years later one fleet dismantled its ships to provide wood for siege engines). The normal conditions for their services came to be one-third of the booty from any city in whose capture they participated, together with a quarter in the bazaar and commercial privileges. In this way much of the potential wealth of the crusader states passed into the hands of the Italian cities. A few examples of Genoese participation will suffice: the conquest of Jerusalem itself was facilitated by the arrival of Genoese sailors at Jaffa with siege equipment; in 1101 a Genoese fleet assisted Count Raymond of Toulouse in taking Tortosa (Tartus), and in 1106 received a third of the town of Jubail (north of Beirut) in exchange for services rendered; in 1105 King Baldwin I entered into negotiations with the same fleet in the port of Haifa, and obtained its aid in the conquest of Acre – which was to become the chief port of the Holy Land. In 1108 Bertrand of Toulouse, the illegitimate son of the then deceased Count Raymond, stopped at Genoa on his way to the East to negotiate with the consuls. He set off with a Genoese squadron added to his fleet of 40 Provençal galleys and 4,000 men, and in the following year conquered Tripoli. The Genoese gained a quarter in the city, a castle some ten miles to the south, and the remaining two-thirds of Jubail. Soon the Genoese had established trading communities at Jaffa, Acre, Caesarea, Arsuf, Tyre, Beirut, Tripoli, Jubail, Lattakieh, Saint Symeon, Antioch, and Jerusalem – where they possessed an entire street.

Genoese merchants imported to Europe both indigenous products and those brought to Jerusalem from the East by Arab traders. Staple imports included pepper, brazil-wood, alum and cotton, all of which were used as currency both by merchants and the city government. A guaranteed supply of alum was vital for tanners, mosaic workers and painters, but above all for the dyers whose skills led to the growth of the Italian textile industry. Other Genoese imports included spices such as cinnamon, nutmeg, cloves; further raw-materials for dye-making like saffron, mastic, gall-nuts and indigo; steel blades, lacquer and incense; silk and cloth from Baghdad; sugar and sugar confections. Most of them were luxury products which had previously been little used in Europe; margins were high, and profits good. But the level of risk was also high, and expanding trade necessitated new financial instruments. A form of 'sea-loan' called the *foenus nauticum* was developed to finance trade with the East: it could be used to make remittances to agents in Jerusalem, to raise money on goods to be exported and used as security for the loan, or as a method of securing investment capital. It was not however cheap: the lender assumed the entire risk on the loan, since repayment was entirely dependent on the safe arrival of both ship and its cargo. Interest payments on the *foenus nauticum* were recorded in 1158 as 33 per cent, but later in the century they varied between this figure as a minimum and 50–60 per cent as a maximum. That such high rates should be acceptable is itself an indication of the potential profits to be made, and of the enormous wealth derived from trade in the eastern Mediterranean.

The second event in which the Muslims were involved was the signing of a treaty in 1161 which allowed Genoa to expand its operations. Fourteen years earlier a new and more powerful dynasty, the Berber Almohades, had displaced the Almoravides who ruled over Spain and whose ships had taken part in Muslim raids on the Italian coast together with the Aghlabids. By 1160 the Almohade leader – and founder of their empire – Abd-al-Mu'mīm (1130–63) had gained effective control of North Africa from Morocco to Tripoli, and his fleets commanded the Western Mediterranean. The treaty negotiated with him enabled the Genoese to sail into the western Mediterranean in safety; such was its success, facilitated by the desire of successive Muslim rulers to encourage trade, that new Genoese trading posts were opened in Ceuta and Tunis. It was renewed in 1176 and 1191 by Abd-al-Mu'mīm's son and grandson respectively. The nascent Genoese merchant fleet was able to expand its operations south-east along the Tyrrhenian coast of Italy and south-west into the French and Spanish Mediterranean.

From a small port in the 1090s, Genoa grew within little more than half a century to become a city which dealt on equal terms with the princes and kings of Europe. The symbol of this new wealth was the new cathedral of San Lorenzo, built with the immense profits of Genoese activity in the Holy Land and consecrated in 1118. But it also filtered down to the merchants and other tradesmen of the city. Private homes were large by medieval standards, with separate apartments for men (the *androniti*) and women (the *gineceo*), and large numbers of well-decorated rooms. Some also had a *loggia* which served as a place for inviting guests. There is evidence of tapestries imported from Egypt in private houses as early as the 12th century, and at least one case of a painted and decorated bed with baldachin. Although the use of oil-soaked linen instead of glass meant that these rooms were often fairly dark, they seem to have been painted. Around 1250 a painter called Baldovino Fornari was commissioned to paint a room vermilion with white roses, and a gallery in the same house white with vermilion roses. The tables were well furnished with game and poultry, which from about 1100 were served with sauces whose ingredients included newly-imported spices like pepper, cloves, nutmeg, ginger and cinnamon. The presence of a celebrated troubadour such as Raimbaut de Vaqueiras in Genoa from around 1190 suggests the existence of a literary and musical life not unlike the noble courts of Provence (the attractive second stanza of his poem 'Eras quan vey verdeyar' – beginning 'Io son quel que ben non aio . . .' – is written in medieval Genoese dialect).

The sudden increase in wealth created internal friction between old power and new money: the former associated with the growing Ghibelline faction in support of the Emperor, the latter associated with the Guelfs. In

The façade of the cathedral of San Lorenzo

Genoa the Ghibellines were the old families loyal to the imperial representatives who had legitimized their power in the past, such as the Spinola and Doria; the staunch Guelfs were the new-rich families whose wealth derived exclusively from trade, such as the Fieschi and Grimaldi. The simmering dispute reached its peak towards the end of the 12th century, when it became necessary to change the system of government to accommodate social change. Once again, a crusade was the key event. When the Third Crusade was declared after the fall of Jerusalem to Saladin in 1187, it was the nobles from the Guelf party who sailed east in support of the Church. The Ghibellines stayed behind – even though their putative leader Frederick Barbarossa himself travelled east – and in the absence of their rivals modified the government of the city. Guelf families lost their hold on power, and it was at this time that the Grimaldi were forced into what remains a gilded exile in Monaco. The *Compagna Communis* were no longer powerful enough to govern the city, the consuls were temporarily abolished, and the new – supposedly neutral – figure of *podestà* appeared as in many other Italian cities at that time. For some decades the tussle between Guelfs and Ghibellines, with often alternating consuls and podestà, racked the city – exacerbated by the absence of so many men in the overseas colonies. Anarchy ruled within the walls. In the picturesque words of Ottobuono, one of the continuators of the annals of Caffaro, in the year 1193 '. . . the Podestà and consuls dozed and slept, while thieves, rogues and parricides kept awake. In a word, the villains and murderers controlled the city.' This confirms the observation of the Rabbi Benjamin of Tudela, who visited Genoa at the beginning of his long fact-finding mission throughout Europe and Asia some 20 years earlier. He noted that each house within the city walls was equipped with a tower, from the top of which fighting took place during civil strifes. By 1216, however, a semblance of order prevailed and the figure of consul disappeared completely from the city government (it survives today as the title of the elected union leader of the *Compagnia unica* into which the dockers are organized). Wealth which had divided and nearly ruined the city was then channelled into strengthening it. But the rivalry persisted. Petrarch was later to describe Genoa as a 'magnificent city' whose very power militates against it and damages it by creating rivalries and jealousies.

The process of political change culminated in the middle of the 13th century with the election by popular acclaim of a *Capitano del Popolo*, who would govern the city for a period of ten years with the help of a council of 32 elders. Such a change reflected a general shift of power in Italy at that time from aristocratic family clans to the emerging form of communal government by the *popolo*, or citizens. In the words of a historian of family structure in Genoa the *popolo* 'championed civic order, curtailed the activities of noble families within the city, and tried to break the cohesiveness of the great households˙. Such a shift was neither immediate nor easy: Guglielmo Boccanegra, who built the Palazzo di Mare to symbolize his role, was elected in 1256 with the blessing of the Ghibelline aristocrats of the Spinola and Doria families; but they soon perceived the genuine popularity of Boccanegra and his equally genuine attitudes in favour of the popolo he was called upon to represent. Recognizing the threat to their own power, the same families that had elected Boccanegra overthrew him six years later. For nearly a decade the city was once again ruled by a Ghibelline *podestà* – at a time when Italy was almost entirely Guelf under the combined pressure of a powerful church and Charles I of Anjou (who had come to Italy ostensibly to recover the peninsula for the Church after the deaths of Frederick II and his immediate heirs). But as so often in Italian history, political expediency and an innate sense of loyalty to the city occasionally overrode the Ghibelline/Guelf divide: when both the papacy and trade in the south had appeared threatened by Frederick II, Genoa had been staunchly Guelf in its support of Rome and had even become a temporary ally of its greatest enemy.

Opposition to Charles of Anjou was to have a more direct effect. In 1269 – a difficult moment after serious military losses to Venice at Acre, and in battles from Constantinople to Trapani – Genoa was to lose its sovereignty for the first time in 300 years. The city was forced to renounce its privileges and independence in favour of Charles, and agreed to be governed by a Guelf *podestà* who was acceptable to the French. But this ignominious situation was short-lived: the following year, in a dramatic show of strength, the Doria and Spinola occupied the palace of the *podestà* and named Oberto Doria and Oberto Spinola as joint *capitani del popolo*. By 1276 Charles had restored the lost privileges to Genoa, and Ghibelline power was such that the *capitani* were able to force local feudal rulers either to declare their loyalty to Genoa or sell their feuds outright. With the enormous wealth then available to its people, Genoa was able to strengthen itself after the momentary lapse of power, and achieve its brief apogee – as we shall see. In this period, the Genoese controlled the Italian coast from its settlement at Porto Venere, on the northern coast of the Gulf of La Spezia, to Nice.

The increasing wealth which provoked internal friction also stimulated reciprocal envy between Genoa and other Mediterranean ports. The history of medieval Genoa is peppered with references to disputes, battles, treaties, alliances and war, especially with Venice and Pisa; eventually this rivalry was to lead to the elimination of Pisa as a serious threat, and then to the primacy of Venice over Genoa and all the minor Italian ports. Violent and lengthy disputes were often the consequence of minor incidents which loomed larger than reality in the participants' minds. What may be described as the First Pisan War – from the Genoese point of view – began in 1118 as the result of Pope Gelasius II's confirmation of Pisan ecclesiastical supremacy in Corsica. On the basis of this 'slight', really unavoidable since Genoa had at that time no archbishop to whom the island could be assigned, a state of war came to exist for 15 years. Gelasius' successor Pope Calixtus II, a Frenchman and better disposed towards Genoa than a southern Italian like Gelasius (who was born in Gaeta, a rival of Genoa), reversed the decision. But the dispute was only resolved by the Salomonic decision of yet another pope, Innocent II (a Roman), who in 1133 divided the island of Corsica into two spheres of influence – much as a later pope was to do with South America.

The 'wars' and 'battles' were often limited in scope. Under the year 1125, in which he says there were many other Genoese victories, Caffaro da Rustico recounts one in which he was personally involved. In late summer eight Pisan galleys sailed out of the River Arno towards Genoa. That there was no standing fleet is suggested by the fact that as soon as the Genoese learned of this expedition they 'armed seven galleys', which then set off under the command of Caffaro. In that year he had been elected consul for the second time, and was accompanied by other noblemen from the city ('cum multis nobilissimis viris'). They chased the Pisans to Corsica, Sardinia and finally Elba, where they engaged the enemy in battle and defeated them off the mainland port at Piombino. That fleets of such limited size were the norm is suggested by a later, and again successful, experience of Caffaro: when he led the Genoese against the Moors in Minorca 20 years later the total fleet under his command amounted to 22 galleys ('galeis') and six supply boats ('galabios').

Hostility with Pisa was the military aspect of a continuous struggle for commercial pre-eminence in the Tyrrhennian Sea. For much of the period between Caffaro's battle off Piombino and the end of the 13th century, the hostility persisted as a background simmering of minor actions between corsairs and privateers; even when it is referred to as a 'war' it was often not much more than a series of skirmishes. The 'First Pisan War' was followed by a Second which lasted from 1165–75, but in spite of the peace which followed this episode the condition of war between Pisa and Genoa became more or less permanent – both in home waters and in the overseas colonies. It was in the 1280s that this brewing hostility boiled up into a violent no-holds-barred war which led to the destruction of Pisa as a maritime power: the climax was a naval battle known as the 'Battle of the Meloria'. The Pisans began the escalation early in 1282, probably convinced that alliances with both Venice and Charles of Anjou would swing the balance in their favour. But luck was against them. On Easter

[169]

Monday the Sicilians rebelled against the tyranny of Charles, opening hostilities with the massacre of the French that was to become known as the 'Sicilian Vespers'. At the same time Venice chose to remain neutral, and allow the rivals on the opposite coast to fight it out between themselves. After two years of desultory skirmishing the Genoese admiral Benedetto Zaccaria left his home port in April 1284 with 30 galleys in an attempt to cut off the Pisan trading routes. He sailed to Porto Pisano at the mouth of the River Arno, and from there patrolled the waters between the islands of the Tuscan archipelago (Elba, Pianosa, Capraia, Giglio, Montecristo), Corsica and Sardinia. While Genoese ships carried on their normal business the Pisan fleet was denied access to the sea for three months.

The Pisans used this hiatus to construct a fleet of 65 galleys and 11 galleons intended to destroy Genoa: the prows of the galleys were equipped with rotating capstans armed with blades and whips to prevent boarding; all the ships carried trebuchets, with supplies of heavy ammunition to be catapulted at the city of Genoa itself. The idea was to attack Genoa while Admiral Zaccaria was in southern Corsica preparing an attack against the Pisan colony at Sassari (in northwest Sardinia). The fleet was commanded in person by the *podestà* of Pisa, the Venetian Alberto Morosini, and its crews were composed of all the leading Pisan nobles and officials. But, in the first of a series of unfortunate coincidences which bring to mind another great Armada, a storm blocked this fleet at the mouth of the Arno as it prepared to sail out, thus losing for the Pisans the advantage of surprise. While Morosini and his fleet sailed across the Ligurian Sea to block the return of Zaccaria's fleet on the normal route to Albenga, the Genoese admiral had been warned in advance and sailed towards the coast south of Genoa. In the city itself there was time to erect extra defences, and to organize a second fleet of 58 galleys under the command of Oberto Doria. By the time Morosini arrived before Genoa a stalemate had been achieved: the Pisan fleet lacked the numbers to attack the well-defended city, while the fleet under Doria's command was too small to sail out of the harbour and attack. This stalemate was broken by the appearance of Admiral Zaccaria south of Genoa. The Pisan commander feared being caught between two fires, and after a half-hearted attempt at bombarding the city retreated to safety behind the heavy chains which closed Porto Pisano.

The Genoese pursued him, and on the evening of 5 August 1284 reached the rock known as 'La Torre della Meloria', about four miles off Livorno (Leghorn) and ten miles south of Porto Pisano. It was there that the brilliant Genoese strategy – probably inspired by Zaccaria – was implemented. While Oberto Doria's fleet rode clearly visible off the Meloria, Zaccaria and his 30 galleys took up position further out to sea with sails lowered so that from the distance they would look like unarmed supply ships. Stung by the ignominy of returning home empty-handed and again having the Genoese block the mouth of the Arno, the Pisan fleet sailed out the next day to attack what Morosini believed to be a fleet of more or less equal size. Admiral Zaccaria, using a tactic he had perhaps learned during his years in the Holy Land, left the burning August sun to take its toll of men forced to manoeuvre heavy and heavily-armed ships into position for attack. His sailors rested, ate, and drank. Then, in the cooler hours of late afternoon, fresh against exhausted men, the combined Genoese fleets attacked. Despite Pisan bravery, it was a débâcle. Seven Pisan galleys were sunk, together with 33 support ships. The remainder, and the bulk of the Pisan nobles, were forced to retreat up the Arno. When the prisoners taken at the Meloria were added to those taken in previous months, the total came to the then enormous figure of 9,000 – including Alberto Morosini. Only severe losses on the part of the Genoese seem to have prevented the immediate sacking of Pisa itself. The combined Genoese fleet sailed home with the chains of Porto Pisano as an ornament for the cathedral of San Lorenzo.

Then the vultures moved in. Within three months of this battle the Guelf cities of Lucca and Florence had made an alliance with Ghibelline Genoa against Pisa. In the early summer of the following year a fleet of 65 Genoese galleys sailed south with the intention of annihilating Pisa. Had Florence and Lucca not in the meantime hastily shifted alliances and sided with Pisa – perhaps fearing Genoese encroachment on the land powers of Tuscany – then all would have been lost. There would have been no leaning tower to visit. As it was, however, the Genoese were not prepared to take on such odds and retreated. So the Pisans, reprieved and to a certain extent revived, continued their independent corsair raids along the Tuscan coast as before, until Zaccaria was forced to attack Porto Pisano yet again. Then, in 1288, Pisan representatives travelled to Genoa and – in Oberto Doria's house – signed a pact in which they renounced their rights to Sardinia, Corsica and their last colony at Acre, and gave Elba to Genoa. When the terms of this pact were not respected, the Genoese destroyed Porto Pisano once and for all. This marked the end of Pisan power, and today nothing remains of the once-famous port – whose site lies under the cement of the modern tourist development of Marina di Pisa.

The collapse of Pisan power was inevitable, but in a sense the victory was Pyrrhic since Genoa too was doomed to decline. In the terms of an economic law propounded by the American historian of Genoese origin Robert S. Lopez, ports nearest to the exporters are the first to benefit from trade but eventually there is a shift towards ports nearer to the export markets than to the exporters. This explains the gradual northward shift of key Tyrrhenian ports from Amalfi to Pisa, and then on to Genoa. It may also be used to explain how the superior communications network of the Po valley made Venice a more natural port for the market created in northern Italy by the growth of cities like Milan, Cremona and Verona in the 13th century. Success in the wars with Pisa was in fact followed by a series of wars with Venice which began in 1293, and which led to the decline of medieval Genoa and the absolute domination of Venice (and indirectly preserved the memoirs of Marco Polo for posterity, since it was after capture in a battle between Genoa and Venice that he dictated them in a Genoese prison). Today, in a modern extension of the process explained by Lopez' law, the port of Genoa seems to be in an irreversible decline as container traffic to Europe – even to northern Italy – moves through Rotterdam.

In 1288 Genoa was at the height of its power and fame. The audacity of its mariners may be symbolized by the voyage of the Vivaldi brothers, Vadino and Ugolino, who in 1291 set off from Genoa and sailed out of the Straits of Gibraltar in search of a route to the Indies – almost exactly 200 years before their fellow citizen Columbus. Although they were never heard of again, the attempt illustrates contemporary Genoese skill and daring. Similar qualities had led to the foundation of colonies and outposts throughout the known world, fuelled as we have seen by the scarcity of cultivable land along the coast of Liguria. Genoa never developed inland as the nobles of the Venetian Empire were later to do, blocked as it was by mountains which rise almost from the sea itself and by the powerful cities of the Lombard League like Pavia and Milan. The Genoese naturally looked seaward for opportunity.

In fact the medieval Genoese seem to have been particularly suited to expatriate life. The anonymous poet of the *Exposicio* emphasizes how able or adaptable ('destexi') they were:

> And so many are the Genoese
> and in the world so adaptable,
> that wherever they go and stay
> they make another Genoa.

('E tanti sun li Zenoexi/e per lo mondo si destexi/che und'eli van e stan/ un'altra Zenoa ge fan.') Contemporary documents show how this was literally true. When they came to receive or request privileges, the Genoese colonies in the Latin Kingdom of Jerusalem (like other Italian colonies) made specific demands for those features which constituted the heart of a medieval Italian town: the *ruga* (square), *funda* (market area), *ecclesia* (church), *furnus* (oven), and *balneam* (bath). Within their

A doorway in Piazza San Matteo, presented to Oberto Doria in 1288 by the commune of Genoa in gratitude for his victory against the Pisans

community the language used was Genoese dialect, and the members had little to do with neighbouring communities. Moreover, they were self-governed, with treaties which meant that Genoese citizens were subject to Genoese law even for business and criminal matters arising in the host country. Notarial records for Tunis in the 1280s show that the community was virtually governed through the joint action of the consul, the priest and the leading merchants under the presiding influence of a Genoese notary. Business was carried out in the main Genoese warehouse, or on important occasions inside the community church. In the 13th century, colonies at Pera or Galata (across the Golden Horn from Constantinople), Kaffa (in the Crimea), and Chios (guarding the approach to the Dardanelles), and smaller settlements in the west at for instance Tunis,

[173]

Malaga, Cadiz and Seville, or further east at Tabriz, were socially and culturally autonomous enclaves. There was a *podestà* at Pera and a *consul* at Kaffa representing the commune of Genoa (although these are rare cases). The colonies became the suburbs of the mother city which the mountains denied to medieval builders.

Pera offered access to the products of Constantinople and the Black Sea, while Kaffa opened up a route to Asia of vital importance. Caravans from Khwarizm, bringing goods from India, reached Kaffa in three months' overland journey. These colonies were well defended: Pera was protected by turreted walls and a seawater moat, and Kaffa was sufficiently fortified to resist a Mongol siege. Their military strength and commercial power were such that these Genoese colonies obtained an absolute monopoly of Black Sea trade in the 13th century. In the words of Gibbon, 'Destitute of a navy, the Greeks were oppressed by these haughty merchants, who fed, or famished Constantinople, according to their interest.' Eastern trade was blocked soon afterwards by the rise of Tamerlane (1336–1405) and the closing of China with the beginning of the Ming dynasty in 1368. But even in its reduced circumstances, Genoa was not lost: trade was simply switched from East to West just as Atlantic exploration was intensified. Even more remarkable was the attempt to introduce eastern products to the west, whence the same items could still be imported to Europe by the Genoese: the Malvasia grape was taken west from the Greek islands, first to Sicily and then on to the Canaries and the island of Madeira which supplied a name for the wine produced from it: sugar followed the same route, and was eventually taken across the Atlantic to the New World by the Genoese. No better justification for the identification of Genoa with Janus could be found.

The social structure of Genoa rendered its colonies anomalous. They might almost be termed 'emotional' colonies, for their link with Genoa derived from language, family ties and membership of compagne rather than direct administrative control. The pattern of division into aristocratic enclaves was repeated in the colonies, with street names and imported social rules enforcing the parallel. With the exception of the later colonies at Pera and Kaffa the strength of Genoese outposts, overseas ports and colonies depended on the power of the families which controlled them, financed trade, and offered military protection; even these exceptions saw members of powerful families like the Doria and Embriaci establish their principal homes in them. But again, the Genoese art of adaptation played a vital role, for they showed a marked willingness to assimilate local conditions, collaborate with foreign states and even to accept the protection of foreign princes. In extreme cases this led to what one historian has termed 'ambivalence': referring especially to Spanish colonies in the 14th century, he argues that the Genoese 'were able to camouflage themselves in local society by intermarriage, formal naturalisation, bilingualism, service to the community and the crown, and even modification of the orthography of their names'. Yet the colonies remained distinctly Genoese, and even in large centres like Seville and Cadiz the merchants managed to create 'another Genoa' of their own. Kinship, common interest and an innate sense of solidarity were the cohesive factors in an otherwise intangible social fabric. Wealth flowed back to the mother city, the mercantile set of mind triumphing over political dissension so that Genoa flourished in spite of war and internecine divisions. Yet in the end this underlying private enterprise nature of Genoese commerce contributed to decline, since no single family or even group of families possessed the capital to compete with Venice in the East or the kingdoms of Portugal and Spain in the West. Genoese admirals led naval powers throughout Europe: Zaccaria sailed for Sancho of Navarre and Philip the Fair of France; Pessagno for Edward I of England. The story of Columbus is too well-known to need repeating.

But Genoa passed: it was never to have an empire such as the 'Serenissima' created, and if the medieval form of the city at its apogee around 1288 may still be discerned beneath later accretions it is at least in part because the irreversible decline of its power cut it off from the main thrust of the Renaissance.

# THE RISE OF THE 'POPOLO' AND 'COMUNE': CREMONA

Tʜᴇ Piazza del Comune of Cremona is one of the finest urban
developments of medieval Italy. On a site which overlapped a corner
of the Roman city and a later episcopal fortress, five monumental
buildings which illustrate the growing power and political development
of Cremona were built between 1107 and 1292: the cathedral, the
baptistery, the *Palazzo del Comune*, the *Torrazzo* or municipal tower, and
the *Loggia dei Militi* built for the militia captains.

According to a surviving inscription, the foundation stone of the
cathedral was laid by Bishop Walterus on 7 September 1107. There had
earlier, however, been a double cathedral as in Pavia, with identical names
but built in line rather than side-by-side: in this case the winter church of
S. Maria Dormiente stood just outside the walls of the Roman city on the
site of the present nave, with a summer church called S. Stefano standing
behind it (across the road from the apse of the present structure). Within
seven years the new cathedral was completed, by architects and masons
who are thought to have belonged to the Third Order of Benedictines
founded by St Benignus of Dijon (later Abbot of Cluny) to be entrusted
with the secret arts of buildings. These so-called *maestri comacini* came
from the abbeys of Campilione, S. Benigno and S. Mailo on the modern
Italian-Swiss frontier near Como, and were the same men who worked on
San Michele and San Pietro in Ciel d'Oro at Pavia. A contemporary seal
shows a building not unlike San Michele, a tripartite basilica with a large
main door, rose window and five circular towers. But the cathedral was
destroyed by an earthquake soon after completion, and a new one started
by Bishop Obertus de Dovaria – member of a wealthy, noble family and the
first of the bishops to define himself proudly in documents as Cremonese.
Work seems to have continued throughout Obertus' long bishopric, from

The façade of Cremona cathedral

1117 to 1162, and the later and more celebrated Bishop Sicar tells us in a letter that he consecrated the new cathedral himself in 1190. A single architrave over the door of the north porch and four statues of prophets now on the main façade are all that remain of Walterus' cathedral, and even the 1190 building has been altered out of recognition in succeeding

[177]

centuries; a fine sculpted version of the months of the year made on the façade by Benedetto Antelami around 1220 is interesting for its similarities with the Bominaco calendar (especially the knight representing May). The façade dominates the piazza, with portal and other sculpture of excellent quality, testifying to the wealth and power of Cremona in the 13th century.

The free-standing baptistery stands to the right of the main façade of the cathedral. A fine brick octagonal structure, with blind arcading and a rib-vaulted cupola, it was completed in 1167 – a date which has led some scholars to suggest that Bishop Sicard's chronology is misleading, and that the cathedral started by Obertus must have been completed by then. The documented existence of a consortium of masons in Cremona as early as 1143, and good city walls by at the latest 1169, suggest that the means to complete it earlier were certainly available.

The piazza is completed by the three lay buildings. The most obviously striking is the red laterite-brick tower known as the *Torrazzo*, which rises dramatically to the left of the cathedral façade. Traditionally the symbol of Cremona, the original square section of this tower was built in 1267. Together with a two-tier octagonal addition made towards the end of the century it reaches a height of 111 metres, offering from its spectacular belvedere views of the entire city of Cremona and countryside surrounding. An arcaded porch known as the 'Portico della Bertazzola' was added to its base in the 16th century as a continuation of the façade of the cathedral – thus providing a misleading illusion of continuity between the two buildings. Between this portico and the clock which is the main visual feature of the lower part of the tower the municipal crest reveals its civic function. Opposite this complex, as if in eternal opposition, is the *Palazzo del Comune*, which was built on the site of an earlier building from 1206 to 1246 but has been substantially modified since then. Aligned both literally and symbolically with the Palazzo del Comune is the smaller gothic *Loggia dei Militi*, erected in 1292 for the militia captains of Cremona. But of these lay buildings it is the massive *torrazzo* which looms over the piazza and draws the attention up and away from the other buildings, as if to stress final victory of secular power against the Church.

For the medieval growth of Cremona was intimately related to the convulsions of the Carolingian kingdom of Italy, to popular resistance against the count-bishops who came to rule many northern Italian cities, and the emergence of the *comune*. The medieval political concepts of commune as a 'free city' and the *cive* or citizen who inhabited it were in fact the consequence of a series of rebellions and autonomous actions roughly contemporary with the popular uprising against Henry II at Pavia in 1004. In the same year, for example, the war which broke out between

A statue of Jeremiah on the façade of Cremona cathedral

Pisa and Lucca implied the existence of organized groups of citizens which had the power to take the decision to go to war and then implement it. In Pavia the demolition of the *palatium* in 1024 had unforseen consequences: the destruction of the legal and financial records on which the Carolingian administration had been based. Suddenly, there was no government. This may have accelerated the desire for a new authority to fill the vacuum caused by the disintegration of the Carolingian kingdom. Already in 945 the lack of a strong central authority had led to a monetary union made with permission of Lothar II between Mantova, Verona and Brescia, showing the way for local political bodies to fulfil functions which were previously the duty of imperial representatives. The absence of central authority was exacerbated by a rapid succession of often-absentee emperors and kings of Italy. Long periods with no resident king weakened the kingdom, because, as we have seen, in the centralized organization inherited from the Lombards responsibility for the entire administrative and legal structure was vested in the physical person of the king. For this reason, since the death of Charlemagne imperial authority had been gradually transferred to the bishops – and great monasteries like Montecassino – by the granting of privileges and immunities. In fact, with few and infrequent exceptions, when the direct Carolingian line came to an end in 887 with the death of Charles the Fat, imperial authority was to a large extent delegated to the bishops. This was partly because the bishops were generally better educated than lay counts, and partly because kings knew that lands granted to them could never become hereditary possessions and therefore gave them preference over secular lords. But in fact one of the long-term – and probably unforeseen – consequences of this was that the clergy became more interested in property and temporal power than in spiritual welfare. It was this fact which ultimately created the need for the 11th century reforms against simony, and led to the Investiture Crisis which broke out between Emperor Henry IV and Pope Gregory VII in 1076 (this dispute, nominally over the imperial investiture of the Archbishop of Milan, derived from the imperial desire to control papal elections and hence the appointment of bishops and abbots).

The story of early medieval Cremona is substantially a record of increasing popular protest against the abuses of episcopal power, an illustration in microcosm of the struggle which led to the Investiture Crisis. For it was with an imperial diploma issued in 882 by Charles the Fat that the bishop of Cremona obtained the right to fortify the cathedral, episcopal residence and other related ecclesiastical buildings. This erection of walls between pastor and flock symbolizes the moment of transition from a pastoral bishop with spiritual functions to a count-bishop with temporal and military power.

Under the first Italian king, Berengar I of Friuli (888–924), the transition was completed. The first intimations of a new role for the cities came as the church, the distribution of feudal power, defences against foreign invaders like the Magyars, and control of economic features such as ports, were organized on a local basis. A capitulary issued by King Lambert (891–8), son and successor of Berengar's rival Guy of Spoleto, contained an important new feature: the organization of church, feudal power, defence against foreign invaders such as the Hungarians, the growth of economic activities such as the ports, *on a local basis*. The city was already beginning, albeit under episcopal control, to replace the central authority of the kingdom. The same capitulary not only sanctioned the passage of comital fiscal duties to the bishops, but re-organized ecclesiastical territory in bishoprics and parishes. This was more important than it might seem today because fiscal and economic privileges were based upon these units. But it was not long before protests at this new arrangement emerged, and there seems to have been a slowly-dawning realization that local autonomy was possible without the count-bishop. There was no sudden general rebellion, but rather a series of uprisings, protests and requests on the part of the civil population for similar privileges. The first sign in Cremona occurred in 924, when the citizens complained to King Rudolf (922–6) about taxes they were forced to pay to their bishop for river transport.

Although this might seem at first sight a trivial matter, it struck at the heart of an economy which had always been based on the fluvial port. A Roman colony had been founded in 218 BC at what was already then perceived as a strategic crossing-point on the River Po, with a garrison of 6,000 colonists to establish a foothold against the Celtic tribes of northern Italy; in the same year troops took refuge there from the advance of Hannibal into Italy through the Alps. Shortly afterwards, around 187–4 BC, it was rebuilt as part of a new chain of frontier fortresses, and a road known as the Via Aemilia was built northwards from the termination of the Via Flaminia at Piacenza. The city was important enough in the 1st century BC to possess a good school, where Virgil studied before moving on to Milan and Rome; it also produced a local poet of some renown in the Furius Bibaculus (or 'little toper') who was an acquaintance of Catullus. The name 'Cremona' probably derives from the Latin underlying root *cremo*, meaning a 'raised place', and the original fortress was built on a terrace inside a wide meander of the Po – which passed within a stone's throw of the later episcopal enclave. Since then the course of the river has moved south, but it can still be seen from the belvedere on top of the *Torrazzo* meandering in great loops through rich agricultural land. Roman Cremona was sacked several times in its early history, and then re-built by

[181]

The civic tower known as Il Torrazzo, seen from behind

[182]

the Emperor Vespasian (68–79 AD). In later Roman times the city gradually lost its importance as the frontier moved towards the alpine passes with cities such as Brescia and Milan.

But the strategic value remained. When Theoderic and the Ostrogoths entered northern Italy in 489 it was at Cremona that Odoacer first made his base. But in the following year Theoderic took Cremona and defeated Odoacer, who then retreated to Ravenna (as we have seen in the chapter on Pavia). Cremona remained in the hands of the Ostrogoths until Totila, their last king (541–52), was defeated by Justinian's general Narsete at the end of the Gothic Wars. In 553, the year before the *Pragmatic Sanction* which formally marked the return of Italy to its status as the Western Province of the Empire, Cremona passed to the Byzantines. Its position on the river route from Ticinum to Ravenna made it a vital city for them, and they established a permanent military base known as the *cataulada* (a hybrid formed from a Greek word meaning walled settlement or camp and a Latin suffix meaning large). At the heart of this area was a Byzantine *praitorion*, almost certainly on the site of the present church of S. Agata. The *cataulada* served the double function of providing a military base on the Po and a bridgehead into pagan northern Italy from which the process of Christianization could be continued. The historian of Cremona Ugo Gualazzini has by a fascinating example of historical detection established the area of the *cataulada* on the basis of toponymy in medieval documents, the location of sacred buildings, and surviving elements of topography. It lay to the north of the Roman city, separated from it by the River Cremonella which then flowed overland into the Po and is now an underground sewer. Thus in early medieval times the city of Cremona was divided into two distinct parts, parallel cities whose separation was to influence later developments. It was only much later, as we shall see, perhaps in the 13th or 14th centuries, that a new road breaking the ancient grid patterns was built to link the political centres of the two parts more directly – on the line of the present Via Garibaldi. Byzantine domination was however short-lived, since in 603 Cremona was taken by the Lombards: Paul the Deacon recounts how King Agilulf departed from Milan in a fury deriving from the imprisonment of his daughter, took Cremona on 21 August that year and 'destroyed it from top to bottom'. The Lombard king's fury was such that today nothing remains of Roman and Byzantine Cremona. For more than a century the city disappeared from view.

Cremona reappears in medieval documents when a pact between the Lombards and the boatmen of Comacchio – to the south of the delta of the Po between Ravenna and Ferrara – was established during the reign of King Liutprand between 715 and 730. The 'Comacchiesi' sailed up the Po

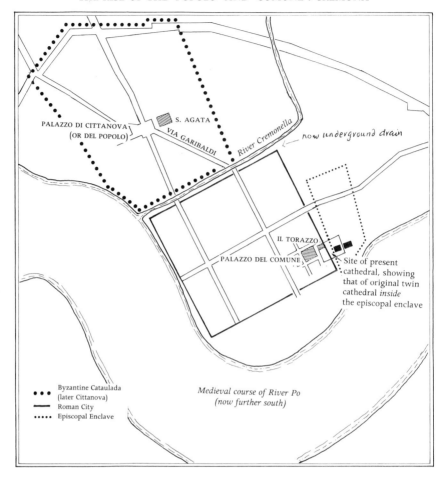

Fig. 10. Sketch map of medieval Cremona showing the twin origin of the city

with salt from their marshes, which they exchanged for cereals. The agreement with the Lombards led to the setting up of delegates called *riparii* who would collect the tolls due to the Lombards at the various ports along the Po. There were to be two of these delegates in the 'port known as Cremona' (*portus qui vocatur Cremona*); but this expression implies that there was no autonomous city at the time, otherwise the port would have been referred to simply as *portus cremonensis*. Thus it was the existence of the port which led to the new growth of the city in the 8th century. The foundation around 750 of a Benedictine *cella* or dependent abbey of Nonantola is a further indication of the renewed importance of Cremona; the Benedictine church was built in the western part of the area of the *cataulada*, but the order possessed lands outside the walls where the bed of

[184]

the Po had retreated southwards. The delegates at the port were to collect a tax on goods transported by river: this was based initially on the Roman 'tenth' of the quantity unloaded in the port, but was soon to become a fixed toll. Around 850 there is evidence that the Venetians had joined the Comacchiesi in the salt trade; about the same time, perhaps even a couple of decades earlier, the people of Cremona themselves entered into the trade – at first in association with the Comacchiesi, later in their own right and with their own boats. At some time in the 10th century the role of the Comacchiesi declined, leaving river traffic in the hands of Venice, Ferrara, Cremona and Pavia.

Thus the potential wealth of Cremona increased steadily from around 750. But at first the principal beneficiary was the Church, since Carolingian policy caused successive kings either to concede to ecclesiastical authorities' complete exemption from the river taxes, or to assign them a portion of the taxes collected. This began with a grant to the Bishop of Cremona by Charlemagne, renewed by Louis II in a decree of 851–2. Soon a process of escalation of grants and privileges began, leading to the dispute of 924 – and eventually to the independence of Cremona. In a diploma dated 12 May 902 issued at Pavia, the Burgundian King Louis III confirmed the ancient rights of Bishop Lando of Cremona, granted him the right to build two towers – which became the nucleus of the later episcopal fortress – and conceded further fiscal benefits. An idea of the imposition involved here may be gleaned from a contemporary diploma issued to the Bishop of Bergamo in which it was made explicit that the bishop's fellow citizens (*concives*) were responsible for the building of similar towers and walls. Then in 910, at a royal court held in Cremona itself, King Berengar I issued a diploma which awarded Bishop Giovanni jurisdiction over several places near Cremona including *porto Vulpariolo* (the port). It also granted him rights over transit on the Po within the territory of Cremona, and over riverside mills upstream to the mouth of the River Adda (about ten miles north). This diploma cited those of Charlemagne and Louis II as precedents in arguing the case, and in 916 was reinforced by a further diploma in favour of the bishop: this granted lordship and fiscal rights both in Cremona and within a five mile radius of the city, renewed the jurisdiction over the Po, and granted fishing rights and markets. In effect it created an episcopal county, and made the bishop a secular lord.

The reaction was immediate, with the *negotiatores* or merchants of Cremona protesting that they should be allowed an advantage over other merchants by not having to pay taxes on what they perceived as *their* stretch of river. Six years later King Rudolf sought to placate the protest with a diploma whose harsh language amounted to a direct threat to the merchants, and asserted in two passages redolent of later inquisitorial

[185]

documents that they had been driven by 'diabolical persuasion' to oppose the fiscal rights of the bishop. It is fascinating to follow the argument with which opposition to the bishop is portrayed as heresy: the merchants are said to have been inspired by the devil, and are compared to the Magyars who in the same year sacked Pavia. The ground was laid for a conflict which was only to be resolved 300 years later.

The population of the city was at that time divided into three social classes: the bishop and clergy, representatives of the emperor, and the *cives*. The largest category of *cives*, or people, included *milites, negotiatores* or *mercatores*, and artisans: the *milites* were nobles whose titles and rights derived from the emperor and who held land outside the city; the *negotiatores* were the merchants; the artisans, already at that time organized into primitive trade associations of butchers, masons, joiners, carpenters and tanners, were the most numerous and natural supporters of the merchants since their trades depended on wealth generated from commerce. The interesting thing about the protest against episcopal privileges is that a numerical majority sought to obtain what they perceived as their *right* to exemptions on the basis of citizenship. For such popular assertion of civic rights was a totally novel phenomenon, powerful enough at the end of the century to lead to the unusual step of organizing a delegation of citizens in 996 to travel to Rome and seek audience with the newly arrived Saxon Emperor Otto III.

In May of that year the delegation obtained a diploma which appeared to give the people of Cremona exactly what they wanted. It stated grandly that 'all free men of Cremona, (*omnes cives Cremonenses liberos*), rich and poor alike,' were, under the emperor's protection, to enjoy free access to the river for all purposes, together with rights of pasture and use of the woods on both banks of the Po within the area previously conceded to the bishop. From the confluence with the Adda to the port. It also threatened severe sanctions against anyone who violated the terms of the decree – including bishops. It was almost too good to be true, and in fact was probably obtained amidst the euphoria which accompanied the coronation of the 17-year-old Emperor Otto; neither he nor his advisers had been in Italy long enough to understand the implications of his action. In August, probably under pressure from the bishop, a second diploma abrogated that of May. Nevertheless, a momentum had been created which episcopal pressure and imperial about-turns could not halt. The culminating point was not far off: at some time between 1027 and 1030, perhaps consciously following the example of the 1024 destruction of the *palatium* at Pavia, simmering discontent at Cremona erupted into violent rebellion. A union of citizens joined by an oath, the *coniuratio*, was more devastatingly successful than earlier protests by the merchants. A diploma

[186]

of the Emperor Conrad II (1024–37) relates how Bishop Landolf was expelled from both palace and city, and stripped of his property; his fortress – described as having a double wall and seven towers – was demolished, and the slaves who survived this assault were sold. Then the entire city was razed to its foundations (*a fundamentis*), and a larger one built in its place 'against the honour' of Conrad. Up to this point many of the merchants, boatmen and artisans who had sustained the struggle against episcopal privilege had been on the outside, looking in; now, quite suddenly, they found themselves – and their homes, warehouses and workshops – within the walls of the new city.

Rebellions similar to that of Cremona occurred in Ravenna, Parma and Milan about the same time, accompanied by the rise of individual noble families who from newly-built castles asserted their rights over vast rural areas of the old *regnum Italicum*. Events in Cremona from about 996 to 1030 were in fact symptomatic of what was perhaps the greatest change in medieval northern Italy: from a single state which enjoyed a certain territorial and administrative continuity with the Roman Empire to a complex of autonomous *castelli* and *comuni* which in varying forms was to last until unification in the 19th century. The same desire for increased autonomy manifested itself in a series of requests from cities within the Lombard kingdom to transfer imperial and royal palaces outside the city walls, one of the most sought-after imperial concessions of the 11th and early 12th centuries. The process may have begun when the new official palace at Pavia was built outside the walls in 1027. Milan and Brescia were granted the privilege soon afterwards, while in Verona (site of the third official residence of Theoderic after Ravenna and Pavia) visiting emperors came to use the monastery of San Zeno instead of the old *palatium*. Local loyalties, to piazza, campanile and cathedral on the model of Pavia, became paramount. For while the bishop was contested as a landowner and tax-collector, his spiritual role was accepted as integral to city life.

Collaboration in the building of the new cathedral of Cremona, begun as we have seen in 1107, symbolizes this new relationship between bishop and the newly-emerged social group known as the *populus* – which replaced the old categories of *milites*, *mercatores*, and artisans. With the *populus* came the first consuls, who had appeared at Pisa between 1081–5 and in 13 other northern cities – including Genoa – by 1149; in Cremona this office appears between 1111 and 1116, while in 1115 the city (together with Mantova and Bologna) had obtained the privilege of building the imperial palace outside the walls. Traditional social distinctions were blurred as the landed aristocracy moved into the city and merchants came to own land; this twin phenomenon was accompanied by an economic boom deriving from the increase of trade between the East and the inland

The north porch of the cathedral

The architrave of the north porch, re-used from the original cathedral founded in 1107

Lombard cities following the First Crusade, and also from increased social mobility. There was a new collective identity between all forms of wealth, status and profession, expressed in the building of the cathedral. Yet it was predominantly an identity of economic interest rather than a fully-fledged political identity. This emergence of a new meaning to the word *populus*, almost contemporary with the *compagne* and consuls in Genoa, is often assumed to represent the appearance of a *comune* – with the local usage of *populus* being synonymous.

But this new condition of collective identity, not yet strong enough to lead to autonomy, created tension between neighbouring cities in Lombardy. Just as the war of 1004 between Pisa and Lucca referred to above implied the existence of organized groups of citizens which had the power to take the decision to go to war and then implement it, so did the first of a long series of battles between Cremona and Milan which took place at Bressanoro in 1110. For Milan was seen to be increasing its hegemony over lands immediately surrounding Cremona. A long-standing feud developed between Milan, which took the part of the Church, and Cremona, which when necessary turned to the Emperor for assistance. A measure of the animosity may be seen in the fact that a thirteenth century extoller of the virtues of Milan like Bonvesin de la Riva, in his *De magnalibus Mediolani* or 'The Wonders of Milan', saw fit to mention

[189]

Cremona three times: each time it was to record an occasion on which the victorious Milanese sacked the entire territory of the *episcopatus* or bishopric of Cremona. This is probably a fair indication of Milanese feeling at the time; ultimately – as we shall see – the conflict was resolved in favour of Milan.

But at the beginning of the 12th century the situation must have seemed quite different to the *populus* of Cremona – and such future defeats inconceivable. A sign of the confidence and fervour of the *populus* may be seen in the new quarter known as Cittanova which had been founded in 1077 around the church of S. Agata on the site of the Byzantine *cataulada*. The same confidence was also expressed through Cremonese enthusiasm for the popular religious movement mainly consisting of priests known as the *Pataria*. In this case the interests of the people coincided with and were sustained by attempts of the Church in Rome to put an end to corruption of the clergy and subtract them from imperial power – linked with the attempts at reform which we have seen during Abbot Desiderius' abbacy at Montecassino. In several cities of Lombardy, for example in Milan, Brescia and Pavia, the *Pataria* fought the battle against simony and concubinage; following the lead of Montecassino the movement was actively supported by the Benedictines, at Cremona by the monks of the abbey of San Lorenzo now inside the area of Cittanova. The people of Cremona gathered together and swore collectively to lend their support to this movement. This oath, together with that of the *coniuratores* or oath-swearers who are referred to in Conrad's diploma of 1030, has often been interpreted as the first sign of a collective political conscience in medieval Italy. The decision of the participants was praised by the clearly biased Pope Alexander II (1061–73), who was from Milan; Bishop Bonizone of Sutri, who was a native of Cremona, wrote with just pride in his *Liber ad amicum* of the leading role played by the entire population of his city ('universus Cremonensis populus . . .). The popular movement thus inaugurated led to a series of uprisings in the decade 1060–70 which further shook the established order. But one effect was the re-integration of the bishop in the life of the city, no longer as imperially appointed count-bishop but as the representative of the pope in Rome. A recent British historian has suggested that while the *patarini* were never united enough to form the basis of the commune, their structure and spirit – especially in the public oath-swearing ceremonies which they used to encourage loyalty – were 'clearly cognate with the early communes'. Cittanova was the centre of this ferment in Cremona, and thus of the development of the *populus* at this early stage: they were the main inhabitants of the new quarter, whose focus was the square in front of S. Agata where later the Palazzo di Cittanova or Palazzo del Popolo was

The Palazzo del Popolo, or Palazzo di Cittanova

constructed on the site of the ancient *praitorion* as an alternative town hall
(today this area, a few minutes walk from the Palazzo del Comune but with
a distinctly different feeling as between two of the inner suburbs – or
'villages' – of London, remains the second focal point of the city with the
interest of the Palazzo di Cittanova, the City Museum and the Stradivarius
Museum). In 1110 the Emperor Henry V (1106–25) stopped at Cremona
during his first visit to Italy. He assumed the protection of the church of S.
Agata, and in so doing offered imperial authority for the expansion of the
land of the *populus* – which necessarily encroached upon land possessed
by feudal counts or ecclesiastical foundations. It may have been this
imperial protection, and even encouragement, which instigated the first
battle with Milan in the same year.

Two minor incidents in the next few years demonstrate the growing
power of the *populus* under the auspices of Henry V. By 1118 they were in
a position to make a feudal grant of the castle of Soncino, and in 1120 a
similar grant of lands south of the Po. Both actions suggest at least tacit
imperial approval. The documents of these grants show that the *populus*
involved in these actions was composed of nobles, merchants and artisans
who are collectively called *boni homines* or 'good men'. At the same time,
however, while there is clearly a collective organization of some kind,

[191]

referred to in the former grant as *comune populi Cremone*, this is still a long way from the later commune: the political activity of the city at this time appears to have consisted of a general assembly or *aringus* (whence 'harangue'), sustained by the élite body of the *populus* which had taken over the military functions of the nobility. The *aringus* and *populus* together constituted the *conscilium civitatis*, which was not far removed from the concept of a town council, and it was in fact at this historical moment that the *populus* was transformed from a social class into a political party. Although it might seem at first sight that this élite body had merely usurped the feudal role of imperial counts and count-bishops, it was in fact nothing more or less than a group of citizens acting in the common interest; or at least in *their* common interests, for in his legalistic analysis of these civic functions, Gualazzini concluded that in the first quarter of the 12th century 'the *populus* was the preponderant part of the commune, but could not be exclusively identified with it'.

Certainly it would be wrong to allow the etymological link with 'popular' to lead us astray. In fact the appearance of the role of 'consul' seems to have coincided with the move into the cities of the nobles, or *milites*. Their inherited social function and experience probably made them acceptable as consuls to the majority of the people, and in the case of Cremona this shift may have been connected with the arrival in the area of the Marquis Alberto Pallavicino – a descendant of Marquis Oberto of the *Terra Obertenga* in the division of the Lombard kingdom we have seen in the chapter on Genoa (his family was to hold an independent state between Parma and Piacenza until it was usurped by the Farnese in the 17th century, and still survives today). The eloquent testimony of this noble warrior's name, which derives from 'pela vicino' or 'neighbour-skinner', suggests qualities which the merchants and artisans needed in their leaders but did not possess themselves. In fact the arrival of noble and *milites* families strengthened the organization of merchants, artisans and professional men, and led to the formation of a new and solid governing class. So powerful did they soon become that, in spite of earlier protests against episcopal power, the people of Cremona welcomed Oberto da Dovara as bishop of the city for the long period from 1118 to 1163. He belonged to a noble family of ancient origins which had entered the city about the same time as Pallavicino, but since he both swore loyalty to the Archbishop of Milan and accepted the authority of Rome he was acceptable to a population with strong leanings towards the *patarini*. Bishop Oberto maintained his credentials with the *populus* by seeking privileges for their churches, such as S. Agata; at the same time the nobles were content to see one of their own in the bishop's palace. During his long rule several members of the Dovara family were consuls or rectors of

Cremona, at least four by one historian's count, and from around 1138 all the rectors of Cremona were from old feudal families.

Just as Marquis Alberto and Oberto da Dovara seem to have coalesced pre-existing tendencies and contributed through their experience to the growth of the *populus*, so two other historical figures of the 12th century were to have an important influence on its development: one was a local man who was to become known as St Homobonus and in tangible recognition of his role become the patron saint of Cremona; the other was the Emperor Frederick Barbarossa.

St. Homobonus, born Omobono Tucenghi, was in many ways an incarnation both of the ideas of the *patarini* and of the civic pride of Cremona. His tendency towards mysticism and nature-worship has led to frequent comparisons with his near-contemporary St Francis of Assisi – who was 15 years old when Homobonus died – but although Omobono was a good, pious and charitable man (the quintessential *Homo bonus*), his activity as a political reformer meant that he was much more than this. He was the son of a merchant family, probably of noble origin, and himself worked as a merchant before entering the Church; thereafter his emphasis on the values of poverty, charity and sacrifice at the expense of simony and corruption gained him a large following amongst the *populus* of Cremona. In this unique combination of noble origins, a successful merchant career, anti-simoniacal piety, and a reciprocal sympathy for the poor which led to him donating his entire earnings to them, the figure of St Homobonus was a perfect symbol for the conflicting interests of Cremona in the 12th century. The powerful features of the face on his statue in the crypt of the cathedral at Cremona, where he is buried, suggest stubborn determination and anxiety. His piety and honesty led to his role as pacifier of both family and municipal strife, gaining him the epithet *pacificus vir* or 'man of peace' from Pope Innocent III. As a point of reference, defender of the rights of the poor and underprivileged, his mediating function played an important part in the development of the collective political conscience in the closing decades of the century. The intensity of religious fervour which he generated can be judged from the enthusiastic response of the people of Cremona to the appeal for crusade preached there in person by Pope Urban II in 1195. Homobonus symbolized the *populus* as no other man, and their sense of identity with his life was expressed by his almost immediate canonization two years after his death in 1197 and elevation to the status of patron saint of Cremona. The rapid canonization was a symptom of the search for local identity in the church and a felt need for local saints remarked in the chapter on Montecassino, a local focus for the patriotism of the commune.

If the personality of Homobonus was strong enough to unite the warring factions of Cremona through his personality and patriotism, the strategy of Emperor Frederick Barbarossa indirectly enhanced the same unity and increased the city's prestige: at first in his generous patronage of the city, and later – paradoxically – in the common ground the citizens found in the formation of the Lombard League *against* him.

For the political acumen required in maintaining a delicate diplomatic equilibrium with Frederick on the one hand, and neighbouring cities on the other, entailed a more sophisticated organization than the loose coalition which had first risen in opposition to the immunities and privileges of the count-bishop. Since the death of Henry IV in 1106 the three German emperors Henry V (1106–25), Lothar II (1125–38) and Conrad III (1138–52) had been hamstrung by factious struggles within Germany and unable to exert their authority in any consistent sense over Italy. It was in the absence of a strong central, or imperial, authority that the *populus* had thrived, and such was the power vacuum in which it developed that a modern biographer of Frederick Barbarossa could observe that at the beginning of the emperor's reign 'it was questionable whether a German emperor could safely venture into Italy to aid a pope'. But the election of Conrad III's nephew Frederick by the German princes was to change that, for on the very day after his coronation – at Aachen in March 1152 – the new Emperor proposed an Italian expedition. At first he was dissuaded from such an action, and simply informed the pope of his election by letter. But later in the same year two events made the matter more pressing: first, in October, plaintiffs from Lombardy met him at Würzburg and pleaded with him to come and subdue the factions tearing their cities apart and confirm some of the bishops in their fiefs; second, a letter arrived from a disciple of the reforming preacher Arnold of Brescia, whose passionate denunciations against clerical corruption made him a rallying point for the rebellious citizens of Rome, suggesting that the new emperor travel to Rome to support the citizens against the pope. Pope Eugenius III (1145–53) was himself equally keen that the emperor come to resolve the situation.

Frederick's own view was that he needed to restore peace and papal power in Rome, otherwise he could not legitimately receive the imperial crown from the pope. He was also under a moral obligation to wage war against the Norman kings of Sicily, since his uncle Conrad had made an agreement with the Byzantine emperor to that effect to which he was heir. In the Treaty of Constance signed by Frederick and papal legates on 23 March 1153 he bound himself formally to these two objectives. Thus on his first journey to Italy at the end of the following year he was well-disposed towards the northern Italian cities; at the same time he did not really understand what was happening in them since his concept of rule was feudal, and founded on precisely that feudal role of the count-bishops against which cities like Cremona had rebelled. But this misunderstanding was at first overlooked in Cremona as the result of his policy: for he took the part of the smaller cities like Lodi, Como and Cremona against Milan. Cremona was in fact granted the right to mint coins, while the same right was denied to Milan. Eventually he put Milan to the ban of the Empire, and took the Milanese possession of Tortona – on the road from Milan to Genoa. Once Tortona had been razed to the ground he held the crown-wearing festival in San Michele at Pavia mentioned in the first chapter.

On his return to Germany in 1155, Frederick launched his audacious plan to create a single imperial territory bestriding several existing states. The emotional centre of this territory was to be the small area of southern Switzerland in which the Rhine, Rhône and Ticino rivers have their sources: for the Rhine flowed into Frederick's homeland of Swabia, the Rhône into Burgundy, and the Ticino – which meets the Po just downstream from Pavia – into Lombardy. Together, these large and wealthy areas were to form the heart of the empire. Frederick's intention was made explicit in decrees promulgated at Roncaglia, near Piacenza, in 1158, when he announced his intention of claiming absolute power over Lombardy on the basis of the conquests of his predecessors. Such a claim implied jurisdiction over everything concerning the life, property and liberty of the population of Lombardy, the sole power to concede noble titles, power over commerce and coinage, the right to demand military service and supplies in his favour, and – fatally as far as Cremona would be concerned – authority over all markets, navigable rivers, ports and tolls. Here, in far more dramatic form, the impositions of the bishops of the 10th century were repeated as a very real and imminent threat with military backing; the imperial declaration of intent threatened to eliminate the progress of over a century of struggle by absolute subjugation. Yet it seems that the advantages to be gained in local rivalries weighed more with the Lombard cities than this greater threat. For when Frederick again went to Italy at the head of a large army in 1158 a contingent of troops from Cremona fought with him against Milan – and distinguished themselves for the fury with which they sought revenge for past depredations. Soon however an unsuccessful siege was to lead to a compromise by which Milan was to remain the leading city of Lombardy, a fact which from the point of view of Cremona altered Milan's status from main enemy to principal ally. But in spite of this change Frederick's presence at first led to greater power for Cremona: his army razed the strongly fortified nearby town of Crema – a Milanese outpost – to the ground in 1160 after payment of a bribe of 15,000 silver marks; in newly changed circumstances two years later the Cremonese participated with enthusiastic abandon in the destruction of the quarter of Milan assigned to them when Frederick ordered the demolition of the city. In such a brief period not only had the fastidious outpost been destroyed, with the prospect for Cremona of territorial expansion to the west, but the centre of evil itself was laid low. Charters were dated on such and such a day 'after the destruction of Milan'. It must have seemed a God-sent opportunity to the citizens of Cremona. For the next few years their city enjoyed a specially-favoured status, received encouragement from the emperor in its policies and privileges, and even obtained large grants of money – such as a sum paid to Cremonese ambassadors at an imperial court in Würzburg in 1165.

Yet within two years of that gift Cremona became the focus of opposition to Frederick, and the conspiracy which led to the formation of the Lombard League began there. On his way through Lombardy at the end of 1166, Frederick took hostages from the towns whose loyalty he suspected; this action – together with continued favour shown to Cremona – caused first Piacenza, then allies of Milan such as Bergamo to reconsider their support for the emperor. But the real revolt originated, ironically, in the imperial stronghold of Cremona: at the beginning of 1167 its citizens opened negotiations with Milan, while the emperor passed his time between Parma and Reggio. Although Cremona had never suffered the destruction and massacres of many other Lombard cities, and had never been intimidated, Peter Munz argues that 'in such a city it was very likely that criticism of the imperial administration in Lombardy should be entertained more openly and more vociferously than anywhere else'. As Frederick's army prepared to move south towards Rome in February to deal with the problem of the pro-Lombard Pope Alexander III (1159–81), the people of Cremona – under the tangible menace of the imperial presence – nurtured the conspiracy. In March the representatives of Cremona, Mantua, Bergamo and Brescia formed an alliance which was the basis of the Lombard League. The idea was to prevent the member cities causing harm to one another, to provide mutual support both militarily and diplomatically, and to prevent non-allied armies from marching through their combined territory; the alliance was to last for 50 years. Later in the same month Milan asked to join the League, and in the following month re-fortification of that city began under its auspices; by the end of September the original cities had been joined by Lodi, Piacenza, and Parma. This rapid success of the Lombard League put unprecedented pressure on the Emperor Frederick. He returned north from Rome with a divisive strategy designed to test the solidity of the alliance: he first pardoned Cremona for its participation, then moved against Milan. The alliance held. Next, he tried Piacenza. Again the alliance held, and the emperor himself came under attack. First he was besieged in Pavia, and then in Susa; finally he was forced to flee the latter town ignominiously in disguise and pass over the Mont Cenis pass into Burgundy. As far as Lombardy was concerned his great design was in ruins, and the role of Cremona had been instrumental.

Emperor Frederick returned in the autumn of 1174 at the head of a largely mercenary army, planning a two-pronged attack against Lombardy from west and east simultaneously. He destroyed Susa, took Asti and besieged the new city of Alessandria – founded in 1168 and named for Pope Alexander – hoping to increase his meagre forces by enrolling Lombard soldiers. The siege halted his march, and when he moved east from Alessandria after Easter the next year a large Lombard army had been put together. This army was encamped near Casteggio, and the imperial army near Voghera; mid-way between them, on flat plains perfect for 12th century warfare, was the small town of Montebello. After days of anxious cat-like advances and retreats, the two forces recognized their mutual unwillingness to engage in battle and signed an agreement known as the Peace of Montebello (on 16 April 1175). This allows a glimpse of the increased prestige of Cremona at this time, for when negotiations between Frederick, Pope Alexander and the Lombard army broke down, it was the consuls of Cremona who were appointed as arbitrators over any disagreement; moreover, their decisions were to be binding on both parties. Unfortunately their arbitration was not decisive, for a diplomatic deadlock followed and it was necessary to fight the Battle of Legnano, near Como, in 1176, where Frederick suffered a famous defeat at the hands of the Lombard League. New negotiations which opened after Legnano were also subject to the arbitration of the consuls of Cremona, and agreement was reached in November of the same year; the final peace, known as the Peace of Venice, was concluded in July of 1177. From that moment Emperor Frederick changed course, seeking to achieve through diplomacy what he had failed to gain by force. Again, from the point of view of Cremona and Lombardy, he failed. It is clear even from the briefest account of those complex negotiations and the importance of the parties involved that the role which the *populus* of Cremona had been able to exert through its consuls was one of absolute international prestige – a remarkable achievement in less than a century since its emergence as a social force.

In passing, it is interesting to note that part of the same attempt to achieve through diplomacy what battle had not gained was Frederick's suggestion to King William II of Sicily that the king's aunt Constance should marry the emperor's son Henry. From that marriage, celebrated in the basilica of Sant'Ambrogio at Milan, was born Frederick II – who was to pursue his grandfather's aims in Italy, as we shall see in the chapter on Castel del Monte.

[197]

The multiple threats and internal dissensions in Cremona might easily have destroyed the nascent *comune*. But in fact, as we have seen, they greatly strengthened the city. Within the terms of the Lombard League larger and stronger city walls were built in 1169. Although the primary purpose was defence against the imperial wrath, they also served to provide better protection for the rapidly growing city in general terms, and increased both the population and the city's sphere of influence in granting to the *burgenses* or inhabitants of the nearby suburbs rights which they had previously not possessed. Thus the city encroached on the district – intended as the area within the five miles radius – increasing physical dimensions and political status, and even in one document of the same year guaranteeing security to the *burgenses* still outside the walls. But, as is often the case, rapid growth created an imbalance which threatened to destroy the previous situation. In the following year the new office of 'consuls of justice' or magistrates appeared, suggesting a lack of equality and rights between cives and *burgenses*, and thus the potential seeds of a social conflict. That such tension seriously threatened the city is shown by the institution of the office of *podestà* in 1182 – although it had existed temporarily when Frederick Barbarossa ordered the institution of the office in 1158. Even though the holder of this office, as we have seen in the case of Genoa and Pisa, was a citizen of another town, the *populus* of Cittanova feared a new hegemony of the nobles. Two years later Cittanova seceded: we find a certain Ambigone dei Guazzoni as podestà in Cittanuova, and Gerardo di Dovara in the old city – this latter noble name demonstrating that the fears of the *populus* had been justified (Guazzoni is probably a trade name). Furthermore, both men were natives of Cremona, a fact which was seen to undermine the supposed impartiality of the role of podestà: in fact the inhabitants of Cittanova in their anger went to the old city in mass and murdered Gerardo di Dovara. Their own podestà remained in his position with jurisdiction over the entire city. But it was no clear victory, since in 1185 the old constitution of the city was re-introduced, and for the next 30 years the city was ruled by an erratic series of consuls and podestà themselves subordinated to the *credentia*, which was a council of about 100 members drawn from the major families of the city. The opposing roles of Guazzoni and Dovara marked the beginning of a century in which Cremona often effectively had two governments: a Guelf government ruling from the Palazzo del Popolo in Cittanova, and a Ghibelline government ruling from Palazzo del Comune in the old city.

In a period which had seen running battles in the street, political murder and the secession of what amounted to half the city, it must have seemed that the *populus* and what it had gained and represented since its victory over the bishop a century earlier was doomed to extinction. But it was precisely at that moment, in the closing years of the 12th century and the first years of the 13th, that a further evolution was to resolve these multiple conflicts. This was the evolution of the *populus* as a political party, a vehicle of consensus which allowed space for each of the conflicting factions to exist and collaborate for the good of the city.

In 1209 Cremona received a new civic constitution, a transitory measure which illustrates the gradual but inevitable development of the *populus*. The full city council was then composed of the *credentia*, which had first appeared around a hundred year earlier, together with consuls representing the artisan guilds, the military societies which were rapidly becoming political parties, and the *vicinie* or neighbourhoods which made up each of the four quarters of the city. Thus each category of citizen was represented, especially since the *vicinie* included people who may not otherwise have been included and would thus have been deprived of their rights. This transitory measure received more detailed explanation in the statutes of the *societas populi* of 1229, which are among the oldest surviving statutes of all Italian cities and are especially interesting as displaying for the first time the concept of loyalty to a *patria* – in the sense of city – rather than a social class or economic interest group. Power was enshrined in a body of men representing the local community rather than an abstract and often distant hierarchy depending on the emperor, pope or their representatives.

The 1229 statutes consist of 18 paragraphs. The first of these specifies that the 'council', based on the earlier *credentia*, will consist of 60 *credenderi* or members – 15 for each quarter of the city. It affirms that the members 'should above all be loyal to their *patria*, always watching over it and seeking to order and perform actions which will be of benefit to the public good'. According to the provisions of the third paragraph, at the head of the council were to be four consuls, again representing the quarters of the city. One of their principal tasks was to ensure that the council met at least once every three months, to check on the health, age and absence through either travel or death of the 60 members. Severe punishments were laid down for actions against the 'honour and usefulness of the Commune of Cremona', including perpetual banishment and death. The council also oversaw the military defence of the city, through a militia organized along the lines of modern military service by a captain elected for each quarter every year, and listed the arms which each man was to keep at readiness in his home; military training was to be carried out once a month under command of the militia captain. Civilian rule was overseen by four standard-bearers, whose duties included keeping copies of the statutes and collecting fines imposed by the consuls. Other officials such as a notary and town-criers were also to be appointed,

[199]

with guarantees to ensure that bad debtors, rumour-mongers and trouble-stirrers be banned from office. The whole council was to operate in harmony with the podestà, and to act in accordance with the statutes for the good of the *comune* and people of Cremona (*Commune et Populo Cremonese*). The final paragraph ensures the integrity of the statutes and prevents their alteration by ensuring the presence of all 60 *credenderi* for any modification to the statute. It therefore represents a sophisticated attempt to guarantee collective rule of the city, and shows the fledgling commune tentatively searching for its final form. It is also fascinating to observe that the period of time necessary for the formal deliberation of the commune through two sets of statutes closely parallels that taken for the building of the Palazzo del Comune to house the meetings of the council.

Yet these statutes were at first to have a limited impact, because the *credenderi* were to be – in the words of the statutes – nobles from the old city, and in 1232 the *populus* of Cremona rebelled against the oligarchy which was in fact established by this primitive commune and asked the Emperor Frederick II to appoint a podestà who would temper the power of the nobles. When a second Lombard League was created against Frederick Barbarossa's grandson, Cremona maintained its ancient imperial loyalty by not participating; in 1237 Frederick defeated the League in battle, and established a northern court at Cremona which was temporarily to match his itinerant court in the Kingdom of Sicily and become the fixed residence of his son Henry (King of Sardinia through marriage). Henry was captured in a battle against Bologna and Mantova in 1249, a year before his father's death, leaving Cremona once more to its fate as a battle-ground between the Guelfs and Ghibellines of Cittanova and the old city. For nearly 20 years the city was ruled over by Uberto Pallavicino, descendant of Alberto, together with Buoso da Dovara, another member of the family of the early 12th century bishop Obertus: two names which clearly indicate the way in which the feudal aristocracy had maintained its power. Then in 1267 the Guelf party of Cittanova inflicted a definitive victory over the Ghibellines: Pallavicino and Dovara were forced to flee the city. It was an important historical victory because it represented a new supremacy of the *populus* over the nobles, or the crafts and trades over feudalism, in the last of three phases identified by J.K. Hyde in the evolution of relations between *popolo* and commune: the *popolo* as a pressure group alongside the commune; the *popolo* as an emerging public force sharing power with the commune; and the ascendancy of the *popolo* over the commune. This triumph was a democratic revolution, for the total number of members of the *popolo* who through their representatives shared in communal power and decision-making in Cremona around 1270 has been estimated as between 7,000 and 8,000 – perhaps 15 or 20 per cent of the population. The

The Baptistery

*Torrazzo* was built as a symbol of the new power, and work resumed on the cathedral during the ensuing period of peace and communal rule.

The new social structure was further elaborated in 1313 by a further series of statutes which listed the *paratici* or artisans' guilds and specified their functions. There were 14 such guilds, the first 13 of which included important categories such as the merchants, cloth-weavers, fishermen, millers and innkeepers. The predominance of textile trades is noteworthy. The cloth-weavers, known as *pignolati* from the similarity of their weave to *pignoli* or pine-seeds, had two separate guilds which emphasized the continuing division of the city: the *Paraticum Pugnolatorum Citanovae* for those from Cittanova and a general *Paraticum Pugnolatorum* for all other cloth-workers; other specialized guilds were devoted to tanners, dyers and drapers. A 14th guild, the *Paraticum et Universitas Mercatindiae*, included all the trades not covered by the previous 13. Thus between commune and guilds a large proportion of the population shared in the running of the city. But it was no sudden or improvised arrangement. For this new political, social and commercial identity of Cremona represented the synthesis of centuries of struggle, and the further elaborated statutes of 1313 represent the high-point of Cremona's medieval history.

The piazza at Cremona, with cathedral, baptistery, campanile, and Palazzo del Comune, was the centre of the struggles, battles and controversies which had racked the city; its buildings – together with the Palazzo del Popolo at Cittanova – represent the triumph of the *popolo*. The complex form of the cathedral betrays its hesitant rise to full power, the persistence of a double commune shows the travail of finding the definitive form of popular government, and the octagonal crown added to the *Torrazzo* symbolizes the final triumph. By the date of the original construction of this tower, in 1267, Cremona was already a fully-fledged medieval city: a compact urban development enclosed and protected by walls and with campanile and towers, a community with laws implying a certain equality between citizens in contrast to those in force beyond the walls, a city with a certain degree of political participation in the life of the community, an autonomous economy governed by the communal authorities, and a well-organized market which functioned as a centre for the surrounding territory. Moreover, it was not merely a local agricultural market. Since the middle of the 12th century Cremona had been important as a market for raw cotton imported via Venice and the Po both from the East and from Sicily and southern Italy, and also as a centre for the transformation of raw cotton into fustian and linen. Merchants came from all over Lombardy to transact business there. By the end of the 13th century it was not only an important centre of transformation, but also a centre for distribution towards the western part of Lombardy and south into Tuscany. These areas had previously been served at least in part by Genoa, but after the fall of Acre in the last decade of the 13th century the Genoese lost their markets in Egypt and were obliged to import lower quality material from north Africa. High quality cotton entered Italy exclusively through Venice, and the major point of distribution into Lombardy was Cremona. The city was also important as a financial market place, converting imperial Cremonese money and other silver coins of Lombardy and Tuscany into Venetian *grossi* which could be used in the cotton market.

From the tiny community which rebelled against successive bishops in the 10th century, Cremona had become one of the most prestigious of the Lombard communes. When advisers of the Emperor Henry VII of Luxembourg made an assessment of the wealth of northern Italian cities for tax purposes in 1311, Cremona was ranked seventh after Genoa, Milan, Venice, Padua, Brescia and Verona. Its growth illustrates perfectly the historical moment at which urban life began to prevail over rural life, a process culminating in the 1180s according to the hypothesis of Georges Duby: a moment at which merchant, financier and middleman replaced the peasant or slave at the heart of the economy. But the newly wealthy city was to enjoy a relatively short period of independence and prosperity, for the age of despots impended. Under the Visconti, who rose to power just as Cremona reached its apogee, the centripetal force of Milan gradually absorbed all the communes of Lombardy. Cremona came under their control in 1334 (as Pavia was to do 25 years later). Such a fate was perhaps inevitable, for as the historian Otto of Freising – the Emperor's uncle – had written perceptively two centuries earlier in his chronicle of the *Deeds of Frederick Barbarossa*: 'Cremona and Milan, ancient enemies, always hostile and jealous of each other, never thought of laying down their weapons until one should completely destroy the other or at least win a decisive victory.' Nothing had changed, and the decisive victory was won by Milan.

# NEW RELIGIOUS FERVOUR: SANTA MARIA DEL MONTE

T HE same religious impulse which drove the *patarini*, produced St Homobonus in Cremona and St Francis in Assisi was manifest in a new kind of monasticism evolved by the Cistercians which was to have effects as profound and long-lasting as the earlier Benedictinism. It is a commonplace that the sites of medieval hermitages and monasteries seem irrational to a comfort-minded modern viewer. Yet Santa Maria del Monte seems more irrational than most, so much so that even the Cistercians abandoned it in later centuries.

The ruins of this grange are spectacularly sited at 1,616 metres on a saddle commanding a broad and well-protected basin on the southern slopes of the Gran Sasso d'Italia, the highest mountain of the Apennines. Set on an east-west axis, the main structure consists of a walled rectangle about 65 by 45 paces in size. At the eastern end, in the south-east corner of the rectangle, are the remains of the chapel. Here the walls reach their highest point, some 10–12 metres above the present ground level; but the position of windows and door-posts indicate that rubble from the long-collapsed roof has raised the floor level considerably. The chapel measures about 10 paces in width and 25 paces in length. Little else is recognizable after the ravages of time and the severe mountain climate. Along the eastern side the roughly-cut limestone walls vary from 4 to 5 metres in height; elsewhere they are virtually non-existent. Beyond the grange, like ancient field-division walls snaking up the slope from its northern extremity, broken lines of stone form an enclosure of about 100 by 50 paces. Along the northern edge of this enclosure are extensive remains of outbuildings and stables, their ceilings collapsed into pits in the mountainside in a way which suggests that cellars and basement rooms had been built under ground level for storage; the base of an observation

A view of Santa Maria del Monte showing its mountain setting

tower is also visible. Beneath the grange, 100 metres lower, a small natural lake formed by water draining off the mountain and melted snow in spring provides water and pasture for animals. One of the valleys nearby is still known as the 'Valley of the Monks'.

Although there was a chapel, and a legal document of 1325 refers to the grange as 'Ecclesiam S. Marie de Monte', the surviving structures are reminiscent of simple rural buildings and stables. According to the normal Cistercian plan, and allowing for variations due to local terrain, next to the chapel along the east wall there must have been a vaulted work-room for the monks with a dortoir above. On the inside of this structure, where in fact the lack of building rubble indicates an open space, would have been the cloister, and beyond that an open passageway leading to the quarters of the *conversi* or lay brethren responsible for much of the manual labour. Now nothing inhabits the site save horse-flies and an occasional viper, but in such a setting even simple unmortared stone-work like this is impressive. In fact, the local historian Alessandro Clementi has argued that the very dimensions of a building like this on such a remote and inhospitable site – above the winter snow-line and distant from good roads even today – is evidence of an extraordinary attempt at land improvement. For this remote monastery may be taken to represent one of the most important developments of medieval Europe: the agricultural colonization of huge tracts of land, in which new tools and techniques dramatically

[205]

changed both landscape and food production and helped to pave the way for a new – and numerically greater – society.

The economic impulse at Santa Maria del Monte was provided by the revival and development of the ancient practice of transhumance, which involved an autumn migration of flocks of sheep south to the plains of Apulia and a return to the high mountain pastures in early summer. The drovers' road or *tratturo* followed a route of great antiquity, used at least since the time of the Second Punic War (218–201 BC) and probably long before. The transhumance was an integral part of the pastoral culture of the Samnite tribes which occupied the area between the Gran Sasso range and Apulia in pre-Roman times, just as it was of other ancient pastoral cultures in the Pyrenees in France, and in Galicia and Extremadura in Spain. The route was then the only well-trodden one between central and southern Italy, and was used by the Romans when they came to develop their network of roads: the later Via Minucia, a continuation of the Via Caecilia which itself led south from the Via Salaria, followed the route of the *tratturo* from Sulmona to the south. Roman control of the entire area enabled large landowners to possess land both in the summer and winter pastures, so that the transhumance became an important factor of pastoral economics.

The Roman writer and scholar Marcus Terentius Varro (116–27 BC), a friend and contemporary of Cicero from the nearby Sabine city of Rieti (Roman 'Reate'), provides fascinating testimony. In Book II of his *De re rustica* he relates that 'the flocks of sheep in Puglia are taken to the land of the Samnites for the summer' and that his 'own flocks, which used to pass the summer in the Mountains of Rieti, spent their winter in Puglia' (it is worth noting that Varro here uses the verb 'to hibernate' in its original sense of passing the winter – *mihi greges in Apulia hibernabant*). Then, with a picturesque turn of phrase, he says that between these two regions the drovers used a public road, the *calles publicae*, which joined them like 'two baskets held together by a yoke'. Varro was himself a large landowner and his book is a treatise in dialogue form on farm management and agriculture, stressing among other things the usefulness of sheep: first, to provide milk and cheese for food; and second, to provide skin and wool for clothing (the book was one of many saved from oblivion by the library at Montecassino). Varro was writing as a man of 80, and therefore referred to customs in the first half of the 1st century BC. It is interesting to observe that while the road was public, the pastures at each end of the 'yoke' were often privately owned. It is likely that the curiously named and beautiful village of Pescocostanzo, whose site south of Sulmona can have no other *raison d'être* than a post on the *tratturo*, derives from the *fundus Costantii* of a similar Roman landowner.

[206]

A passing reference by Varro to the fact that the drovers were punctilious in their payment of the required dues for fear of committing a violation of the law is sufficient to suggest both the importance of the transhumance in the Roman economy, and the degree of organization. Indeed, an Italian archaeologist has speculated that the rite of transhumance may be at the very heart of the myth of the foundation of Rome. According to this argument, the absence of weapons in Bronze Age sites of the indigenous tribes of the Apennines can be explained by a period of relative peace which allowed them to concentrate on their primary activity of breeding sheep and cattle; during this period they migrated southward and westward as a consequence of finding more amenable places to live during the transhumance. The rites of departure and the annual custom of leaving the settlement rendered migration easier, for permanent migration is no more than a one-way transhumance. Rites associated with spring departures led to the Roman idea of a sacred spring with its offerings (the *ver sacrum*). Thus entire family groups migrated and formed new tribes like the Marsi, Peligni and Vestini who later became the peoples of the medieval transhumance; these migrations also underlie the tradition of the *veria sacra* of the Sabine tribes towards Rome. On this view the transformation of a seasonal migration into a permanent one led to the foundation of Rome itself (until recent times an alternative transhumance from the Montereale area – on the western slopes of the Gran Sasso range and once within Sabine territory – was to Viterbo, north of Rome). The presence of the she-wolf which nurtured Romulus and Remus is thus explained by the transfer of pastoral traditions to the newly founded city since the wolf, still present in the Apennines, was never native to Rome. The simple huts of Sabine settlements on two of the hills of Rome, the Quirinal and the Esquiline, may represent no more than the temporary homes of a migrating people. If this is the case, then the legend of the Sabine women who were 'invited' to Rome by Romulus may be read as a mythological explanation of that one-way transhumance.

The twice-annual migration continued throughout Roman history, and in fact the medieval word *tratturo* derives from the laws of Justinian (527–565) where the privilege to use the *calles publicae* is referred to as a *tractoria*. But the transhumance fell into disuse when the endemic unsafety of long-distance routes together with the dispersal of large holdings of land made the longer *tratturi* obsolete. It was with the Norman domination of the Kingdom of Naples – and of the Abruzzo region around 1140 – that the whole of southern Italy was once again ruled by a single power. One of the immediate consequences was the reopening of the ancient *tratturi*, just as the Cistercians were expanding into the area. In 1155 William I of Sicily issued a decree which regulated the rights of

[207]

pasture along the route, and punishment for offenders including confiscation of their property and even death. As we shall see in the next chapter, both the breeding of sheep and the foundation of Cistercian monasteries were encouraged by Frederick II. It was under his rule that the 'Demanio del Tavoliere' or 'Demesne of the Plain' was introduced in the lower part of the Capitanata; this was achieved by uniting land belonging to throne and church with private land, and was intended to facilitate the collection of taxes from the owners who sent their flocks on the transhumance. Frederick also emanated the 'Mena delle Pecore in Puglia', which organized and distributed the pastures, and instituted two annual fairs. The fair in Foggia, which was held in the first half of May when the flocks left for the journey north, survived into the 20th century.

In their heyday, there were 12 main *tratturi* and innumerable minor tracks known as *tratturelli* which converged with them; the longest was that from L'Aquila to Foggia, a distance of nearly 300 kilometres. The main *tratturi* consisted of broad swathes of land '60 trapassi' or about 110 metres wide, while the smaller ones were from 15 to 20 'trapassi'. At regular intervals along the main routes were stopping-places with protected places for both shepherds and their flocks, often with a rustic chapel, where forage was available at carefully regulated prices and safety guaranteed in exchange for the taxes paid. Statistics from the 12th and 13th centuries do not exist, but under the rule of King Alfonso of Aragon (1442–58) the larger flocks consisted of 10,000–15,000 sheep and the smaller ones of 200–300 with a total of between two and three million sheep over the 12 *tratturi*. The taxes which then flowed into the coffers of the Kingdom of Naples have been said to have constituted 'one of the most conspicuous sources of revenue'.

Santa Maria del Monte was at the source of this great flow of sheep, men and money. Sited at an ideal gathering place and control-point for flocks which grazed on the enormous and excellent summer pastures of the high plateau known as Campo Imperatore, one of the few amenable routes down from the plateau to the L'Aquila-Foggia *tratturo* passed by the grange. The outbuildings and folds above the grange probably served both for gathering flocks ready for departure in autumn, and for mass shearing on their return in early summer. The monks' skill in breeding and curing sheep made the grange a vital centre for the pastoral life of the mountains. In this way, as we shall see, the Cistercian presence played a vital role in generating new wealth which transformed the entire area of south-central Italy and established an economy which sustained its population until the present century. Following the precepts of St Bernard of Clairvaux, an early and seminal recruit to the new Order, that 'woods and rocks will teach [you] more than any master', they had come to live in a

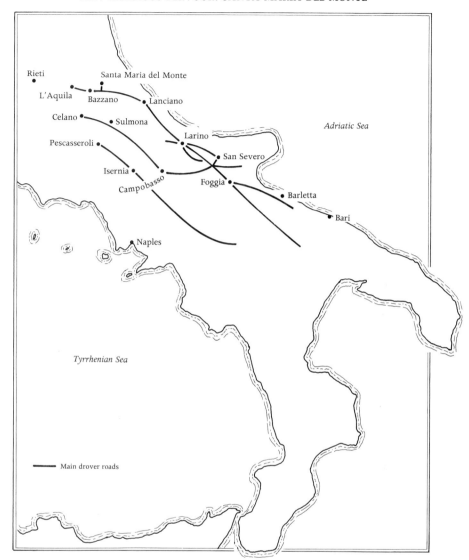

Fig. 11. The main drover roads of the transhumance between the central Apennines and the plains of Apulia

barren wilderness; by their industry, the wilderness was transformed into a fount of great wealth.

The expansion of the Cistercians from their foundation at Cîteaux in 1098 – and virtual refoundation with the arrival of St Bernard in 1112 – is one of the great success stories of medieval Europe. It has been argued by Albert D'Haenens that their abbeys 'functioned as laboratories in which

[209]

solutions to the problems posed by man's relationship to space, time and his body were elaborated and tested as prototypes or prospective models.' In other words, the organization of the monastery was a prototype for the organization of the new cities. Parallel in a sense to the emerging consensus which government by the *populus* implied, life within Cistercian abbeys was based upon common acceptance of and obedience to a law; elements of monastic life which may seem less attractive to the modern layman, such as delation and public confession of guilt in chapters, were themselves models of group behaviour. Within this context, regular chapter meetings and daily discussions, together with a daily check on individual obedience to the *Rule* of the Order, may be said to have constituted a prototype of collective political participation. As early as 1115, contemporary with the earliest communes, a chapter-general known as the *parliamentum* was evolved at Cîteaux; the Cistercian constitution, the *Carta Caritatis*, was written about the same time by the third abbot of Cîteaux, the Englishman Stephen Harding. This charter, which was probably begun in 1113 and was confirmed by Pope Calixtus II six years later, created an intricate governmental system for the Order. All electoral, legislative, administrative and judicial power, together with spiritual supervision, was overseen by the *parliamentum*, which was at first held at irregular intervals but eventually became a triennial meeting of up to 300 abbots. That the mechanism of the *parliamentum* was used as a blueprint for lay political organizations, at least in England, is strongly suggested by the important role of the Archbishop of Canterbury Stephen Langton in drawing up the Magna Carta just over a century later. For he was much influenced by Cistercian practice, and when on his consecration at Viterbo in 1207 he was prevented from travelling to England by King John he spent six years at the abbey of Pontigny (one of the first four daughter houses of Cîteaux, founded in 1114). In Italy, as we shall see, the ruler most willing to learn from Cistercian experience was the Emperor Frederick II.

The practical organization of life for a large body of men in remote areas such as that of Santa Maria del Monte entailed new methods of production, distribution and preservation of food, especially since the special requirements of taboos and fasts often rendered traditional methods unsuitable. For instance, the ban on eating the meat of quadrupeds directed special attention to pisciculture, poultry breeding, dairy produce, and the increased production of vegetables and fruit. This in turn led to improved fishing methods, the construction of ponds and water barriers, and the development of techniques of artificial fecondation. Within the monasteries the preparation of large quantities of raw produce necessitated changes in kitchens: this resulted in new designs for architectural elements such as ovens and chimneys, and improved

[210]

The ruins of S. Maria del Monte

drainage, such as may be seen at Fontevrault (such large abbeys often had as many as 500 monks, up to 300 *conversi*, plus regular visitors). Architectural change was also necessary to improve methods of long-term storage and cellarage of excess produce for leaner seasons: the huge vaulted cellars at Clairvaux or Fountains Abbey were up to 70 metres long. Improved techniques were devised for the production of cheese from surplus milk, cider from apples, and especially wine from grapes: from 1115 onwards at the Cistercian house at Clairvaux the wine-making brothers were required to undergo a three year apprenticeship. Celebrated Burgundies such as Clos-Vougeot, Vosne-Romanée and the Bonnes-Mares were developed at Nuits – where they were established in 1098 – by the Cistercians. This vast improvement in the quality of foodstuffs in 12th and 13th century monasteries has led to the assertion that monastic cuisine was at the origin of modern gastronomy. Similar improvements in animal husbandry and breeding were also of great importance, especially in the case of the development of sheep breeding and the wool trade both in southern Italy and East Anglia. Frederick II drew on Cistercian experience and skill in his search for the improvement of horse- and sheep-breeding techniques.

Other innovations came from special conditions of monastic hygiene, such as increased personal hygiene resulting from sexual abstinence, and

[211]

the skilled use of running water in the development of communal lavatories. At the abbey of Grande Chartreuse there was already in the 12th century running water inside to sluice the lavatories; an interesting surviving example may be seen in the external reredorter, or latrine, at Muchelney Abbey near Langport in Somerset. The barn-like reredorter with its individual compartments is not only detached from the main buildings of the abbey and supplied with running water: it is situated at the south-east corner so that sewage drained away from the abbey. As in great Benedictine abbeys like St Gall and Cluny, the infirmaries of Cistercian abbeys were always set apart from other buildings to eliminate easy contagion. The earliest civic hospitals, such as the Ospedale Maggiore founded by Francesco I Sforza in Milan, were organized on the Cistercian model. In fact the monastic plan as developed in the 12th century, with walls, streets, gates, open spaces within, and carefully-planned distribution of buildings in the greater abbeys, made the Cistercian abbeys microcosms of urban life. Monks and *conversi* specialized in the building trades necessary for the construction of the new planned cities, as masons and architects or in gardening and irrigation. The inhabitants of the abbeys were aware of this similarity: the Cistercian monk Guerric d'Igny, who died in 1157, wrote in one of his sermons that 'we live as if in a town'. Outbuildings such as granaries, stables, presses, guest quarters, or the fine forge at Fontenay, were built as proudly as similar buildings on great estates or in wealthy cities.

At a site such as Santa Maria del Monte the Cistercian predilection for remote and uncultivated terrain made virtue out of necessity: they soon became leading experts in forest clearance, land reclamation, drainage, damming, the construction of dykes, aqueducts, and irrigation channels, and in obtaining increased power for mills and forges. The fact that the Cistercians were organized in large, stable and determined communities provided the necessary intelligence, application and man-power for innovation, and they became pioneers in both large-scale agricultural production and detailed aspects of farming, such as the improvement of agricultural implements. These improvements included advances in the use of metals in their forges, better harnesses and ploughs, the introduction of crop rotation, the use of marl as a fertilizer, and advances in management techniques and the keeping of accounts – in which their warrior branch of the Knights Templar excelled. The production of parchment from animal skin and textiles from wool are examples of secondary activities in which the Cistercians made improvements. Less predictable advances were made in the production of musical instruments. Above all, unlike later innovators, they were liberal with advice, and provided information to farmers, artisans and even rulers like Frederick II.

Surviving walls of the chapel at S. Maria del Monte

Cistercian abbeys became renowned for their expertise: Chiaravalle, just south of Milan, was famous as the place where they built the first permanent irrigation system; the houses of Casamari and Fossanova south of Rome specialized in horse-breeding; in the same way the mother house of Casanova (founded just inland from Pescara in 1191) and its dependencies like Santa Maria del Monte specialized in sheep-rearing.

Life in a monastery at the frontiers of civilized life like Santa Maria del Monte was hard; still today the nearest asphalted road is closed by snow for several months a year and the nearest village of Santo Stefano Sessanio is regularly isolated. It might best be compared to that of highland crofters: in winter the grange looks across the mist in neighbouring valleys as crofts on Skye across the promontories and bays of the Atlantic; the monks and *conversi* hewed a living from similar unpromising rocky soil; their creature comforts were equally minimal. Yet it was an ideal site for the new Order, since within the severe asceticism of St Bernard the pains and injuries of manual labour were to be equated with physical mortification – even though the Cistercians were quick to develop the use of *conversi*, who first appeared in the eremiticial foundations of the early 12th century. The *conversi* were lay brothers usually of peasant origin, subject to monastic discipline but whose main task was manual labour. They represented one of the great inventions of the middle ages: cheap, totally loyal and totally owned labour in large numbers. The *conversi* were one of the vital

[213]

elements of the rapid growth of Cistercian wealth: in large French monasteries they numbered as many as 300, and were usually found in a proportion of three or four to each monk. They endured a year-long novitiate before being admitted to the Order, dressed as monks, and made a lifelong vow in the same way; their life was governed by the scansion of the monastic day, with the sole provision that they were to follow divine offices wherever they happened to be working. To a modern mind the most astonishing fact about these *conversi* was that they could never aspire to genuine monastic status, and were doomed to remain illiterate in the midst of a community in which reading was one of the main activities. As one historian has remarked, they were a kind of celibate monastic vassal which constituted 'a disciplined labour force which required no wages, had no families to support, and could not withdraw its labour.' Like other slaves they later rebelled, so that the system came to an end by about 1300; but by that time the Cistercians had been able to create a formidable economic empire.

Daily life was conditioned by the exigencies of manual labour and agricultural production. Given the strict rules and hierarchical structure of the Order the same procedures would be carried out in such a remote house as in the greater French houses of Clairvaux and Fontenay, or the strangely Burgundian abbey of Fossanova just south of Rome (which we shall see in the chapter on Frederick II). After Prime all monks within the monastery would go to the chapter, where they would salute the East and then sit on a stone bench which ran round the room. Then they would listen to readings from the *Rule*, make confession and listen to announcements concerning special events, feast days or any special prayers requested by the brothers – such as for a deceased relative. Then, after saluting the East again, they would return upstairs to the communal dortoir: there they would find tools such as shovels and hoes for the day's work laid out on the beds. A large wooden block known as the *tabula* would then be sounded by the prior, and the monks would return down to listen to the distribution of tasks for the day. This would be at around 6 a.m. in summer, later in winter. Tasks would include hay-making, sheep-shearing or specialized jobs such as work in a forge, and would continue for about three hours. Then the tools would be cleaned, the monks would wash and dust their working habits, perhaps return their tools to the dortoir, and attend Terce. The rest of the morning would be devoted to reading, meditation, the office of Sext, and perhaps a meal and/ or a rest (in summer). The *tabula* would be sounded again after Nones, about 3 p.m., when the monks would return to work with the same procedure until the sounding of the bell for Vespers. For the *conversi* the day was much the same, with extra work replacing the hours devoted to reading and meditation. In a particularly harsh climate such as that of Campo Imperatore, we may imagine winter working hours severely curtailed, and compensated by the increased seasonal labour at the departure and return of the transhumance, and moments such as sheep-shearing. The high altitude meant that vines and olives needed to be transported from lower monasteries – such as the parent house at Casanova. Local crops such as lentils and other legumes, still a feature of the area, were probably produced together with the by-products of sheep rearing. Some parts of the statutes of the Cistercians read like an agricultural manual, or Varro's *De re rustica*, for it is as precise on the care of animals and land as on the performance of divine office: it is difficult to imagine St Benedict specifying the distance of pigsties from a grange, or allowing for the fact that even shepherds must get their daily food from the monastery.

The exact foundation date of the grange at Santa Maria del Monte is unknown, but must have occurred at some time between 1191 and 1289. For it is known that the Cistercian Order first appeared in this part of central Italy in the former year, when Countess Margherita of Loreto Aprutino sponsored the foundation of Casanova. Today no more than the chapel of this monastery survives, on the eastern slopes of the Gran Sasso range between the villages of Civitella Casanova and Villa Celliera. At about the same time the Countess appears to have made a grant of land 'near Santo Stefano' in the same year; the 18th century historian Antonio Ludovico Antinori notes that this 'seems to have been in the place called *Cambradore*', which is Campo Imperatore – thus coinciding with the position of S. Maria del Monte. Like many Cistercian abbeys, Casanova soon ramified into five dependent branches: Ripalta (near San Severo, Apulia) in 1201; S. Matteo, now called S. Pastore (in the diocese of Rieti) in 1218; S. Spirito d'Ocre (near L'Aquila) in 1222; S. Maria (on the Tremiti Islands) in 1236; and S. Bartolomeo di Carpineto (near Penne) in 1259. Under the third of these foundations, Santo Spirito, were two dependent granges; S. Benedetto delle Cafasse (now known as S. Nicola, ten kilometres north of L'Aquila), and Santa Maria del Monte. They first appear in a document of 1303 where the prior of Santo Spirito, Giacomo di Valle, solicits a sentence from the Bishop of L'Aquila concerning the exemption of the granges from the tax known as the 'tenth' of their mill, fishing and pasture rights. So although the land was granted earlier it would appear the buildings of the grange were erected after the foundation of Santo Spirito in 1222; the first certain documentary mention was in 1289, by which time it was already prosperous. But there is a possibility that it was founded as soon as the land was given, *before* Santo Spirito: in fact a document of 1196 records the gift of some land to the church of S. Maria della Carità by a certain Tommaso de' Barili and his wife

Mobilia di Ceccano for the redemption of their souls, and those of their immediate family members. The land amounted to 'a bushel of seed', that is, the amount of land which could be sown with eight gallons of seed, and Antinori claimed that this church may be identified with Santa Maria del Monte.

The use of monastic foundations for strategic purposes was a long-consolidated practice. The Lombard kings Ratchis and his brother Aistulf encouraged the foundation of the monasteries at Sesto, Nonantola and Monte Amiata, and one of the few land grants made by Charlemagne during his brief visits to the Italian peninsula was the gift of two strategic alpine valleys, the Valcamonica and Valtellina, to the French monasteries of St Martin of Tours and St Denis respectively. In fact control over remote areas of Italy had been achieved by the establishment of great frontier monasteries throughout the period of Lombard and Carolingian rule, notable examples being the already cited Benedictine houses at Bobbio, Farfa, Montecassino, S. Vicenzo al Volturno and S. Clemente in Casauria. In the chapters on Montecassino, Pavia, Bari and Cremona we have seen how these Benedictine foundations contributed to the local economies of their region. But the Cistercian practice was something quite new, above all in their policy of earning income by direct exploitation of the land instead of the more traditional means of tithes and rents for the *curtis*, and the performance of holy offices such as confession, absolution and burial rites. To take one instance of traditional practice, a *curte* of San Vincenzo al Volturno was defined as an area of 270 paces square, complete with church, peasant hovels and store-rooms, with one-third of the land given to the leaseholder free of all charges to support the agricultural labourers, and a tax of one-half of the production of wine and grain to be paid to the abbey. The direct management of thousands of acres of pasture and the enormous numbers of sheep involved in the transhumance was quite a different proposition; together with constant attempts at improving crop yields and the breeds of animal, it required the evolution of totally new skills and procedures. The workforce provided by the *conversi* enabled the Cistercians to engage in labour-intensive projects such as land reclamation, forest clearance, irrigation systems and the development of previously unused land. Thus the new centres of production which they created became the generators of the local economy and acted as magnets to agricultural workers, masons, and tradesmen of all kinds who were introduced to new techniques and implements imported from France. This distinction between local people and the newly-arrived foreigners is made explicit by Buccio di Ranallo, a poet who wrote a verse history of the city of L'Aquila in the mid-14th century, who refers to the Cistercians as 'Francisci' or Frenchmen.

[216]

The success of new farming methods and land reclamation soon produced a surplus of goods. Since the monks did not eat meat, used relatively little of the non-edible products of animal husbandry such as wool and leather, the surplus was often considerable. Although St Bernard himself made severe strictures against usury and forbade personal property to his monks, the use of cash by the monasteries following his *Rule* grew rapidly in the 12th century. With large properties and the frequent possession of dependent houses at some distance, it was much easier in the growing monetary economy to transport cash than goods. The Cistercians became wealthy almost in spite of themselves, since with the money they gained there was little to do but purchase more land or improve already existing abbeys and their lands. A surviving parchment document written for the Abbot of Casanova not only authorises Jacobi de Carpineto, prior of Santo Spirito, to act as factor and grants him and Brother Nicolae de Asserico to purchase some land in Bazzano (a vital point at the beginning of the main *tratturo* just outside L'Aquila), but permits them to make a down payment of 600 ducats and acts as a guarantee for the remaining 1,000 ducats of debt which they incur. In England at the same time it was common practice, despite St Bernard's strictures, to borrow against the following year's wool crop, and we may assume that the Cistercians of Central Italy were no different. Similar early prohibitions against the decoration of Cistercian churches and the use of luxuries also fell by the wayside: abbeys were embellished with books, altar cloths, plates, pitchers, candle holders, retables and reliquaries. From their point of view, cash enhanced liturgy; from the point of view of their many enemies, the Cistercians were referred to as the new Jews of Europe.

Their success however generated wealth for others as well, and in this area the expansion of the transhumance and sheep-related activities had consequences beyond the enrichment of the Order. It was almost as if the ever-increasing numbers of sheep and men along the *tratturi* spread wealth as they passed – as on the more famous pilgrim routes, to Rome or Compostela. One recent author has suggested that as many as 300 'urban complexes' came into being as the result of the presence of the *tratturi*. This building falls into three distinct categories: the first consists of the customs houses and official resting places (established later by Alfonso of Aragon); the second category includes chapels and churches built along the route for prayer and shelter, which on a bright day seem almost like mirages amongst fields of grain miles from any village and often distant from the modern road; and the third category comprises the monasteries and granges such as S. Maria del Monte purpose-built in function of the economy of the transhumance. The wayside chapels, some of which reached the dimensions of a large parish church, had folds and other

[217]

outbuildings to provide shelter built against them: placed at intervals of a day's march, they fulfilled a multiple role as landmarks, places for prayer, and refuge from the elements. At the beginning of each *tratturo* were even larger churches: an example is the magnificent Romanesque basilica of Santa Giusta in the tiny village of Bazzano a few miles south of L'Aquila. Today it stands incongruously in an exceptionally bland village, ludicrously oversized as far as present pastoral needs are concerned in the manner of the Suffolk wool churches, but once the fields below Bazzano were the principal gathering place for the start of the autumn *tratturo* to Foggia (as we have seen, the Cistercians possessed land in Bazzano). Santa Maria del Monte was the gathering place for the principal tributary of this *tratturo*, while on the plains of Apulia were other monasteries – including some founded by Frederick II – where the flocks were blessed on safe arrival and then departed again the following spring.

Apart from these solitary buildings, numerous villages and towns along the route prospered as the result of the transhumance. Some, like Scanno or the Pescocostanzo already mentioned, possess churches and palaces of surprising elegance for such remote and apparently poor areas. It has also been shown how the important city of L'Aquila itself came into being as the result of the increased wealth, rapid increase in population and need for a new urban centre under the impulse of the Cistercian economic thrust in the mid-13th century. Inexistent in 1250, by 1294 it was rich enough to host the coronation of Pope Celestine V and a crowd which contemporary chronicles put at over 100,000 – including bishops, cardinals, nobles, and the Kings of France and Hungary. In the 14th and 15th centuries it was a major centre of the international wool trade, with elegant palaces and courtyards testifying to great wealth accumulated from nothing in a short period of time.

A further – and equally unexpected – by-product of the transhumance was the exportation of patron saints along the route of the *tratturo*. For instance, the early Christian saints of Siponto (modern Manfredonia) on the coast of Apulia to the east of Foggia, were honoured by a series of important churches and cults in the valleys near the northern end of the main *tratturo*. One notable example was Santa Giusta: as we have seen, the basilica at Bazzano was dedicated to her, as was the first church to be constructed in the new city of L'Aquila. Another patron saint who originated from Siponto, where he had been the bishop, was San Eusanio: his route northwards from his home town may be followed by tracking the churches and villages named for him, at Lanciano (near the coast between Siponto and Pescara), the village of San Eusanio south of L'Aquila, a hamlet of San Eusanio north of L'Aquila, and another church in Varro's hometown at Rieti. Since he was responsible for the conversion of

*Above:* One of the surviving transhumance churches on the main *tratturo*, with the depression made by the drover's road clearly visible. *Below:* Outbuildings of the transhumance church

[219]

numerous villages still then pagan, it is a curious confirmation of a phenomenon we have observed in the history of Bari: that Christianity followed the ancient Roman trade routes from the East rather than the more direct, and nearer, route from Christian Rome itself.

The revival of this ancient route was one of the key factors in the medieval economic development of a large part of central and southern Italy. The Cistercians were, in the words of Sir Richard Southern, 'the greatest organizers of economic forces before the Fuggers and Medicis'. But the emergence of new 'organizers' and of the great new merchant cities rapidly undermined their importance. From its heyday in the 13th and 14th centuries the grange at Santa Maria del Monte went into a steady decline as the Spanish rulers of the Kingdom of Naples gradually assumed control of the transhumance. Documentary evidence of 1592 shows that it was still in existence as a monastery, but at some stage in the next two centuries it was abandoned. In a record of land ownership dating from 1753 the site is referred to dismissively as a pasture within the bounds of nearby Santo Stefano 'commonly known as' the 'meadow' of Casanova. Then it disappears from historical records, and we may assume that the roughly-hewn limestone blocks were plundered by shepherds for the walls, folds and shelters which are dotted over Campo Imperatore. But this was by no means the end of Cistercian land ownership in the area: as late as 1807 a Napoleonic suppression order names possessions of the Cistercians in as many as 16 villages in the valley, including all the most important ones.

Thus the economy into which they breathed new life still flourished 600 years after the arrival of the first Cistercians in the area. The transhumance itself survived into the 20th century: what had once been a 'conspicuous source of revenue' continued to perform a vital role until recent years. It was only with economic changes following the Second World War that the medieval transhumance ended. The few animals which make the journey today do so by lorry, save those of a single shepherd who makes the annual journey from his village in Molise down to the plains of Apulia. The Cistercian presence in the valleys below the Gran Sasso is reduced to a series of spectacular ruins.

# 9

# *THE EMPEROR FREDERICK II AND*
# *CASTEL DEL MONTE*

T HE unique, perfectly octagonal structure known as Castel del Monte sits at 540 metres on the summit of a rounded hill in the range known as the Murge to the east of Bari, as if it were a crown surveying the land that Frederick II loved. For although his father was the German Emperor Henry VI, Frederick's first royal title was 'King of the Romans and of Sicily' and as a child he was known as 'the boy of Apulia' (*puer Apulie*) because of his Norman heritage. The future emperor was born on the move, at Jesi (near Ancona) in 1194 while his mother was travelling from Regensburg to Palermo, and he spent much of his life as an itinerant king, moving almost incessantly from castle to castle, and from city to city. Frederick never had a fixed capital, but seems to have been happiest and to have come closest to a stable residence in Apulia: it was there that he built his favourite residence, his hunting lodges and a series of massive castles; it was also in Apulia that he died – at Castel Fiorentino, now little more than a ruined wall eight miles north-west of Lucera, in 1250. More than any of his other buildings Castel del Monte symbolizes the austerity and grandeur of Frederick II, and the perception of the imperial role which motivated him in the heroic but ultimately impossible task he set himself: to be the 'transformer of the world', as the epithet *Immutator Mundi* used by his contemporaries expresses it. One of the many curious facts about Frederick II is that although his frenetic building activity peppered the countryside of southern Italy with castles, towers and palaces, he never built a church. Perhaps in this sense we may consider Castel del Monte as his 'temple': an architectural hymn in praise of the arts he loved.

Superficially, the description of such a regular building is simple. It is a two-storeyed octagonal structure of fine limestone with an octagonal tower at each of the eight angles, and inside an octagonal courtyard; above

Castel del Monte seen from below

is a flat roof terrace. Each floor has eight vaulted trapezoidal rooms of identical dimensions. The structure is 24 metres in height, with walls varying from 2.20 to 2.40 metres in thickness; each of the eight external façades is 16.30 metres in width, and the total diameter from the furthest corners of the towers is 56 metres.

Yet Castel del Monte is far more than the sum of its parts enumerated in this stark manner. First of all it is an astonishing *mélange* of architectural style. The main entrance to the castle is by a double staircase leading to a severely classical portal: this is sustained by pilasters with Corinthian capitals, and surmounted by a tympanum which was probably decorated by relief sculptures of Frederick and his son Manfred – rather like the Parthenon. Within this portal is a smaller doorway with a curiously undecided arch which is part-Gothic and part-Arab in form; fluted columns on either side of the door bear Hohenstaufen lions in place of the expected capitals. This eclecticism, typical of Frederick II and his architecture, is emphasized by the incongruous mullioned and traceried Gothic window which sits improbably almost on the point of the severely classical tympanum. Yet, as in later Renaissance 'compositions' of elements of diverse architectural provenance, the effect is harmonious: grand, imposing, and uncluttered. Furthermore, this architectural perfection masks the scale of the building: on approaching it seems larger and more massive than any photograph can suggest. The portal, which in a

[222]

photograph seems just an elegant classical doorway as the result of its superb proportions, in fact fills an entire 16 metre façade of the castle. A complete circuit of the building on foot is some 300 paces.

The windows of the lower floor are simple in design, made of red breccia, while the more elaborate double-mullioned windows of the upper floor suggest the idea of a *piano nobile* for the Emperor and his court. These are a delicate composition of red breccia and white marble, each one surmounted by a lunette with a rose window on coloured marble columns that were removed to the later palace of the Neapolitan kings at Caserta. The only exception is that between the second and third tower, which looks towards Andria, where there is a treble-mullioned window. Legend has it that this exception to the rule was requested by Frederick himself, since his second wife Yolanda de Brienne and third wife Isabella of England (King Henry III's sister) were both buried in the crypt of the cathedral at Andria. If this is the case, then it suggests that this room was a personal room of the Emperor himself, a hypothesis strengthened by the extraordinary nature of the third tower – which lies between this room and the fourth room of the *piano nobile*. It has traditionally been known as the 'falconer's tower', and is in fact quite different to the others. It ends abruptly at the level of the first floor, and access to the upper part of the tower and a small totally dark room within it can only be gained by means of a trap-door and ladder. This conforms perfectly to the description which Frederick wrote in his manual on falconry of the ideal place to keep newly-captured baby falcons: in an isolated building or tower, far from the noise of people, in a place which is difficult of access, and totally dark. Moreover this tower possesses direct access to the roof-terrace, which could have been used for training the birds. Once again the personal interests of the emperor seems to have conditioned the structure of his castle, which appears to have been conceived as a purpose-built hunting lodge with imperial quarters on the upper floor. All these rooms are well-lighted, and have elegant marble columns and capitals supporting the vaults; the walls were faced in marble up to the mouldings which ran round the rooms at the height of the capitals. Above the marble, the walls were made of stone in Roman 'opus reticulatum' – a clear indication of Frederick's classical taste since such stone decoration had been in disuse for centuries. The floors were decorated with multi-coloured mosaics, while travertine benches ran round just above the floor. Five of these upper rooms have fireplaces, compared with only two on the lower floor which were probably for the use of kitchens.

Technically, the castle is also fascinating. The carefully planned water supply and inclusion of flushing lavatories are reminiscent of the attention to these details paid by the Arabs, as we have seen in Palermo (and al-

[223]

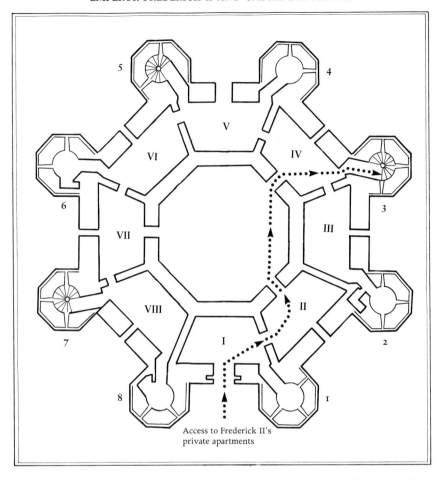

Fig. 12a. Ground floor plan of Castel del Monte, showing the well-defended access to Frederick II's private apartments

Qahîra). Five of the towers contain small, private cubicles with water supplied from the roof, and broad stone seats in the Roman fashion, while drains also carried water from the roof to an octagonal basin placed in the centre of the internal court and to the giant cistern beneath it. The other three towers contain spiral staircases leading to the upper floor, and although from a distance the towers appear solid the numerous loopholes with embrasures in each of them provide sufficient light for the stairs and lavatories within. Also, the apparently small windows on the ground floor are so dramatically bevelled that the window area inside is twice that of the external aperture, thus providing sufficient light. The distribution of loopholes over the towers is moreover irregular, following internal

[224]

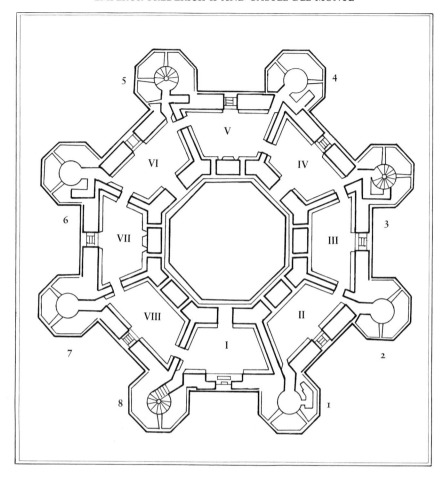

Fig. 12b. Upper floor of Castel del Monte, showing the imperial apartments (I, II, III) and the falconer's staircase (3)

structure rather than external appearance. Similarly the arrangement of doors, and thus of possible routes through the castle, is irregular: for instance, entering on the ground floor access is provided only to the first room on the right, and thence to the internal courtyard; but neither to the left nor to the third room on the right – which corresponds to what we have suggested may be the emperor's private room on the upper floor. In fact the only way to get to this 'private room' was to re-enter the building from the courtyard into the fourth room on the right, ascend the third tower, and turn left; the toilet facilities in the second tower (whose only access was from the third room, itself only attainable from the fourth) were only available from this private room, and were in fact the most

[225]

sumptuously decorated of all – including carefully placed ventilation loopholes. There is also evidence that there was once a bath. Once on the *piano nobile*, however, access to the rooms was facilitated by a now-disappeared wooden gallery which ran around the courtyard at the level of the doorways opening within. Both the security and the privacy of the emperor could therefore be maintained by controlling access through the indirect route from main entrance to his private quarters. Such care is evidence of skilled planning, and the capacity of the architect to reconcile practical exigencies within and the rigid symmetry of the building's exterior. All qualities consonant with the expertise of Cistercian masons.

For the technical excellence, classical features, possibly Arabic geometrical perfection, Norman Romanesque appearance of the towers, and elements of Gothic in this unique structure are blended with an ease reminiscent of the simplicity and beauty of Cistercian architecture. A fact so simple – and obscured by the evident "rightness" of the building – that it has been overlooked by historians. The site itself is one that Cistercians could have chosen, and was in fact previously occupied by a church known as Sancta Maria de Monte – a foundation of Benedictine construction but possibly taken over by the Cistercians like many other possessions in southern Italy. Even more important is the predilection which Frederick II showed towards the Cistercians. Frederick himself often stayed in the Order's abbey at Casamari, in the Liri valley north of Montecassino, where it may be assumed that he wore the garb of a *converso* like other noble guests. Tradition has it that three heads sculpted on decorated capitals on the south side of the cloister at Casamari represent Frederick II, his chancellor Petrus della Vigna, and the abbot John, and that they were intended to celebrate the admission of Frederick into the order of St Bernard as a lay brother. The link with this monastery was maintained, for Abbot John of Casamari became responsible for the royal chancery in 1221 and exercised considerable influence over Frederick – who was impressed by the practical spirit of the Order. Frederick always maintained friendly relations with the Cistercians, who during his reign enjoyed their maximum moment of splendour in southern Italy and came to possess 22 monasteries within his Sicilian kingdom. It was probably the result of Abbot John's influence and persuasion that in the early 1220s many Cistercian abbeys received imperial gifts. More remarkable, and specific, is the brief but informative paragraph written under the year 1223 by an anonymous chronicler in the Cistercian monastery of Santa Maria di Ferraria (in the 'Terra di Lavoro' in Apulia): 'At the same time the Emperor received permission from the council of the Roman Curia to use *conversi* from all the abbeys of the Cistercian Order in the Kingdom of Sicily and Apulia and in the Terra di Lavoro to work in these places as

The main entrance to Castel del Monte

[227]

master of the flocks and herdsmen, to do various other jobs, and to build castles and homes for the inhabitants of the kingdom who possess no home of their own.' This affirmation provides explicit evidence for the employment of Cistercians in Frederick's building projects. The date of this chronicle entry coincides with the beginning of work on Frederick's first large project in Apulia, his residential palace at Foggia (of which only a single arch remains, incorporated into the wall of the city museum). Thus the Cistercians came to play an important role in the building career of Frederick, and facilitated the introduction of elements of the newly developed Gothic style from France into southern Italy. That the close affinity never slackened is suggested by a comment of the chronicler Matthew Paris, who wrote in his *Chronica majora* that Frederick 'died in Apulia . . . clothed as a Cistercian'.

We have seen in the previous chapter that Cistercian building and technical skills were unrivalled. Apart from this direct testimony of 1223 we know that the only building of Frederick II considered on a par with Castel del Monte, the now-ruined triumphal gate-tower at Capua, was constructed under the supervision of a Cistercian referred to in documents as 'Domnus Bisancius'. Nothing is known of the building history of Castel del Monte, but the elements common to Cistercian skills such as the wall-building technique, vault structure, specialized plumbing, window decoration and regular plans, together with the very high quality stonework which all visitors note, suggest that these highly skilled workers were employed here as well. But there is also another parallel: comparison has often been made between the monumental portal at Castel del Monte and another Cistercian abbey at Fossanova, which is about 50 miles south-east of Rome (near Priverno) and even in Frederick's time less than a day's journey from Casamari (both monasteries were specialized in horse-breeding, an imperial passion; the enormous stone stable building with its original troughs may still be seen in the former). Fossanova was originally a Benedictine house but passed into the hands of the Cistercians around 1135; the present monastery was built in the early Gothic style from 1187 to 1208, and possesses among other things a fine octagonal tower above its chapel. There was also a powerful family link for Frederick II: an inscription on the architrave over the main door states that the church was built with a donation by Frederick Barbarossa. A recent author has convincingly argued that the portal dates from around 1222 – exactly when Abbot John was the head of the royal chancery and Frederick's interest in the Cistercians seems to have been at its peak. Less elegant than that of Castel del Monte, this portal consists of a Gothic doorway set into a classical portal surmounted by a tympanum. Other details also suggest affinities: Antonio Cadei has shown strong similarities

The façade of Fossanova Abbey, showing the same combination of
Romanesque doorway and classical tympanum found at Castel del Monte

between the particular four-leafed capitals of the cloister of the finely
preserved Cistercian abbey at Fontenay founded by St Bernard himself
near Montbard in Burgundy (completed in 1147), those of the chapel at
Fossanova, and those at Castel Del Monte – especially in the corridors.
Certainly the interior of the rooms on the upper floor at Castel del Monte
*feel* like the cloister or perhaps even more the so-called copying room at
Fontenay. The fantastic Atlas figures squashed and contorted under the
weight of the corbels high up at the beginning of the vaults of the seventh
tower of Frederick's castle resemble the figures at Reims more than
anything else. What has happened here is a curious personalization of the
Cistercian ideal which only a man like Frederick could achieve: utilizing
the skills of *conversi* designed for self-sufficiency, and exalting a style
conceived as humble and austere into a symbol of temporal power and
elegance – from the dank earthen floor of the chapel at Fontenay to the
marble and presumed silks of Castel del Monte.

Moreover, the site of Castel del Monte rendered it an intensely personal
place. From the roof-terrace there are views to the mountains 30 miles
away to south and south-west, and to Trani on the Adriatic coast 15 miles
to the north-east. To the east and north-east the extraordinary series of

[229]

The scriptorium at the Cistercian abbey of Fontenay (Burgundy), with vaulting similar to that at Castel del Monte

Norman cathedrals of Apulia is visible, together forming a triangle which may be represented schematically as follows:

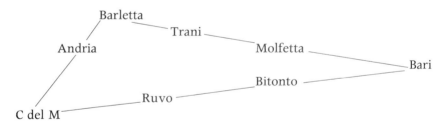

Given Frederick's astronomical and geometrical predilections, and the fact that Castel del Monte was orientated according to the cardinal points, this may be no accident. Certainly these sites played an important role in the emperor's life: it was from Barletta that he departed for his crusade in 1228; the castle at Bari was rebuilt by Frederick 1233–40; the importance of Andria we have seen as the site of the tombs of his later wives; after his death at Castel Fiorentino Frederick's own body was taken to Bitonto on its way to Taranto to be shipped to Palermo for burial.

[230]

The octagonal form of the castle is also thought to be a reflection of the personal taste for perfection and symbolism of Frederick II, with several possible symbolic interpretations. Perhaps the most plausible is linked to the search for legitimacy by imitating past models which we have seen in the chapter on Pavia. For the octagon may derive from the chapel built by Charlemagne at his palace in Aachen (now the octagon gallery in Aachen cathedral), where Frederick himself was crowned in 1215, and that in turn from the shape of the German imperial crown; Frederick's veneration for his great predecessor was also shown in his commission for a gold and silver sarcophagus for Charlemagne's remains. Another 'imperial' interpretation derives from the stylized octagonal shape with which the vision of celestial Jerusalem was represented, or of the eight-sided mosque known as the Dome of the Rock (or Mosque of Omar) built by the Muslims on the site of Solomon's temple – which Frederick had admired in Jerusalem while on crusade. The materials used for this mosque, porphyry columns, breccia and other coloured stone retrieved from the ruins of Roman Jerusalem, are also similar to those employed on the Apulian castle (in either case, the severely geometrical design of Castel del Monte foreshadows the star-shaped cities of the Renaissance, or Leonardo's sketch of Florence modified as the ideal city). Yet the austerity of these materials, and of the present state of Castel del Monte, contradict what we know of Frederick's personality. During his lifetime he was credited with a love for the exotic comforts of the harem and Arabic luxury, and when his sepulchre was opened in the 18th century his body was found 'to be wrapped in rich Arabic fabrics of red silk embroidered with cryptic arabesque designs'. It is therefore probable that the formal elegance of columns, doorways and vaults was complemented by rich materials and colours, and possibly tapestries on the bare walls; surviving fragments of coloured marble and mosaic floors support such a hypothesis.

Yet there is no evidence that Frederick II ever used his castle. The only documentary mention of the building is dated 1240, just ten years before his death, when reference is made to a 'castle near *sanctam Mariam de Monte*'; but the context of the letter in which it appears, written by Frederick to an official in the Capitanata, suggests that although work had already begun it was only at a preliminary stage. It is generally agreed however that the castle was completed by 1246, and that he may have resided there in that year. The enchantment of place casts a spell over rational distinction between fact and legend: after visiting Castel del Monte many writers have managed to convince themselves that the emperor *must* have written his treatise on falcons there. But his possession of so many other castles, palaces and hunting lodges, even in the relatively small area of northern Apulia, and the fact that he died so soon afterwards, means that opportunities for residence were necessarily limited. At most, he could have made very occasional use of the castle for about three years. But this does not detract from its value in representing Frederick's personality: the very perfection of the building bears the imperial stamp, and there can be no doubt that it was one of his favourite castles; it is often thought that Frederick himself conceived the building, even though he may not have been responsible for the details of the final design. For although Frederick II was born in the 12th century and belonged to a twin line of distinctly 'medieval' kings – his paternal grandfather Frederick Barbarossa misunderstood the emergence of new social forces, and his maternal forbears were archetypal medieval adventurers – his own mind and mental attitude were often surprisingly 'modern' and he has been said to foreshadow the much later concept of a 'Renaissance man'.

The premises were both auspicious and ominous: a wealthy man born into the twin cultures of Germany and Norman Sicily, with the influences of Byzantium, Islam and Rome constantly in sight; but with danger always near, from the threat of the heirs of the illegitimate King Tancred (natural son of Roger, William I's brother) in Messina to that of Otto of Brunswick's attempt to usurp Frederick's uncle Philip of Swabia in Germany. Frederick's first coronation, as 'King of the Romans and of Sicily', in May 1198 at the age of four, in fact represented a renunciation imposed upon his mother Constance in her desire to make him heir to the Norman Kingdom of Sicily. For she had virtually sacrificed her son's right to the German throne: there is powerful irony in the fact that Barbarossa's dream of adding Sicily to his kingdom should be realized in this way. But although the young Frederick inherited both crusading zeal and the desire to conquer Constantinople from his grandfather and father, he was hardly German at all. In November of the year of his coronation as King of Sicily his mother died and Frederick became ward of Pope Innocent III – which would have been an inconceivable situation for such a vigorous opponent of the papacy as Barbarossa. His infancy was spent in Palermo as hostage to the papal, German and Norman factions which desired to exercise control over the Kingdom of Sicily. Eventually he assumed the responsibilities of kingship on attaining his majority at 14, in 1208. But he was still not independent: the following year Innocent III's diplomatic activity resulted in Frederick's marriage to Constance of Aragon, sister of King Pedro II (1196–1213), widow of the King of Hungary and ten years older than the Sicilian king. A letter of this period describes the young king as of medium height, well-built, with mobile features and a friendly ruddy face; he was already an excellent horseman, and skilled with both sword and bow.

In 1212 envoys of the German princes travelled to Palermo to persuade

A miniature showing Pietro da Eboli presenting his *Liber ad Honorem Augusti* to the Emperor Frederick II

[233]

the young king to accept the royal and imperial crowns in the stead of Otto of Brunswick, who as Otto IV had been sole emperor since 1208 after a period in which he contested the throne with Philip of Swabia (rival emperor 1197–1208). Frederick's infant son Henry was crowned King of Sicily under the regency of Queen Constance, and in March 1212 Frederick travelled north as 'Emperor Elect' – although Constance and Henry were to join him four years later. He remained in Germany until 1220, when he returned to Italy and was crowned Holy Roman Emperor by Pope Honorius III. Yet this was hardly a great success, for Frederick had gained the support of the German princes by a policy of granting them territorial rights and sums of money with such lavishness that he effectively conceded them complete autonomy; this almost suicidal generosity weakened his treasury to such an extent that he was forced to look back to Sicily for his future.

On his return to the Kingdom of Sicily, Frederick found that much of his power and lands there had been usurped by local barons. He set about destroying castles which they had built in the previous 30 years or so and examining royal decrees in their favour. Obstinate nobles were defeated and sent into exile, and he worked at establishing the basis of a stable kingdom. It was also as this time that he managed to dominate the Muslim bands which threatened southern Sicily and made the extraordinary decision to transfer 16,000 of them with their families to Lucera in the Capitanata and allow them to live there freely with their own legal and administrative officials. By this unusual measure – which only an Emperor such as Frederick could have conceived – in the long term he created a loyal reservoir of Muslim troops and also of Muslims for his household servants. It was one of many long-sighted moves. In 1224 he founded a university at Naples on the model of Bologna. The idea this time was to create a legal and administrative élite for the running of his kingdom, but the syllabus included the teaching of philosophy and natural sciences (its most famous student was to be Thomas Aquinas). The preliminary moves were thus made with great care. At Easter two years later he summoned the Diet of Cremona in order to re-establish imperial authority in Lombardy. Apart from Cremona itself, traditionally loyal to the emperor (and a decade earlier a strong opponent of Otto IV), all the Lombard cities rejected the imperial authority and attempted to create a new Lombard League. Opponents seemed to proliferate even as he defeated old enemies, and in the next year a new pope was elected in the person of Gregory IX (1227–41), a nephew of Innocent III, who was determined to resist imperial expansion. Pope Gregory was particularly concerned with potential encroachment by such a powerful monarch on the territory of the papal state, and his shrewd legalistic mind perceived an ideal opportunity to

[234]

remove Frederick from the scene by demanding that he fulfil a vow to go on crusade made 12 years earlier.

Thus, in 1228, Frederick departed on the most anomalous of all the crusades. The first anomaly derived from the fact that he was under excommunication, a punishment imposed by Pope Gregory the year before after a farcical departure on crusade and immediate return; clergy throughout Europe were obliged to pay a tax destined in the mind of Pope Gregory to finance a *crusade against Frederick II*. The idea of an excommunicated emperor fighting a holy war for the Church and seeking to recapture Jerusalem was at best bizarre. Moreover, he actually succeeded. What must have been most galling for the Pope to digest was that Frederick managed to negotiate a ten-year truce and the return of Jerusalem to Christian hands, in a treaty signed on 18 February 1229. This Arabic-speaking, harem-keeping Christian king, whom the Arab chronicler Ibn Wasil speaks of admiringly as 'friendly to philosophy, logic and medicine, and favourable towards the Muslims', maintained good personal relations with Fakhr ad-Din, son of the Sultan of Egypt. Such relations and his personal qualities enabled him to succeed where many others had failed. On 17 March 1229 he was crowned King of Jerusalem.

During his absence Pope Gregory had sent troops to Sicily to conquer the imperial lands for the Church, but Frederick returned sooner than he had been expected and managed to complete the reconquest of his kingdom by the end of 1229. The following year he placated papal opposition by making a formal renunciation of imperial control over the Church within his kingdom, a real thorn in the side of the pope. The year 1231 opened with Frederick in Apulia as victorious King and Emperor, with 20 years of active life ahead of him in which he was to become the Emperor Frederick II known to history and legend. They were to be what a modern biographer of the Emperor has described as 'the years of Frederick's mature statesmanship, the years witnessing his greatness as legislator, as administrator, as poet, philosopher, and scientist – above all, as the patron of a unique cultural revival.'

Frederick's first significant action was the preparation of the *Liber Augustalis*, which was promulgated at Melfi in 1231 and became known as the 'Constitutions of Melfi'. These constitutions represented his desire to impose a new legal and administrative order on his kingdom, and were based on the nucleus of the assizes which had been drawn up at Capua in 1220 and Messina in 1221 as part of his first attempt to create order in the Kingdom of Sicily. They were written under the supervision of the imperial chancellor Petrus della Vigna, who had studied at the law school in Bologna, and represented a development of the earlier code of laws of Pavia. Like the *Liber papiensis*, Frederick's constitutions consist of a

[235]

One of the vault keystones at Castel del Monte

synthesis of Lombard, Byzantine and Norman laws on the solid foundation of the laws of Justinian, together with the incorporation of the common law of the Kingdom of Sicily. This compilation of laws, with an extremely practical bias, constituted such a complete civil code that it continued to serve as a fundamental body of law for the Kingdom of Sicily until the time

[236]

of Napoleon. The *Liber Augustalis* consists of a *Prooemium* or preamble and three chapters: Chapter I begins with a discussion of heresy, delineates the limits of imperial power, and sets out clearly the duties and responsibilities of imperial officials; Chapter II contains procedural law for both criminal and civil cases; Chapter III deals with feudal and private law, and specifies punishments for the crimes listed. Later laws promulgated by Frederick were added as necessary in the form of 'novels'. Thus the work was an up-to-date and practical synthesis of past learning, incorporating the laws of Roger II, William I and William II (who are given due credit at the head of the relevant paragraphs). In fact some of the most interesting paragraphs are those dedicated to the local and specific problems of Sicilian society: several of them, for instance, deal with the prohibition of the use of arms to visitors within the kingdom, including such passive armour as breastplates and mailcoats as well as the more obvious category of knives and swords. Concern for the permanence of documents is shown in the command to write them legibly – not in the elaborate script of monastic copyists – and to use parchment rather than the more perishable Sicilian papyrus. Other local difficulties are suggested by intriguing paragraphs on punishment for people who shave imperial gold and silver coins, and for those who prepare and sell love potions.

Yet of greater interest than the legal details of these constitutions is the concept of imperial power and the person of the emperor which transpires from the brief *Prooemium*. It begins with the grand and at first apparently tangential affirmations that 'After Divine providence had formed the universe . . . he made man in his own image and likeness . . .', and that since men 'conceived hatred' among themselves the same providence saw that princes were created 'through whom the license of crimes might be corrected'. After this explanation of divine authority for the emperor, the imperial grandeur reaches its apex: 'Thus we, whom He elevated beyond hope of man to the pinnacle of the Roman Empire and to the sole distinction of the other kingdoms at the right hand of the divine power, desire to render to God a two-fold statement for the talent given to us . . .'. In effect, this amounted to 20 years of absolute tyranny based upon the contents of the laws to which the *Prooemium* was an introduction. Frederick's intentions (and no doubt the tyranny) were clearly based on past experience, for he goes on to state that the kingdom 'has until the present been harassed quite often because of the weakness of our youth and because of our absence by the assaults of past disturbances' and that his intention is to provide through these laws for the 'peace and justice' of his kingdom. This topical reference to the usurpations and threats against both imperial person and kingdom in Frederick's youth emphasize the underlying purpose of the *Liber Augustalis*.

[237]

The same motivation was also behind the frenetic period of castle-building which began in the same year, once the administrative, judicial and economic systems which sustained the kingdom had been thoroughly overhauled. In the immediate area of Apulia near Melfi castles were built at Gravina (1231), Castelfiorentino (c.1233), Lucera (1233), Bari (1233–40), Lagopesole (1242–50), and of course Castel del Monte (c.1240–6); Melfi itself had been rebuilt in 1229. This was also the period in which Frederick's almost unprecedented intellectual curiosity and skill, which was manifest in such diverse fields as falconry, science, mathematics, poetry and architecture, seems to have been allowed full leash.

Frederick's castles in Apulia were sited at the crossroads of learned and scientific tradition. Greek culture flourished in Calabria, as we have seen in the chapter on Bari, with abbeys and centres such as S. Nicola di Casole near Otranto – which had been patronized by Roger II and perhaps supplied the tutor to his son William – possessing a large collection of Greek and Latin manuscripts, and the birthplace of St Nilus at Rossano. An indication of the extent of such libraries may be given by the fact that on his death in 1131 the Basilian monk Scholaricus had bequeathed a private collection of over 300 manuscripts to the monastery of S. Salvatore di Bordonaro, near Messina. The importance of these libraries and centres of Byzantine culture was increased after the loss and consequent sacking of Constantinople in 1204. Such vast learning does not match the common concept of the period, and we must remember that a powerful man like Frederick II had privileged access to these collections and had many copies made for his own library. To the north-west of his kingdom were the medical school at Salerno, Frederick's own university at Naples, and the abbey of Montecassino with a tradition in scientific study that we saw beginning with Alphanus and Constantinus Africanus in the 11th century. The Emperor himself had spent his infancy in Palermo, where the traditions of scholarship established during the reign of Roger II were still strong, and where Frederick appears to have received an excellent basic education in spite of the political struggles which characterized his regency. His linguistic and literary gifts in particular were legendary. Even a hostile chronicler such as Salimbene states that 'he could speak many different languages' and that 'he could read, write, and sing, and he could compose music and songs'. The Emperor knew vulgar Italian, Latin and Arabic well, learned at least spoken German while in that country, probably knew Greek fairly well, and had a smattering of Hebrew, Provençal and French (which had been the language of the Norman court). The imperial library included codices in Arabic and Greek as well as the basic Latin collection, with works on such varied subjects as mathematics, astronomy, astrology, medicine, law and natural history. In a letter sent

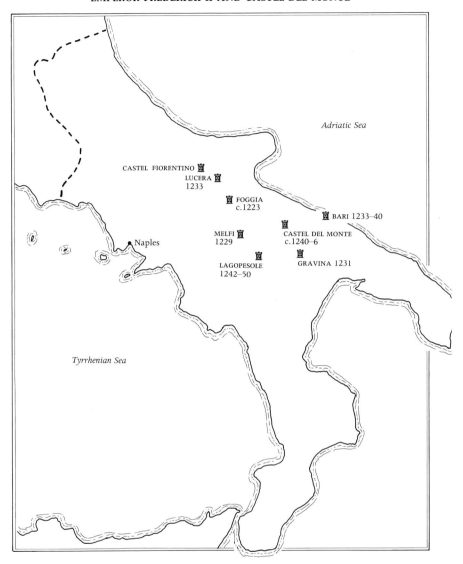

Fig. 13. Sketch map showing Frederick's II's castles in Apulia

by Frederick to the University of Bologna in 1232 with some Latin translations he stresses the importance of knowledge (*scientie*) and refers to 'the volumes and books written in diverse characters and diverse languages which enrich the cupboards where our treasures are kept'. He refers specifically to Greek and Arabic works on mathematics.

It is no surprise to see that translation was one of the principal activities in this polyglot court. Translations of the works of Aristotle, Averroes (Ibn

[239]

Rushd) – who exercised a profound influence on the emperor's thinking – and Avicenna were made, and copies sent to the universities of Bologna and Paris; other translations were made from Arabic to Hebrew, from Hebrew to Latin, from Greek and Arabic to Latin. One of the main artificers of this production was Michael Scot, a scholar and translator of Scottish origin who was court astrologer to Frederick from about 1227 to his death in 1236. Scot knew Hebrew as well as Arabic, had already been involved in the translation of Arabic works and Aristotle at Toledo, had taught at Bologna and was credited by his contemporaries with reintroducing Aristotle into western culture. He dedicated to Frederick a Latin translation of Avicenna's *De animalibus*, which introduced Aristotle's thought on zoology to western Europe, and composed works on astrology, meteorology and an influential treatise on physiognomy, all of which drew deeply on Arab and Greek sources. The employment of such an eminent scholar – who was like many such men of the time considered a magus, and consequently finished in the eighth circle of Dante's *Inferno* – and the large number of works prepared for Frederick, is an index of the imperial curiosity and genuine interest in scientific subjects. One of Frederick's practices was to send lists of scientific questions to leading scholars. One such letter shows the restlessness of the imperial curiosity: it consists of a list which included questions concerning matters like the creation of the earth, the dimensions of the earth, the difference between fresh water and sea water, the nature of hot springs, winds, and volcanoes, and was probably sent from Pozzuoli (near Naples, and Vesuvius), which suggests that the questions were stimulated by his presence at the natural baths there. He could in this case be compared to a schoolboy writing a series of scientific questions to his master during the summer holiday.

During the same period Frederick patronized Leonardo of Pisa, the foremost mathematician of the period, who participated in open discussions of problems of arithmetic and geometry at the imperial court. Leonardo's book called the *Liber abaci*, in which he introduced Arabic methods of calculating into Europe, was dedicated to Michael Scot; a later work, the *Liber quadratorum* was dedicated to Frederick II. A permanent and serious interest in mathematics is shown by the fact that Frederick took with him on crusade a Muslim tutor in logic called Ibn-al-Giuzi, and astonished his contemporaries by discussing mathematical problems with the 'enemy' during negotiations for the liberation of Jerusalem with Sultan al-Kamil of Egypt. His tastes were well-known to Arab rulers, and in 1232 the Sultan al-Ashraf of Damascus sent him as a gift a planetarium with figures of the sun and moon marking the hours as they moved round the sphere. Four years later al-Kamil, himself a learned man, patron of Sufi poets and interested in agriculture and irrigation, sent to the emperor an

[240]

astrologer known as Master Theodore of Antioch. Theodore had studied at Baghdad, and succeeded Michael Scot as court astrologer: he corresponded with famous Arab mathematicians, cured ailments of leading court officials with syrups and herbal medicines, translated from Arabic to Latin, and composed a treatise on hygiene for the emperor – whose unusual interest in the matter was certainly part of his Arabic culture and can be seen in the lavatories and baths of Castel del Monte. It was Sultan al-Kamil's shrewd practice to send scientists and literary figures as ambassadors to Frederick's court, doubtless imagining the immediate favour they would find. The result was that we find in a single court in the 1230s the meeting point of two diverse cultures: a scholar born in Fife, student at Oxford, Paris and Toledo, teacher at Bologna; and his successor another scholar born in Antioch, student at Mosul and Baghdad, and teacher at Cairo. Moreover these two men are merely the most famous, and were part of a large body of scholars who seem to have travelled with Frederick on his peregrinations from castle to castle; others visited the court for shorter periods. Even more interesting was the spirit of discussion, observation and experiment which seems to have pervaded the court. Not content with mere translations, these scientists improved on their sources by adding personal observations, as can be seen in Frederick's own insistence that 'one should accept as truth only that which is proved by nature and by the force of reason'. In this he anticipated the later writers of the century like Albertus Magnus and Roger Bacon, who are often credited with having introduced the experimental method into science, and sponsored the production of important practical manuals. The work on veterinary medicine written by the imperial farrier Jordanus Ruffus, the *De medicina equorum*, was the first treatise on the treatment of horses. It was written on express imperial command and contained chapters on horse diseases, possible injuries, and treatment, which a horseman like Frederick would find invaluable. Jordanus states in his work that he had been able to learn from the expertise of Frederick himself – and it would be fascinating to know what the emperor had learned from the Cistercians at Fossanova and Casamari. In fact, when Frederick travelled east his Arab hosts had been astonished at his knowledge of both human and veterinary medicine, and he founded a chair of anatomy at Salerno which used human corpses for dissection long before the celebrated anatomical studies of Leonardo da Vinci. Jordanus's book exercised an influence on similar works for centuries: it was printed in an Italian translation at Venice in 1492, and several times in the 16th century.

The same spirit is present in Frederick II's passion for falconry, which may be considered part of the general interest in animals that he demonstrated throughout his life. His passion for hunting was part of his restless curiosity and love for the exotic and extravagant display. He kept and bred large numbers of exotic animals, making exchanges of Indian animals which al-Kamil sent him with peacocks and bears native to Europe. The animals he took with him on royal progresses throughout Europe aroused the astonishment of medieval chroniclers. In 1231 he visited Ravenna with 'many animals unknown to Italy: elephants, dromedaries, camels, panthers, gerfalcons, lions, leopards, white falcons, and bearded owls'. The chronicler Salimbene records a similar procession in Parma five years later, and Frederick even travelled over the Alps into Germany with an exotic menagerie of camels, monkeys, leopards and the first giraffe to be seen in medieval Europe. Near his palace at Foggia he kept a zoo furnished with various natural environments for aquatic birds and animals. His interest in falconry, cultivated since his infancy at the court in Palermo, was genuinely scientific and resulted in one of the most celebrated of all books on that art.

Frederick's *De arte venandi cum avibus*, or treatise on falcons, was written between 1244 and his death six years later and therefore could plausibly have been composed at Castel del Monte. The six surviving books are probably incomplete, and no manuscript by Frederick himself or his own copyists survives. That it was a long-term project is shown by his statement in the preface that this work designed to replace the 'falsity and inadequacy' of earlier treatises had been in his mind for about 30 years, amidst the 'arduous and intricate affairs of state'. Amongst these earlier treatises was an Arabic work which had been translated for him by Theodore. He also had a good knowledge of Aristotle's treatises on natural science, but remarks in the preface with truly astonishing scepticism for a man of his age that 'we discovered by hard-won experience that the deductions of Aristotle, which we followed when they appealed to our reason, were not entirely to be relied upon'. There are frequent references to local experience, to the then heavily forested Apulia and the Capitanata. Such passages, for example when he describes the summoning there of experts from Egypt to carry out an experiment on the incubation of ostrich eggs, impart a strongly personal and direct flavour to the book, and suggest that the book was written in Apulia – possibly between Castel del Monte, his residential palace at Foggia, and a hunting lodge at nearby Gravina. Local experience was enriched by the gathering of information wherever Frederick travelled or had contacts, employing the research techniques used by al-Idrîsi in his geographical compilation for Frederick's Norman grandfather. He brought experts from Arabia to answer his questions, but at the same time never accepted their theories without trying them out for himself. In addition he sought information from

A detail from a manuscript page of Frederick II's book on falconry

England, France and Spain, using diplomatic contacts to further his research, and imported exemplars of various types of falcon from even further afield: he himself cites Ireland, Spain, Bulgaria, Asia Minor, Egypt and India. This world-conquering emperor held the more humble falconer's art in great esteem, stressing that great skill and study were indispensable to achieve the best results. A register for the years 1239–40 provides some idea of the extent of his interest: it names as many as 50 falconers in the service of the emperor, who were in charge of birds kept throughout his kingdom from Cremona to Malta. A legend recounts that when the Great Khan tried to order Frederick to become one of his subjects and accept court office, the European emperor replied jokingly that an ideal post for him would be that of court falconer.

The book opens with a systematic discussion of the different species of bird, and then deals with the physical structure and habits of falcons. It thus moves in scholastic fashion from the general to the particular, from considerations on species to detailed aspects such as capture, breeding, migration, flight and training. Some of the most interesting passages are those in which he discusses technique, matters like the best lures to use or how to encourage the birds by singing to them at feeding time; further details concern the perfect diet for newly captured birds, the legs or eggs of chickens cooked in milk. Genuinely scientific experiments recorded in the book include that with ostrich eggs already referred to, the sending to northern Europe for limpets from ship's timbers to see if barnacle geese were actually hatched from them as many people then believed, establishing the nesting habits of the cuckoo, and putting masks over the eyes of vultures to see whether they sought food by sight or by smell. The observation that falcons 'cannot find meat thrown to them even if their sense of smell is not impeded' led to the important innovation of the use of hoods, until then unknown in Europe. These sections of his work bring to mind an enquiring mind of later centuries such as Leonardo da Vinci (a comparison made by Nietzsche), or an earlier figure like Aristotle. It is in the spirit of such men that Frederick insists upon the importance of observation, personal experience and experiment. The uniqueness of his book was such that it was printed over 300 years later, in 1596, and saw several editions and translations in later centuries.

In addition to his scientific interests Frederick also patronized poets and himself wrote Italian poetry. Here, as in other spheres, he was heir to a triple tradition: German, Arabic (and Provençal), and Greek. In Germany the Hohenstaufen were intimately connected with the emergence of courtly romance in the 12th century and the apogee of German heroic and lyric poetry. In 1184 Frederick Barbarossa had attended at the Diet of Mainz the first public reading of courtly poetry in Germany by visiting

[244]

troubadours and native minnesingers; it has been suggested that he would not have understood much of it, but none the less he was there and it happened. His grandson Frederick II was recognized and admired as a generous patron of the poets during his eight-year residence in Germany from 1212 to 1220. The most celebrated of the minnesingers was Walther von der Vogelweide (*c*.1170–*c*.1230), an intimate of the Hohenstaufen and writer of works dedicated to Frederick – who assigned a feud to the poet just before leaving Germany in 1220, an action which drew a poem in praise of the king. Two other German poets were also at their prime: Wolfram von Eschenbach (*c*.1170–*c*.1220), who was the author of the grail poem 'Parzival' and a poem entitled 'Willehalm' which was inspired by the aura of crusade surrounding Frederick; and Hartmann von Aue (*c*.1170–*c*.1215), who adapted French courtly romances. That Frederick himself learned from them is suggested by the fact that he began composing poetry immediately after his return from Germany.

It was under the influence of Arabic poetry that Frederick's interest seems to have developed, and we have seen in the chapter on Palermo the extent to which it had flourished in Sicily. The use of vulgar Italian rather than Latin for poetic expression derived from Arab poets and singers, and it has been shown that the early popular poetry of Italy like the ballata share the same metrics as popular Arabic verse in Andalucia – for example the *zajal* and *muwashsháh*. These brief forms, consisting of a few stanzas with strict metrical form and sophisticated rhyming schemes are reminiscent of the tightly controlled poems of the troubadours and the early Italian lyric poets. An example of this involves the use of a master-rhyme ending each stanza as a refrain, interrupted by subordinate rhymes, as in the poem *En cest sonet coind' e leri* by Dante's *miglior fabbro* Arnaut Daniel. An even more pertinent example is the tightly controlled and famous poem against Rome *D'un sirventes far* by Guilhem Figueira, who travelled to Apulia to seek Frederick's patronage, where a poem of 20 stanzas is bound by the intricate rhyming scheme. In fact the very division of lyric poems into stanzas was derived from the Arabic *bayt*, meaning 'house' or 'strophe'. One of the elements which has been identified in the Arab love-songs of Spain and Sicily is a tender romantic feeling, which is found together with what one historian of Arabic literature described as 'an almost modern sensibility to the beauties of nature'. This element, as we shall see, prevails in the poems attributed to Frederick II himself.

The third element in the poetic ferment of Frederick's court was Greek. Monks and scholars from abbeys like S. Nicola di Casole, who were employed as translators and secretaries, brought with them a strong literary culture. Some, now forgotten like George of Gallipoli and John Grasso, were poets whose work in praise of the emperor was important

[245]

because it continued to draw on the myths of classical Greece. While at Frederick's court, for instance, John Grasso wrote a poem titled *Lament of Hecuba at the Fall of Troy*. Such writers and their work provided the emperor with purchase on yet another culture.

Frederick himself was both an accomplished orator and a gifted poet. He was an admirer of the *ars dictaminis* or study of epistolary composition established, as we have seen, by Albericus of Montecassino. The appreciation of good prose was one of the elements of the legal culture of Bologna, where the law schools inspired a new interest in rhetoric and *belles-lettres* among its students – including Frederick's chancellor Petrus de Vigna (who also wrote Latin poetry). Fluency and refinement in Latin prose were seen as essential qualities of lawyers, of diplomatic envoys and the *podestà* who governed over the northern Italian cities; stylistic manuals were written to encourage such refinement. The grandiose rhetoric of the *Prooemium* to the Constitutions of Melfi is an example of this style, and although the chancellor was usually responsible for making imperial speeches Frederick is known to have spoken himself on several important public occasions and to have shown interest in literary style. The study of grammar and rhetoric was included in the curriculum of his university at Naples. A further measure of the emperor's interest in style may be seen in the fact that on the occasion of his son Henry's funeral he is said to have been so moved that he later asked for a copy of the oration.

The poetic influence of his court was even more marked. Indeed the emperor acted as a direct link between the courtly tradition of the north and the southern kingdom, and it is interesting to note that his first Italian poem 'Dolze meo drudo' was probably written in 1220 – the year he returned to Apulia and Sicily from his eight-year residence in Germany. Frederick II is usually accredited with four poems, of which two in particular can be asserted with some certainty to be his: 'De la mia disïanza' ('Of my desire') and the leave-taking poem 'Dolze meo drudo e vatene;' ('My sweet love', which uses the ambiguous term 'drudo' whose primary meaning is vassal and is today considered disparaging). Two others, 'Oi llasso, nom pensai' ('Alas I did not think . . .') and 'Poi ke tti piace, Amore' (Because I love you, Love) are not today generally considered to be authentic – although the latter is interesting because it resembles a German *lied* in form. But the first two are sufficient to demonstrate that Frederick was a fine, if neither profound nor especially serious, poet. One example will suffice: 'Dolze meo drudo' is a leave-taking poem written as a dialogue; the first two stanzas are spoken by a lady to her departing lover, and the last three contain the lover's reply. It is translated here by the author from the southern Italian text published in 1926 by Hermann H. Thornton, with slight alterations to make sense of what remains a difficult text:

'Dolze meo drudo e vatene;
meo sire, a Dio t'acomando
che ti diparti da mene
ed io tapina rimanno.
Lassa! la vita m'e noia,
dolze la morte a vedere
ch'io nom penssai mai guerire
menbrandome fuor di gioia.

'My sweet love, you are leaving;
my lord, I recommend your soul to
   God,
because you are leaving me
and I wretched remain here.
Let it be! Life is boredom to me,
and death is so sweet to see,
that I think I will never recover,
remaining without happiness.

Membrandone che ten vai,
lo cor mi mena gran guerra;
di cio che piu disiai
il mi tol lontana terra!
Or se ne va lo mio amore
ch'io sovra gli altri l'amava;
biasmo la dolze Toscana,
che mi diparte lo core.'

Reflecting that you must leave,
my heart endures great suffering;
for what I most desired
is taken from me by a distant land!
Now my love is leaving
who I loved above all others;
I blame sweet Tuscany,
which has taken my love from
   me.'

'Dolcie mia donna, lo gire
nonn e per mia volontate,
che mi convene ubidire
quelli che m'a 'm potestate.
Or ti comforta s'io vaio
e gia nom ti dismagare,
ca per null'altra, d'amare,
amor, te nom falseragio.

'My sweet lady, this journey
is not made of my will,
but I must obey
those who lord over me.
Now take comfort even as I leave
and do not despair,
since by loving no other woman,
love, will I betray you.

Lo vostro amore mi tene
ed ami in sua sengnoria,
ca lealmente m'avene
d'amar voi sanza falsia.
Di me vi sia rimembranza,
non mi pigliate 'n obria;
c'avete in vostra balia
tutta la mia disianza.

Your love holds me,
and I love in its thrall;
so I am bound by loyalty
to love you without betrayal.
Let me be remembered
and don't let me be forgotten;
because you have at your mercy
all my desire.

Dolze mia donna, 'l commiato
domando sanza tenore;

My sweet lady, I request
a farewell without fear;

[247]

| | |
|---|---|
| che vi sia racommandato | let it be recommended |
| che con voi riman mio core: | that my heart stays with you: |
| cotal' e la 'namoranza | So much am I enamoured |
| degli amorosi piacieri | of the pleasures of love, |
| che non mi posso partire | that I cannot remove from |
| da voi, donna, il leanza.' | you, lady, my loyalty.' |

Poetry was never intended by Frederick as a serious enterprise, as it was to become for Dante within half a century; he appears to have seen it more as a light-hearted pastime, a courtly exercise in forgetting reality in troubadour style. But it was practised at the court with sufficient assiduity to influence the emperor's four sons: Henry, Enzo, Frederick of Antioch, and his heir Manfred are all known to have composed lyric poems, and the tradition was carried into the next generation by his grandson Conradin. In the end, however, the precise attribution of poems to Frederick II and his sons is irrelevant; the undeniable fact is that his personality and learning were such that an authority such as Dante could associate lyric poems with him. The fact is that he appreciated artistic excellence and liked to surround himself with the most eminent poets of his time.

Frederick II's promotion of translations from Arabic and Greek, his own Italian poems, and his patronage of the sciences and mathematics all attest to his restless intellectual curiosity and his role as a focal point for the developing Italian culture of the 13th century, as we shall see in the Epilogue. These aspects of his personality have traditionally been associated in the imagination – if perhaps not in reality – with Castel del Monte as a resort of brilliance, stimulating intellectual conversation, hunting with falcons, and the more austere pursuits of mathematic and scientific investigation. The whole life of the Emperor Frederick II may be seen as a constant, restless quest for perfection which was never satiated, either politically or intellectually. But it was always to Apulia that he returned, and the Kingdom of Sicily was always at the centre of his plans and affections: he referred to it as 'the most brilliant of our possessions' and even more picturesquely as 'a garden of pleasure in the midst of thorns'. Frederick's concept of Empire began with the area of the old Norman kingdom, then worked outwards to include central Italy and Lombardy, and finally Germany – the exact opposite of the concept of his grandfather Barbarossa. It is easy to postulate that at the very centre of this enterprise was to be Castel del Monte, just as Aachen had been the spiritual centre of his greatest predecessor Charlemagne.

It is in what one biographer has referred to as the 'majestic loneliness' of Castel del Monte when seen from the distance which provides the clue to the way in which this astonishing building stands for the mind of

The head of Frederick II on his gold coin known as the *Augustalis*

Frederick II. For it was his own conception of himself as Emperor, as a man apart from others, which was his most remarkable characteristic, and which stimulated the immense yearning which he nurtured for the glory and majesty of ancient Rome. The boy who was first named Constantine had himself portrayed on his gold coin, the *Augustalis*, in classical mode and dress which unequivocally recall the sedate Roman *gravitas* and even the physical features of the statue of Augustus as Pontifex Maximus in the Museo Nazionale in Rome. The verses which were composed for his tomb:

> If probity, wit, the grace of each virtue, magnificence
> And the nobility of his stock can resist death,
> Then Frederick, who lies here, is not dead.

recall the words of the *Prooemium* to the Constitutions of Melfi. In this metaphoric and nostalgic sense Frederick II represents continuity between the last of the Roman Emperors and the 13th century; none of the future claimants to the title of Holy Roman Emperor was to match his achievement until the 16th century Hapsburg King of Spain and Emperor Charles V, who had himself crowned in Frederick's coronation robes. After that the title became increasingly honorific until its demise in 1806. But the social and economic changes which we have seen in earlier chapters rendered the role of emperor as originated by Augustus obsolete with Frederick's death; his was an impossible task from the outset, for the geometrical and artistic perfection which the Emperor's mind could demand of a structure such as Castel del Monte could not be imposed upon the emerging 'Italian' society.

# PART III

## Epilogue

## 1250–1300

# AN 'ITALIAN' CULTURE AND THE ORIGINS OF THE RENAISSANCE

T HE death of the Emperor Frederick II in 1250 marked the eclipse of medieval plans for a united kingdom of Italy on the model of the Roman Empire. Following the pattern of autonomy we have seen develop in the communes in the absence of an effective external power, Italy was soon to fragment into the duchies, republics and principalities whose military and artistic rivalries characterized the Renaissance. The most important political development in succeeding decades was the transfer of power from commune to a single family or individual: the *signoria*. The rise of families like the Visconti in Milan, the Este in Ferrara and the Montefeltro in Urbino occurred in these years, placing power and the necessary capital for artistic patronage into the hands of the rulers of relatively small parts of the peninsula. Yet, ironically, this loss of the possibility of a united Italy – lamented by Dante in his *De monarchia* and only fulfilled 600 years later – was paralleled in the same period by the elaboration of a culture which was distinctly 'Italian'.

The name for the country *Italia* and description of it as the *Italian peninsula*, probably of Sicilian origin, derived from Greek usage of the fourth century before Christ. At first referring only to the limited area from the Straits of Messina to a line drawn from Taranto to Posidonia (just south of Paestum), it was expanded by the Romans first to a line beginning at the mouth of the Arno and then eventually to the Alps as they conquered the entire peninsula. The Romans used Italia as Gallia or Hispania to denote a province of the Empire, and in Pliny's *Natural History* the adjective appears in the phrase *bellum italicum*. Still at the time of Theoderic the court writer Cassiodorus uses the expression *regnum italicum* to refer to the whole peninsula in opposition to the threat from Justinian at Constantinople to return Italy to the Empire. But under the Lombards and Carolingians this same expression came to refer to the area ruled by them, thus central and northern Italy: 'Italian' and 'Lombard' were more or less synonymous. It was only in the 12th century that 'italiani' became used in an ethnic and geographical sense instead of the

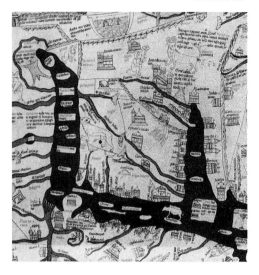

Italy as shown around 1200 on the Hereford *Mappamundi*

ancient usage of 'italici' or 'italienses', an important historical shift which coincided with the decadence of the use of 'Lombardi' in connection with the old *regum italicum*. Then in the 13th century the adjective 'italiano' entered literary and common usage in the modern sense, first in the *Tresor* of Brunetto Latini as 'Ytalien' between 1260–6 and about the same time as 'ytaliano' in an anonymous compilation of *exempla* (or models) of prose. This development was closely associated with Frederick II, and marks a vital shift in the process of melding the discrete elements of the past of the peninsula into a characteristically 'Italian' culture.

Frederick was instrumental in this shift because his Italian court was the first in Europe to adopt the vulgar tongue as its official language in the place of Latin. Furthermore, apart from his own poetic talent, there was a new flowering of lyric poetry based on the poems of the troubadours of Provence but often quite distinctively Italian. The poetic dialogue 'Rosa fresca aulentissima' (translated as 'Thou sweetly-smelling fresh red rose' by Dante Gabriel Rossetti) by the imperial notary Cielo d'Alcamo is generally considered to be the first poem written in the Italian language, and is remarkable for the way in which it presents two sides of the case – like Frederick's 'Dolze meo drudo'. Moreover the poetic excellence of this dialogue was by no means isolated at the imperial court, which provided a focal point for some of the finest poets of the 13th century: Rinaldo d'Aquino (who may have been brother to Thomas Aquinas, and whose 'Gia mai non mi conforto' still reads with astonishing freshness), Giacomino Pugliese, Giacomo da Lentini (who is credited with the invention of the sonnet form), and Guido delle Colonne. Their works are the germ of Italian poetry.

[254]

Dante, in the 12th book of his defence of vernacular expression and thus of the Italian language, *De Vulgari Eloquio* (written in 1303–4 just 50 years after Frederick's death), stresses the importance of what he referred to as the Sicilian 'school' in the development of Italian poetry. After a historical account of the formation of languages and the reasons for there being so many, he provides a classification with examples of the most important 'idioms' of Italy; his purpose, albeit a foregone conclusion, is to identify the idiom most suited to be the language used throughout Italy. The first one he chooses to discuss as worthy of consideration is the Sicilian idiom, because 'the Sicilian vernacular has assumed greater fame than the others' through the poems which have been written in it. According to Dante, men of 'noble heart and endowed with graces' naturally gravitated to the court of Frederick II and his son Manfred, and 'since the royal throne was in Sicily it came to pass that whatever our predecessors wrote in the vernacular was called Sicilian, and we too shall use this name, and our successors will not be able to change it'. The expression 'Sicilian school' meant for Dante the court of Frederick II, even though it might have been more apt to call it the 'Apulian school' and thus avoid the confusion of generations of Italian schoolchildren; but in fact he was careful in giving the 12th chapter the title *De idiomate siculo et appulo*, and does refer to 'Apulum' as well as 'Siculum'. At the end of his brief discussion of this school Dante dismisses 'Sicilian' as rough and unrefined (it is worth observing that he quotes the third line of Cielo d'Alcamo's poem as an instance – among others – of the infelicities of the style). But his formulation of its historical primacy led to the canonical history of Italian literature beginning with the lyric poets of the 'Sicilian school'. The style was immediately taken up and improved upon by the Tuscan poets of the *dolce stil nuovo*, and of course perfected by Dante himself.

Italian prose had a more ancient lineage. It is interesting to note in the context of this book that the earliest known example is to be found in a *iudicatum* or judgement pronounced at Capua in 960 by Abbot Aligern of Montecassino (948–85). The court of Frederick II played no direct role in the development of Italian prose, but the Emperor appears as a model of courtly manners in what is considered the first narrative work of Italian literature, the collection of brief fables and stories designed to present 'flowers of speech' and elegant use of language known as the *Novellino*. These anonymous stories can be dated between 1281 and 1300 on internal evidence; in 1525 a selection of a hundred of them was printed as *Le Cento Novelle Antiche*. The collection presents an idea of courtly gentility and courtesy which is epitomized by the person of Frederick II. The second novella is in fact an imaginary account of an embassy from the fictitious Prester John to Frederick's court: the opening sentence praises the emperor as 'truly the mirror of the world both in speaking and in his morals', and as a man who loved 'speaking delicately and [was] skilled in giving wise answers'. Some of the stories are evidently based on popular traditions and legends, such as this one concerning the embassy of Prester John or another on a presumed visit by Frederick to the Old Man of the Mountains, but the very geographical extension of the settings would not have been possible without the crusades and the example of cosmopolitan atmosphere at his court. For there are stories of oriental origin, about events in Byzantium and Egypt. But beyond these specific tales and references, Frederick's is the presiding genius of the collection. Although only eight of the hundred stories are directly about him, his presence dominates for two reasons: first, because he is cited as a model; and second, because stories about him open and close the collection (II and C). Novella XXI provides an echo of Dante's idea about the imperial court as a centre of patronage when it states that 'men of genius (*bontade*) came to his court from everywhere'. All in all, the *Novellino* offers an intriguing glimpse of the enduring importance of Frederick's court in the mind of a Florentine writer – or compiler – half a century after his death.

In the history of art Frederick's influence is of less immediate importance than in the history of literature and language; yet the synthesis of different styles which we saw in Castel del Monte anticipated the synthesis of classical and Byzantine continuity with barbarian and Gothic novelty which formed the new tradition of 'Italian' art – as opposed to medieval art – in Tuscany towards the end of the 13th century and in the early years of the 14th. Furthermore there is an often unremarked link between Frederick's court and the mainstream of Tuscan art. The litany of the founders of Renaissance art usually includes Dante, Giotto (cited by Dante himself in *Purgatorio*, XI, 94–6), Cimabue, the father-and-son team of Nicola (or Nicolo) and Giovanni Pisano, and Nicola's pupil Arnolfo di Cambio, an apparently Tuscan sextet. Yet the attributed family name Pisano disguises the fact that Nicola – whose work influenced that of Giovanni, Arnolfo and probably Giotto – was almost certainly born in Apulia, for in two non-Pisan documents he is described as Nicolo 'de Apulia'. In fact the strength and maturity of his first signed work in Pisa in 1260 presupposes a long apprenticeship and career as a sculptor earlier. Little is known of his life, and the date of his birth has been placed anywhere between 1205 and 1225, but the hypothesis that he learned the art of sculpture with the masters who worked for Frederick II is fascinating (though anathema to those who seek to accord the primacy in 'modern' sculpture to Tuscany). If, as seems likely, Nicola moved to Pisa in the 1240s – when his son Giovanni was born there (a man bearing the most typical name of the area near Bari giving to his son the most typical name of

Tuscany) – then it is possible to formulate a direct link with the classical and Gothic sculptures made for Frederick II at Castel del Monte and on his now-lost triumphal gate-tower at Capua. Although it is impossible to demonstrate, the hypothesis that Nicola Pisano may even have worked at Castel del Monte makes sense: first because it is inconceivable that such a talented sculptor in Apulia should not be employed by the emperor, and second because the 'Gothic' of the pulpits made by Nicola and his assistants in Pisa and Siena is a Gothic *sui generis* in the same way as that of the southern buildings. It is a peculiarly Italian blend of classical and Gothic evolved in the south as the result of Frederick's deliberate attempt to revive Roman grandeur with the aid of Cistercian architects and masons; neither French nor Tuscan.

In painting the term 'Italian' art is first used of Giotto (1267–1337), who is credited with the birth of 'modern' painting parallel to the achievement of Nicola Pisano. Indeed the much praised heaviness and reality of Giotto's figures in such works as the 'Madonna Enthroned' (c.1310), painted for the Florentine church of Ognissanti and now in the Uffizi Gallery, clearly derive from sculpture – as a glance at Pisano's marble pulpit for the baptistery in Pisa shows (with the same classical technique of showing the forms of the body, in this cause the knees, under the drapery instead of allowing them to fall shapeless to the floor). Frescoed figures like 'Faith' in the Arena chapel (c.1305) at Padua also possess the solidity of sculptures, but in fact create the illusion of depth by the techniques of foreshortening, use of shadow and modelling of rounded forms which characterize Italian Renaissance painting. This was absorbed from the twin traditions of Roman and Byzantine art, which was nowhere easier to see than in Apulia although similar effects had also been achieved in Italian sculpture further north. An exhibition of the work of Benedetto Antelami (fl.1178–1225) at Parma in the summer of 1990 illustrated at eye-level and in photographs how Antelami achieved the same effects in his sculptures for the cathedral and baptistery at Parma as early as 1215–20. This success can be seen most clearly in his figures of Solomon and Sheba (the latter figure recalls the Padua 'Faith'), where the form of the body is seen clearly beneath the drapery. It may also be seen in the smaller figures for the frieze of the months which Antelami made on the façade of the cathedral at Cremona, of which Frederick II and his court certainly knew and may even have financed. Although the lack of documentary evidence makes it hard to pin down the degree of direct influence of Benedetto Antelami on Apulian sculpture or Apulian sculpture on Nicola Pisano, the presence of such a powerful centripetal force as Frederick II – which Dante and the *Novellino* acknowledge – make it likely that his court was the catalyst for future developments. For it was the solidity and sense of real presence in 13th

[257]

The sculpted pulpit at Pisa, by Nicola Pisano

The fresco of *Faith* by Giotto, in the Arena Chapel (Padua)

century sculpture which was new, and which Giotto successfully transferred to painting.

As far as Florentine architecture is concerned, sufficient finance and manpower could be devoted to large-scale public building projects when in 1289 a series of wars with Siena, Pisa and Arezzo came to an end and was followed by a period of peace. The frenzy of activity in literature and painting was paralleled by the civic pride in Florence which resulted in the construction of the Palazzo Vecchio, the Bargello, the new cathedral, the campanile for which Giotto himself provided the first design, and the new city walls. In Siena, slightly later although Nicola Pisano had already worked in the old cathedral in the 1260s, a new baptistery was begun in 1317 and ambitious plans for an immense new cathedral began to circulate, culminating in the laying of the foundation stone in 1339. Then the frenzy was truncated.

There were several reasons for this. From around 1340 a series of factors contributed to an unprecedented decline: an economic recession caused in part by the closure of northern markets due to beginning of the Hundred Years War (1338), the closing of eastern trade routes as a result of the rise of the empire of Timur the Lame (1336–1405), the wars which proliferated with the aid of the new-formed mercenary companies of *condottieri* (the Company of St George, 1339; the Great Company, 1442); and finally a series of natural disasters. These latter included a dramatic famine in the crop season 1339–40, the destruction of crops by heavy rain in 1345–6, and the Black Death which decimated the population of Italy in 1348 – and was followed by a series of lesser plagues until the end of the century. Contemporaries put the deaths as high as 80 per cent in Venice, 68 per cent in Genoa, and 50 per cent in Siena; in Florence the population is thought to have declined from between 80,000–100,000 to about 30,000, and at the time of Cosimo 'the Elder' de' Medici (1389–1464) rose to between 40,000–50,000. The effects on art were devastating: artists such as Pietro and Ambrogio Lorenzetti probably died in the plague, which in fact carried off most of Siena's artists. It is impossible to name a cluster of artists in the second half of the 14th century to compare with those of 1290–1320 or the 1440s. An eloquent symbol of this dramatic rupture is the unfinished cathedral of Siena, whose present – and imposing enough – nave was to have been merely the *transept* of a much larger construction. Many cities of Tuscany and Umbria owe their present – and to us attractive – late medieval appearance to this sudden halt in building and urban expansion, for example Volterra, San Gimignano, Spoleto, Gubbio and Orvieto. Neither manpower nor money existed after 1348 to complete the projects in hand on the original scale; nor did diminished populations necessitate new building for centuries.

[260]

The recovery of artistic activity is generally associated with the competition for the decoration of the bronze doors of the Baptistery in Florence, announced in 1401 and won the next year by Lorenzo Ghiberti. From that moment the Renaissance of classical values is said to begin, with Ghiberti's assistants Donatello, Masolino and Paolo Uccello – whose scientific perspective is the really new phenomenon. But a fascinating thesis propounded by the Italian art historian Giovanni Previtali, in an essay on the division of the history of Italian art into periods, coherently suggests that the success of this commission was in fact a resumption of activity after the disruption of the 1340s. On this reading the 're-naissance' was a resumption of the 'naissance' which occurred in Tuscany and especially in Florence between roughly 1290 and 1320, not simply the revival of classical values mythicized by Giorgio Vasari in the famous passage of his *Lives of the Artists* where he describes Brunelleschi and his friend Donatello in Rome measuring buildings in pursuit of the former's ambition to 'restore the practice of good architecture' and Donatello imitating 'as many as possible of the works of the ancient world', both going without food and sleep in their utter concentration. Previtali argues that classicism only became an element of the work of Brunelleschi and Donatello in the 1430s, well after the revival had begun. The painting of Masaccio, for instance, who flourished in the 1420s, was heavily indebted to Giotto (as can be seen in the 'Madonna and Child' in the National Gallery in London), occasioning Bernard Berenson's unconsciously pertinent comment that he was 'Giotto born again, starting where death had cut short his advance'. The rebirth had therefore already begun before the two 'treasure-hunters' – as Vasari says they were known in Rome – left Florence around 1431. The work on the Baptistery doors commission (on which Donatello himself worked as apprentice to Ghiberti) may be seen as a re-birth of values temporarily lost, a resumption of work in progress that began with Nicola Pisano, his assistants, and Giotto.

This brings us back to Frederick II, for the birth of a truly 'Italian' literature and possibly art at the end of the 13th century was indirectly associated with his person, as we have seen. The elements of the diverse cultures represented by means of the cities and places whose histories have been told in this book, the Roman, Lombard, Carolingian, Arab, Byzantine, Norman, and German, blended in him as in no other man. They consolidated in the brief period from his death in 1250 to around 1290 into forms of literature and art which were recognizably 'Italian' and represented the *naissance* of an Italian culture. The important point about Frederick is the way in which his person and mind represented a drawing together of the many strands which came to make up Italian culture: in the literary sense the Arab, modern Greek, Latin, German and French traditions; in the legal sense the Roman, Byzantine, Lombard and Norman traditions; in science the Arab, Hebrew and classical Greek traditions; in architecture the Roman, Norman Romanesque and Cistercian Gothic. It is in this sense that around the time of his death in 1250 he stands as a focal point for the future development of Italian culture, as Dante was quick to realize in literary terms. It was on this gathering together of diverse cultures, symbolized by Frederick II, that the Renaissance drew.

At the end of the 13th century it is possible to speak of Italian literature, Italian painting and Italian sculpture, indelibly marked by Dante, Giotto and Nicola Pisano. The culture of the peninsula had begun its rise towards the glories of the 15th and 16th centuries. While it is futile to portray Frederick II as a Renaissance man when he was very much a man of his own time and place, it is none the less true that in his interests in the ancient world, his recognition of the importance of law, his detached attitude towards personal religion, his keen interest in aesthetics, and his understanding of the usefulness of a knowledge of history, he shared at least some of the interests which characterized the humanists of the 15th century. In the end Frederick II overreached himself in the unlimited ambition of his imperial imagination, but he was reaching in the right direction. It was for this reason that his presence endured after his death, and that legends about his immortality proliferated.

In 1300 Frederick had been dead for 50 years, and Hohenstaufen power was dissipated. The political map of Italy had on the basis of previous centuries stabilized into three major sections: the Kingdom of Naples and Sicily to the south, the papal state dividing the peninsula on a broad swathe which ran roughly from Terracina to Rimini, and a series of independent states in northern Italy. This division was to last more or less unchanged for half a millennium, until the unification of Italy was completed by the breach of Porta Pia in Rome in 1870. The modern state managed to revive the unity of Roman 'Italia' where Justinian, Liutprand, Barbarossa and Frederick II failed. But beneath this apparent unity the strands which together formed Italian culture are still a tangible legacy. It is for this reason that Renaissance and Modern Italy can only be comprehended on the basis of an understanding of the unique continuity and multiple influences of the country's medieval history.

# SELECT BIBLIOGRAPHY

CHAPTER 1: PAVIA

ARNALDI, GIROLAMO, 'Pavia e il "Regnum Italiae" dal 774 al 1024', in *Pavia capitale di regno: Atti del 4° Congresso Internazionale di Studi sull'Alto Medioevo*, Pavia-Scaldasole-Monza-Bobbio 10–14 settembre 1967, Spoleto: CISAM, 1969, pp. 175–89.

BARNI, GIANLUIGI, *I Longobardi in Italia*, Novara: De Agostini, 1987.

BOGNETTI, GIAN PIERO, *L'Età Longobarda*, Milan: Giuffré, 1966–8 (4 vols.).

BERTOLINI, OTTAVIO, 'La data dell'ingresso dei Longobardi in Italia', in *Scritti Scelti di Storia Medievale*, Livorno: Il Telegrafo, 1968, vol. I, pp. 19–64.

BLAKE, HUGO, *Lancaster in Pavia: Archaeological research undertaken in 1977 by the Dept. of Classics and Archaeology in the Italian city of Pavia*, Lancaster: University of Lancaster, 1978.

— 'Pavia', in *Lancaster in Italy: archaeological research undertaken in Italy by the Dept. of Classics & Archaeology in 1979*, Lancaster: University of Lancaster, 1980, pp. 5–12.

BOORSTIN, DANIEL J., *The Narrators of Barbarian History (AD 550–800): Jordanes, Gregory of Tours, Bede, and Paul the Deacon*, Princeton: Princeton UP, 1988.

BRÜHL, CARLRICHARD, 'Das Palatium von Pavia und die Honorantiae Civitatis Papiae', in *Pavia capitale di regno*, cit., pp. 189–220.

BULLOUGH, DONALD, 'The Ostrogothic and Lombard Kingdoms', in D. Talbot Rice (ed.), *The Dark Ages*, London: Thames & Hudson, 1965, pp. 157–74.

— 'Urban Change in Early Mediaeval Italy; the example of Pavia', *Papers of the British School at Rome*, XXXIV (1966), pp. 82–131.

CAGIANO DE AZEVEDO, M., 'Esistono una architettura e una urbanistica longobarde?', in *Atti del Convegno Internazionale sul tema 'La Civiltà dei Longobardi'*, Roma 24–26 maggio 1971, Rome: Accademia Nazionale dei Lincei, 1974, pp. 289–329.

CALMETTE, JOSEPH, *Charlemagne, sa vie et son oeuvre*, Paris: A. Michel, 1945.

CESSI, R., 'Pavia capitale di regno', *Ricerche Medievali*, II (1967), pp. 3–30.

CHIERICI, GINO, *Le sculture della basilica di San Michele Maggiore a Pavia*, Milan: Edizioni de L' 'Arte', 1942.

DE FRANCOVICH, GEZA, 'Il problema delle origini della scultura cosidetta "Longobarda"', in *Atti del 1° Congresso Internazionale di Studi Longobardi: Spoleto 27–30 settembre 1951*, Spoleto: L'Accademia Spoletina, 1952, pp. 255–73.

DELL'ACQUA, CARLO, *Dell'Insigne Reale Basilica San Michele Maggiore in Pavia*, Pavia: Fratelli Fusi, 1875.

DELOGU, PAOLO, 'Il regno longobardo', in Delogu, P., Guillou, A., Ortalli, G., *Longobardi e Bizantini*, Turin: UTET, 1980, pp. 2–216.

DREW, KATHERINE FISCHER (ED.), *The Lombard Laws*, Philadelphia: University of Pennsylvania Press, 1973.

GASPARRI, S., *La cultura tradizionale dei Longobardi: Struttura tribale e resistenze pagane*, Spoleto: CISAM, 1983.

HALLENBECK, JAN T., *Pavia and Rome: The Lombard Monarchy and the Papacy in the Eighth Century*, Transactions of the American Philosophical Society, Vol. 72, Part 4, 1982.

HUBERT, JEAN, 'Les "Cathédrales doubles" et l'histoire de la liturgie', in *Atti del 1° Congresso Internazionale di Studi Longobardi*, cit., pp. 167–76.

KRAUTHEIMER, RICHARD, 'The Twin Cathedral at Pavia', in *Studies in Early Christian, Medieval, and Renaissance Art*, London: University of London Press, 1971, pp. 161–80.

MOR, C.G., 'Pavia Capitale', in *Pavia capitale di regno*, cit., pp. 19–31.

PAUL THE DEACON, *Historia Langobardorum*, Trs. in Barni, *I Longobardi in Italia*, pp. 197–360.

PORTER, ARTHUR KINGSLEY, *Lombard Architecture*, New Haven: Yale UP, 1915–17, 4 vols.

RADDING, CHARLES M., *The Origins of Medieval Jurisprudence: Pavia and Bologna, 850–1150*, New Haven: Yale UP, 1988.

VACCARI, PIETRO., *Profilo storico di Pavia*, Pavia: La Tipografia Ticinese, 1950.

— *Pavia nell'alto medio evo e nell'Età communale, Profilo Storico*, Pavia: Busca, 1956.

— 'Pavia nell'alto medioevo', in *La Città nell'Alto Medioevo: Settimane di Studio del Centro Italiano di Studi sull'Alto Medioevo*, VI (1958), Spoleto: CISAM, 1959, pp. 151–92.

VERZONE, PAOLO, 'Architettura longobarda a Spoleto e Pavia', in *Pavia capitale di regno*, cit., pp. 221–9.

WARD-PERKINS, BRYAN, 'The towns of northern Italy: rebirth or renewal?', in HODGES, Richard & HOBLEY Brian (ed.), *The Rebirth of towns in the west AD 700–1050*, London: Council for British Archaeology (CBA Research Report 68), 1988.

WICKHAM, CHRIS, *Early Medieval Italy: Central Power and Local Society 400–1000*, London: Macmillan, 1981.

— 'The Other Transition: From the Ancient World to Feudalism', *Past & Present* 103 (May 1984), pp. 3–36.

— 'L'Italia e l'alto Medioevo', *Archeologia Medievale*, XV (1988), pp. 105–24.

ZIMOLO, GIULIO, C., 'Pavia nella storia della navigazione interna', in *Atti e Memorie del Quarto Congresso Storico Lombardo, Pavia 18–19–20 maggio 1939*, Milan: Giuffré, 1940, pp. 493–531.

ACOCELLA, NICOLA, *La decorazione pittorica di Montecassino dalle Didascalie di Alfano I (Sec. XI)*, Salerno: Di Giacomo, 1966.

ANTHONY, EDGAR, *Romanesque Frescoes*, Westport, Conn.: Greenwood Press, 1971.

BERTAUX, ÉMILE, 'Due tesori di pittura medioevale: S. Maria di Ronzano e S. Pellegrino di Bominaco, con appendice del Calendario Valvense', *Rassegna abruzzese di storia ed arte*, III (1899), No. 8, pp. 107–29.

— 'Gli affreschi di S. Vincenzo al Volturno e la prima scuola d'artefici benedettini nel IX secolo', *Rassegna abruzzese di storia ed arte*, IV (1900), No. 11–12, pp. 105–26.

— *L'Art dans l'Italie Méridionale de la fin de L'Empire Romain a la Conquête de Charles d'Anjou*, Paris: Fontemoing, 1903, (3 vols.; reprint 1968).

BLOCH, HERBERT, 'Monte Cassino, Byzantium and the West in the Earlier Middle Ages', *Dumbarton Oaks Papers*, 3 (1946) pp. 163–224.

— 'Monte Cassino's Teachers and Library in the High Middle Ages', in *La scuola nell'Occidente latino dell'alto medioevo: Settimane di Studio del Centro Italiano di Studi sull'Alto Medioevo*, XIX (1971), Spoleto: CISAM, 1972, pp. 563–613.

— *Monte Cassino in the Middle Ages*, Rome: Edizioni di storia a letteratura, 1986 (3 vols.).

CARLI, ENZO, 'Affreschi benedettini del XIII secolo in Abruzzo', *Le Arti*, I (1938), No. 5, pp. 442–63.

CARAVITA, ANDREA, *I codici e le arti a Montecassino*, Montecassino: The Abbey, 1869–70 (2 vols.).

COWDREY, H.E., *The Age of Abbot Desiderius: Montecassino, the Papacy and the Normans in the Eleventh and Early Twelfth Centuries*, Oxford: Clarendon, 1983.

DANDER, MARILENA, *I Tesori di Bominaco*, L'Aquila: EPT, 1979.

DE DOMINICIS, A., *Bominaco e la sua abbazia*, L'Aquila: Japadre, 1971.

DEL TREPPO, MARIO, 'La vita economica e sociale in una grand abbazia del Mezzogiorno: San Vincenzo al Volturno nell'alto Medioevo', *Archivio Storico per le Province Napoletane*, LXXIV (1955), pp. 31–110.

DUNN, MARILYN, 'Eastern Influence on Western Monasticism in the Eleventh and Twelfth Centuries', in Howard-Johnston *Byzantium and the West*, cit., pp. 215–33.

FRUGONI, C., 'Chiesa e lavoro agricolo nei testi e nelle immagini dall'età tardo-antica all'età romanica', in *Medioevo rurale. Sulle tracce della civiltà contadina*, Bologna: Il Mulino, 1980, pp. 321–41.

KITZINGER, ERNST, *The Art of Byzantium and the Medieval West: Selected Studies*, Bloomington: Indiana UP, 1976.

LE GOFF, JACQUES, 'Calendario', in *Enciclopedia Einaudi*, Vol. II, Turin: Einaudi, 1977, pp. 501–34.

— *Tempo della Chiesa e tempo del mercante*, Turin: Einaudi, 1977.

LENTINI, ANSELMO, *La Regola di San Benedetto*, Montecassino: The Abbey, 1979.

[265]

MORISANI, OTTAVIO, *Bisanzio e la pittura cassinese*, Palermo: Istituto della Storia dell'Arte, Palermo University, 1955.

— *Gli affreschi di Sant'Angelo in Formis*, Cava de Tirreni: Di Mauro, 1962.

PANTONI, ANGELO, *Le Vicende della basilica di Montecassino attraverso la documentazione archaeologica*, Montecassino: The Abbey (Miscellanea Cassinese 36), 1973.

PRIORI, DOMENICO, *Badie e conventi benedettini d'Abruzzo e Molise*, Lanciano: Carabba, 1950 (Vol. I); Lanciano: Mancini, 1951 (Vol. II).

RASETTI, GERARDO, *Il calendario nell'arte italiana e il calendario abruzzese*, Pescara: De Arcangelis, 1941.

SETTIS, SALVATORE, 'Iconografia dell'arte italiana, 1100–1500: una linea', in *Storia dell'arte italiana*, Part I, Vol. III: *L'esperienza dell'antico, dell'Europa, della religiosità*, Turin: Einaudi, 1979, pp. 175–270.

SOUTHERN, R. W., *Western Society and the Church in the Middle Ages*, Harmondsworth: Penguin, 1970.

STERN, H., 'Poésies et representations carolingiennes et byzantines des mois', *Revue Archéologique*, 7th series, 1955, pp. 141–86.

WEBSTER, *The Labours of the Months in Antique and Medieval Art to the End of the Twelfth Century*, Evanston: Northwestern UP, 1938.

WILLARD, HENRY M. & CONANT, K.J., 'A Project for the Graphic Reconstruction of the Romanesque Abbey at Monte Cassino', *Speculum*, X (1935), pp. 144–6.

CHAPTER 3: PALERMO

AHMAD, AZIZ, *A History of Islamic Sicily*, Edinburgh: EUP, 1975.

AMARI, MICHELE, *Storia dei musulmani di Sicilia*, Catania: Romeo Prampolini, 1933–9 (5 vols.).

ARATA, GIULIO V., *Architettura arabo-normanna e il Rinascimento in Sicilia*, Milan: Bestetti & Tumminelli, 1913.

DE SETA, CESARE, & DI MAURO, LEONARDO, *Palermo*, Bari: Laterza, 1980.

DI GIOVANNI, VINCENZO, *La Topografia Antica di Palermo, dal secolo X al XV*, Palermo: Tipografia e Legatoria del Boccone del Povero, 1889–90 (2 vols.).

— 'Il Castello e la Chiesa: della Favara di S. Filippo a Mare Dolce in Palermo', *Archivio Storico Siciliano*, Nuova Serie, XXII (1897), pp. 301–74.

FAZIO ALLMAYER, V., 'Gli arabi e l'arte in Sicilia', *Rassegna d'Arte*, VIII (1908), pp. 37–9.

GABRIELI, FRANCESCO, & SCERRATO, U., *Gli Arabi in Italia: Cultura, contatti e tradizioni*, Milan: Garzanti/Scheiwiller, 1979.

HITTI, PHILIP, *History of the Arabs*, London: Macmillan, 1970.

HOURANI, A.H., & STERN, S.M., *The Islamic City: A Colloquium*, Oxford: Bruno Cassirer, 1970.

IBN HAUKAL, *The Oriental Geography of Ebn Haukal, an arabian traveller of the tenth century*, ed. and trs. Sir William Ouseley, London: Oriental Press, 1800.

MONNERET DE VILLARD, UGO, *Monumenti dell'arte musulmana in Italia*, Rome: Collezione Meridionale, 1938.

— *Le Pitture musulmane al soffitto della Cappella Palatina in Palermo*, Rome: La Libreria dello Stato, 1950.

STASOLLA, MARIA GIOVANNA (ed.), *Italia euro-mediterranea nel Medioevo: testimonianze di scrittori arabi*, Bologna: Patron, 1983.

THUCYDIDES, *The Peloponnesian War*, trs. Rex Warner, Harmondsworth: Penguin, 1959.

WAERN, CECILIA, 'Some notes on mediaeval Palermo', *Burlington Magazine*, No. XXXI, Vol. VIII (1905), pp. 23–32.

— *Mediaeval Sicily: Aspects of Life and Art in the Middle Ages*, London: Duckworth, 1910.

WATT, W. MONTGOMERY, *The Influence of Islam on Medieval Europe*, Edinburgh; EUP, 1972.

## CHAPTER 4: BARI

AMBROSI, ANGELO, 'Il Convento delle monache benedettine di S. Scolastica, Bari', in Calò Mariani, Maria Stella (ed.), *Insediamenti Benedettini in Puglia: Per una storia dell'arte dall'XI al XVIII secolo*, Galatina: Congedo, 1980 (2 vols.), vol II, pp. 163–84.

BELLI D'ELIA, PINA, *La Basilica di San Nicola a Bari*, Galatina: Congedo, 1985.

BELTING, H., 'Byzantine Art among Greeks and Latins in Southern Italy', *Dumbarton Oaks Papers*, 28 (1974), pp. 1–29.

BLATTMANN, IDA, 'Sulle strutture medievali del monastero di S. Benedetto, Bari', in Calò Mariani, *Insediamenti Benedettini*, cit., Vol. II, pp. 193–202.

BROWN, T.S., 'The Background of Byzantine Relations with Italy in the Ninth Century: Legacies, Attachments and Antagonisms', in Howard-Johnston, *Byzantium and the West*, cit., pp. 27–45.

BURGARELLA, FILIPPO, 'Bisanzio in Sicilia e nell'Italia meridionale: i riflessi politici', in GUILLOU, André et al., *Il Mezzogiorno dai Bizantini a Federico II*, Turin: UTET, 1983, pp. 129–248.

CALASSO, FRANCESCO, 'La citta nell'Italia meridionale dal sec. IX al XI', in *L'Italia meridionale nell'alto medioevo e i rapporti con il mondo bizantino: Atti del 3° Congresso Internationale di Studi sull'Alto Medioevo*, Benevento-Montevergine-Salerno-Amalfi, 14–18 October 1956, Spoleto: CISAM, 1959, pp. 39–63.

CHARANIS, PETER, 'On the Question of the Hellenization of Sicily and Southern Italy during the Middle Ages', *American Historical Review*, Vol. LII, No. 1 (1946), pp. 74–86.

CORSI, PASQUALE, 'Dalla riconquista bizantina al catepanato', in Tateo (ed.), *Storia di Bari dalla Preistoria al Mille*, cit., pp. 315–50.

FALKENHAUSEN, VERA VON, *La dominazione bizantina nell'Italia meridionale dal IX all'XI secolo*, Bari: Ecumenica, 1978.

[267]

FERLUGA, JADRAN, 'L'Italia bizantina dalla caduta dell'Esarcato di Ravenna alla metà del secolo IX', in *Bisanzio, Roma e l'Italia nell'Alto Medioevo: Settimane di Studio del Centro Italiano di Studi sull'Alto Medioevo*, XXXIV (1986), Spoleto: CISAM, 1988, Vol I, pp. 169–93.

GAY, JULES, *L'Italie méridionale et l'empire byzantin depuis l'avènement de Basile Ier jusqu'à la prise de Bari par les Normanni (867–1071)*, Paris: Albert Fontemoing (Bibliotèques des Écoles Françaises D'Athènes et de Rome, Fascicule 90), 1904.

GUILLOU, ANDRÉ, *Studies on Byzantine Italy*, London: Variorum Reprints, 1970.

— *Culture et Societé en Italie Byzantine (VI–XI siècles)*, London; Variorum Reprints, 1978.

— 'L'Italia bizantina dall'invasione longobarda alla caduta di Ravenna', in DELOGU, GUILLOU, ORTALLI, *Longobardi e Bizantini*, cit., pp. 219–338.

— 'L'Italia bizantina dalla caduta di Ravenna all'arrivo dei Normanni', in GUILLOU et al., *Il Mezzogiorno dai Bizantini a Federico II*, op. cit., pp. 3–126.

HOWARD-JOHNSTON, J.D. (ED.), *Byzantium and the West c.850–c.1200, Proceedings of the XVIII Spring Symposium of Byzantine Studies, Oxford 30 March–1 April 1984*, Amsterdam: Adolf H. Hakkart, 1988.

MILELLA LOVECCHIO, M., 'La scultura bizantina dell'XI secolo nel museo di San Nicola di Bari', in *Mélanges de l'École Française de Rome: Moyen Âge – Temps Modernes*, 93 (1981), vol. I, pp. 7–87.

MUSCA, GIOSUÉ, *L'emirato di Bari 847–871*, Bari: Dedalo, 1967.

— 'L'espansione urbana di Bari nel secolo XI', *Quaderni Medievali*, 2 (1976), pp. 39–72.

PERTUSI, AGOSTINO, 'Contributi alla storia dei ''temi' bizantini dell'Italia meridionale', in *L'Italia meridionale nell'alto medioevo e i rapporti con il mondo bizantino*, cit., pp. 495–517.

— 'Bisanzio e l'irradiazione della sua civiltà in Occidente nell'alto medioevo', in *Centri e vie di irradiazione della civiltà nell'alto medioevo: Settimane di Studio del Centro Italiano di Studi sull'Alto Medioevo*, XI (1963), Spoleto: CISAM, 1964, pp. 75–133.

PETRIGNANI, MARCELLO, & PORSIA, FRANCO, *Bari*, Bari: Laterza, 1982.

PORSIA, FRANCO, 'Il primo secolo di vita dell'Abbazia di S. Benedetto a Bari', in Calò Mariani, *Insediamenti Benedettini*, cit., Vol. I, pp. 153–65.

PSELLUS, MICHAEL, *Fourteen Byzantine Rulers: The 'Chronographia' of Michael Psellus*, trs. E.R.A. Sewter, Harmondsworth: Penguin, 1966.

SALVATORE, MARIAROSA, & LAVERMICOCCA, NINO, 'Sculture altomedievali e bizantine nel Museo di San Nicola a Bari; Note sulla topografia di Bari bizantina', *Rivista di Archaeologia e Storia dell'Arte*, 3 (1980), pp. 93–135.

SCHETTINI, FRANCO, *La basilica di San Nicola di Bari*, Bari: Laterza, 1967.

TATEO, FRANCESCO (ED.), *Storia di Bari, Vol I: Dalla Preistoria al Mille*, Bari: Laterza, 1989.

ABULAFIA, DAVID, *The Two Italies; Economic relations between the Norman Kingdom of Sicily and the Northern Communes*, Cambridge: CUP, 1977.

AGNELLO DI RAMATA, GIOVANNI, 'La Domus Regia di Ruggero in Cefalù, in *Atti del Congresso Internazionale di Studi Ruggeriana, 21–25 aprile 1954*, Palermo: Boccone del Povero, 1955, Vol. II, pp. 455–63.

AMATUS OF MONTE CASSINO, *Storia dei Normanni*, ed. V. de Bartholemaeis, Rome: Istituto Storico Italiano (Fonti per la Storia d'Italia), 1935.

BELLAFIORE, GIUSEPPE, *La Cattedrale di Palermo*, Palermo: Flaccovio, 1976.

BROADHURST, R.J.C. (TRS.), *The Travels of Ibn Jubayr*, London: Jonathan Cape, 1952.

CAPITANI, OVIDIO, 'Specific Motivations and Continuing Themes in the Norman Chronicles of Southern Italy in the Eleventh and Twelfth Centuries,' in *The Normans in Sicily and Southern Italy*, Lincei Lectures 1974, Oxford: OUP (Published for the British Academy), 1977, pp. 1–46.

CARAVALE, MARIO, *Il Regno Normanno di Sicilia*, Milan: Guiffré, 1966.

CHALANDON, FERDINAND, *Histoire de la Domination Normande en Italie et en Sicile*, New York: Burt Franklin, 1960 (reprint of 1904 Paris edition), 2 vols.

CURTIS, EDMOND, *Roger of Sicily and the Normans in Lower Italy 1016–1154*, New York & London: G.P. Putnam's Sons, 1912.

DELOGU, PAOLO, *I Normanni in Italia: Cronache della conquista e del regno*, Naples: Liguori, 1984.

DEMUS, OTTO, *Byzantine Art and the West*, London: Weidenfeld & Nicolson, 1970.

DI PIETRO, FILIPPO, *La Cappella Palatina di Palermo: I Mosaici*, Milan: Sidera, 1954.

DI STEFANO, GUIDO, *L'Architettura Gotico-Sveva in Sicilia*, Palermo: F. Ciuni, 1935.

— *Il Duomo di Cefalù: Biografia di una cattedrale incompiuta*, Palermo: Quaderni della Facoltà di Architettura dell'Università di Palermo, 1960.

— *Monumenti della Sicilia Normanna*, Palermo: Società Siciliana per la Storia Patria, 1965.

DOUGLAS, DAVID, *The Norman Achievement*, London: Eyre & Spottiswoode, 1969.

GALASSO, GIUSEPPE, 'Social and Political Developments in the Eleventh and Twelfth Centuries', in *The Normans in Sicily and Southern Italy*, cit., pp. 47–63.

GELFER-JØRGENSEN, MIRJAM, *Medieval Islamic Symbolism and the paintings in the Cefalù cathedral*, Leiden: E.J. Brill, 1986.

GIUNTA, FRANCESCO, *Bizantini e bizantismo nella Sicilia normanna*. Palermo: G. Priulla, 1950.

IDRISI, *L'Italia descritta nel 'Libro del Re Ruggero' compilato da Edrisi*, ed. M. Amari & C. Schiaparelli (Arabic text and translation), Rome: Salviucci, 1883.

JORANSON, EINAR, 'The Inception of the Career of the Normans in Italy – Legend and History', *Speculum*, XXIII (1948), pp. 353–96.

KITZINGER, ERNST, *The Mosaics of Monreale*, Palermo: Flaccovio, 1960.

LOUD, G.A., 'How "Norman" was the Norman Conquest of Southern Italy?' *Nottingham Medieval Studies*, XXV (1981), pp. 13–34.

— *Church and Society in the Norman Principality of Capua 1058–1197*, Oxford: Clarendon, 1985.

— 'Byzantine Italy and the Normans', in Howard-Johnston, *Byzantium and the West*, cit., pp. 245–59.

MARONGIU, ANTONIO, 'A model-state in the Middle Ages: the Norman and Swabian Kingdom of Sicily', *Comparative Studies in Society and History*, Vol. VI (1963–4), pp. 307–20.

— 'I due regni normanni d'Inghilterra e d'Italia', in *I normanni e la loro espansione in Europa nell'alto medioevo: Settimane di Studio del Centro Italiano di Studi sull'Alto Medioevo*, XVI (1968), Spoleto: CISAM, 1969, pp. 497–552.

MENAGER, L.-R., *Hommes et Institutions de l'Italie Normande*, London: Variorum Reprints, 1981.

NORWICH, JOHN JULIUS, *The Normans in the South 1016–1130*, London: Longman, 1967.

— *The Kingdom in the Sun 1130–1194*, London: Longman, 1970.

PONTIERI, ERNESTO, 'Il capitolo sui normanni nella storia d'Italia', in *I normanni e la loro espansione*, cit., pp. 15–34.

RESTA, GIANVITO, 'La cultura siciliana dell'età normanna', in *Atti del Congresso Internazionale di Studi sulla Sicilia Normanna*, Palermo 4–8 dicembre 1972, Palermo: Istituto di Storia Medievale,Università di Palermo, 1973, pp. 263–78.

RIZZITANO, UMBERTO, 'La cultura araba dell'età normanna', in *Atti del Congresso Internazionale di Studi sulla Sicilia Normanna*, cit., pp. 279–97.

SALVINI, ROBERTO, 'Monuments of Norman Art in Sicily and Southern Italy', in *The Normans in Sicily and Southern Italy*, cit., pp. 64–92.

TRAMONTANA, SALVATORE, 'La monarchia normanna e sveva', in Guillou et al., *Il Mezzogiorno dai Bizantini a Federico II*, op. cit., pp. 437–810.

WHITE, LYNN TOWNSEND JR., *Latin monasticism in Norman Sicily*, Cambridge, Mass: The Medieval Academy of America, Publication No. 31, 1938.

WIERUSZOWSKI, HELENE, 'Roger II of Sicily, Rex-Tyrannus, in 12th century Political Thought', *Speculum*, XXXVIII (1963), pp. 46–78.

## CHAPTER 6: GENOA

BELGRANO, LUIGI TOMMASO, *Della Vita Privata dei Genovesi*, Genova: Reale Istituto di Sordo-Muti, 1875.

— (ed.), *Annali Genovesi di Caffaro e de' suoi continuatori, da MXCIX al MCCXCIII*, Rome: Istituto Storico Italiano (Fonti per la Storia d'Italia: Scrittori, secoli XI e XIII), 1890, Vol I.

BIANCHI, LUCIANO GROSSI, & POLEGGIO, ENNIO, *Una Città Portuale del Medioevo: Genova nei secoli X–XVI*, Genoa: SAGEP, 1987.

BYRNE, E.H., 'Genoese Trade with Syria in the Twelfth Century', *American Historical Review*, XXV (1919–20), pp. 191–219.

CANALE, MICHEL-GIUSEPPE, *Nuova Istoria delle Repubblica di Genoa, del suo commercio e della sua letteratura dalle origini all'anno 1797*, Florence: Felice le Monnier, 1858 (2 vols.).

DAY, GERALD W., *Genoa's Response to Byzantium 1155–1204: Commercial Expansion and Factionalism in a Medieval City*, Urbana and Chicago: University of Illinois Press, 1988.

FERNANDEZ-ARMESTO, FELIPE, *Before Columbus: Exploration and Colonisation from the Mediterranean to the Atlantic, 1229–1492*, London: Macmillan, 1987.

HEERS, J. 'Urbanisme et Structure Sociale à Gênes au Moyen-Âge', in *Studi in onore di A. Fanfani*, Milan: Giuffré, 1962, vol. I, pp. 369–412.

HUGHES, DIANE OWEN, 'Urban Growth and Family Structure in Medieval Genoa', *Past and Present*, No. 66 (Feb. 1975), pp. 3–28.

— 'Kinsmen and Neighbours in Medieval Genoa', in MISKIMIN, Henry A., HERLIHY, David, & UDOVITCH, A.L., (eds.) *The Medieval City*, New Haven: Yale UP, 1977, pp. 95–111.

KRUEGER, HILMAR C., 'Genoese trade with Northwest Africa in the twelfth century,' *Speculum*, VIII (1933), pp. 377–95.

— 'Wares of exchange in twelfth-century Genoese-African trade', *Speculum*, XII (1937), pp. 57–71.

*La Cattedrale di Genova 1118–1918*, Genova: Tip. della Gioventù, 1918.

LOPEZ, ROBERT S., *Genova Marinara nel Duecento: Benedetto Zaccaria Ammiraglio e Mercante*, Messina-Milan: Giuseppe Principato, 1933.

— 'Market Expansion: The Case of Genoa', *Journal of Economic History*, 25 (1964), pp. 445–64.

MANFRONI, CAMILLO, *Genova*, Rome: Edizioni Tiber, 1929.

NADA PATRONE, ANNA MARIA & AIRALDI, GABRIELLA, 'Genova e la Liguria nel medioevo', in *Comuni e signorie nell'Italia settentrionale: il Piemonte e la Liguria*, Turin: UTET, 1986, pp. 365–547.

PISTARINO, GEO., 'Genova medievale fra Oriente e Occidente', in *Rivista storica italiana*, LXXXI (1969), pp. 44–73.

POLEGGI, ENNIO, & CEVINI, PAOLO, *Genova*, Bari: Laterza, 1981.

PRAWER, JOSHUA, 'Crusader Cities', in MISKIMIN, Henry A., HERLIHY, David, & UDOVITCH, A.L., (eds.) *The Medieval City*, New Haven: Yale UP, 1977. pp. 179–205.

PRYOR, JOHN H., *Geography, Technology, and War; Studies in the maritime history of the Mediterranean 649–1571*, Cambridge: CUP, 1987.

SLESSAREV, V., *'Ecclesiae Mercatorum* and the rise of merchant colonies', *Business History Review*, XLI (1967).

TUDELA, B. ben Jonah da, *The Itinerary of Benjamin of Tudela*, Trs. & Comm. M.N. Adler, New York: Philipp Feldhein, 1907.

ASTEGIANI, LORENZO, (ed.), *Codice Diplomatico Cremonese 715–1334*, Turin: Fratelli Bocca (Historiae Patriae Monumenta, Third Series, vols. XXI, XXII), 1895–98 (2 vols.).

BARRACLOUGH, GEOFFREY (TRS.), *Medieval Germany 911–1250: Essays by German Historians*, Oxford: OUP, 1938.

— 'Frederick Barbarossa and the Twelfth Century', in *History and a Changing World*, Oxford: Blackwell, 1955.

BERNARDI, AURELIO, 'Cremona, colonia latina a nord del Po', in PONTIROLI, G, (ed.), *Atti del congresso storico archeologico per il 2200 anno di fondazione di Cremona*, Cremona: Libreria del Convegno, 1985.

BOSL, KARL, *Il risveglio dell'Europa: l'Italia dei Comuni*, Bologna: Il Mulino, 1985.

BONVESIN DE LA RIVA, *De Magnalibus Mediolani*, Ed. Maria Corti, Milan: Bompiani, 1974.

BREZZI, PAOLO, *I comuni medioevali nella storia d'Italia*, Turin: ERI, 1959.

BUTLER, W.F., *The Lombard Communes: A History of the Republics of North Italy*, London: T. Fisher Unwin, 1906.

DENTI, GIANNINA, *Storia di Cremona*, Cremona: Turris, 1985.

FASOLI, GINA, *Dalla 'civitas' al comune*, Bologna: Patron, 1961.

GOETZ, WALTER, *Le origini dei comuni italiani*, Milan: Giuffré, 1965.

GUALAZZINI, UGO, *I mercanti di Cremona 1183–1260–1927*, Cremona; Soc. Ed. 'Cremona Nuova', 1928.

— 'Dalle prime affermazioni del *Populus* di Cremona agli Statuti della *Societas populi* del 1229', in *Archivio Storico Lombardo*, 1937, pp. 3–66.

— *Il "Populus" di Cremona e l'Autonomia del Comune*, Bologna: Zanichelli, 1940.

— *Ricerche sulla formazione della "Città Nova" di Cremona dall'età bizantina a Federico II*, Milan: Giuffré, 1982.

HYDE, J.K., *Society and Politics in Medieval Italy: The Evolution of the Civil Life, 1000–1350*, London: Macmillan, 1973.

LOFF, FABRIZIO, *Il Torrazzo di Cremona*, Cremona: Turris, 1987.

LUCCHINI, LUIGI, *Il Duomo di Cremona: Annali della sua fabbrica dedotti da documenti inediti*, Mantova: G. Mondovi, 1894.

MANINI, LORENZO, *Memorie Storiche della Città di Cremona*, Cremona: Fratelli Manini, 1819 (2 vols.).

MIGLIOLI, GUIDO, *Le Corporazioni Cremonesi d'arti e mestieri nella legislazione statutaria del Medio Evo*, Padua: Fratelli Drucker, 1904.

MONTEVERDI, MARIO, *Storia di Cremona*, Cremona: Libreria del Convegno, 1979.

MONTORSI, WILLIAM, *Cremona: Dalla Città Quadrata a Cittanova*, Modena: Aedes Muratoriana, 1981.

MUNZ, PETER, *Frederick Barbarossa: A Study in Medieval Politics*, London: Eyre & Spottiswoode, 1969.

PIVANO, SILVIO, *Stato e Chiesa: da Berengario I ad Arduino 888–1015*, Turin: Fratelli Bocca, 1908.

PUERARI, A., *Il Duomo di Cremona*, Milan: Cariplo, 1971.

RACINE, P., 'A Cremona, à la fin du XIII siècle', in *Studi in Memoria di Federigo Melis*, Naples: Giannini, 1978, vol. I, pp. 527–41.

SALVATORELLI, L., *L'Italia comunale del secolo XI alla metà del secolo XIV*, Milan: Mondadori, 1940.

SCHIAPARELLI, LUIGI, (ed.), *I Diplomi di Berengario I*, Rome: Istituto Storico Italiano (Fonti per la Storia d'Italia), 1903.

— (ed.), *I Diplomi italiani di Lodovico III e di Rodolfo II*, Rome: Istituto Storico Italiano (Fonti per la Storia d'Italia), 1910.


CHAPTER 8: SANTA MARIA DEL MONTE


BONANNI, TEODORO, *Le antiche industrie della Provincia dell'Aquila*, L'Aquila: Grossi, 1888.

CLEMENTI, ALESSANDRO, *Momenti del Medioevo Abruzzese*, Rome: Bulzoni, 1976.

— *L'Arte della lana in una città del Regno di Napoli*, L'Aquila: Japadre, 1979.

CODA, MARC'ANTONIO, *Breve Discorso del Principio, Privilegii, et Instruttioni della Regia Dohana della Mena delle Pecore in Puglia*, Naples: Geronimo Fasulo, 1666.

COLAPIETRA, RAFFAELE, *La dogana di Foggia: Storia di un problema economica*, Bari/Santo Spirito: Edizioni del Centro Libraio, 1972.

— *L'Aquila e Foggia: Transumanza e Religiosità nella societa pastorale*, Foggia: Società Dauna di Cultura, 1981.

— 'Gli itinerari della transumanza', *Studi Storici Meridionale*, IV (May–Dec. 1984), pp. 253–70.

D'HAENENS, ALBERT, 'Le projet monastique de Benôit comme matrice culturelle', in *San Benedetto nel suo tempo: Atti del 7° Congresso Internazionale di Studi sull'Alto Medioevo, 29 September–5 October 1980*, Spoleto: CISAM, 1982, vol. 2, pp. 429–47.

FARINA, FEDERICO, & FORNARI, BENEDETTO, *L'Architettura cistercense e l'abbazia di Casamari*, Frosinone: Casamari, 1978.

FRANCIOSA, LUCCHINO, *La Transumanza dell'Appennino centro-meridionale*, Naples (Centro di studi per la geografia economica, Univ. of Naples): Memorie di Geografia Economica III (Jan.–June 1981), Vol. IV.

LEYSER, HENRIETTA, *Hermits and the New Monasticism: A Study of Religious Communities in Western Europe 1000–1150*, London: Macmillan, 1984.

LITTLE, LESTER K., *Religious Poverty and the Profit Economy in Medieval Europe*, London: Paul Elek, 1978.

MANIERI, GIOVANNI BATTISTA, *Il sistema della mena della pecore in Puglia*, L'Aquila: Arte della Stampa, 1934.

NEGRI, DANIELE, *Abbazie Cistercensi in Italia*, Pistoia: Tellini, 1981.

PUGLISI, SALVATORE M., *La civiltà appenninica: Origine delle communità pastorali in Italia*, Florence: Sansoni, 1959.

SABATINI, F., *La regione degli altopiani maggiori d'Abruzzo*, Genoa: Sigla Effe, 1960.

VARRO, MARCUS TERENTIUS, *De re rustica*, in *Opere*, ed. A. Traglia, Turin: UTET, 1974, pp. 581–877.

WICKHAM, CHRIS, *Studi sulla Società degli Appennini nell'alto medioevo: Contadini, signori e insediamento nel territorio di Valva (Sulmona)*, Bologna: CLUEB, 1982.


CHAPTER 9: CASTEL DEL MONTE


ABULAFIA, DAVID, *Italy, Sicily and the Mediterranean, 1100–1400*: London: Variorum Reprints, 1987.

— *Frederick II: A Medieval Emperor*, London: Allen Lane, 1988.

CADEI, ANTONIO, 'Fossanova e Castel del Monte', in Romanini, *Federico II e l'Arte del duecento italiano*, cit., pp. 191–215.

DE STEFANO, ANTONINO, *La cultura alla corte di Federico II imperatore*, Palermo: F. Ciuni, 1938.

DE VITA, RAFFAELE, *Castelli, torri ed opere fortificate di Puglia*, Bari: Mario Adda, 1974.

FASOLI, GINA, *Aspetti della politica italiana di Federico II*, Bologna: Patron, 1966.

GABRIELI, FRANCESCO, 'Frederick II and Moslem Culture', *East & West*, IX (1958), pp. 53–61.

GAUDENZI, AUGUSTO (ED.), 'Ignoti Monachi S. Maria de Ferraria Chronica ab anno 781 ad annum 1228', in *Ignoti Monachi Cistercensis S. Mariae de Ferraria Chronica et Ryccardi de Sancto Germano Chronica Priora*, Naples: Giannini (for Società Napoletana di Storia Patria), 1888, pp. 3–46.

GÖTZE, HEINZ, *Castel del Monte*, Milan: Hoepli, 1988.

HASKINS, CHARLES H., *Studies in the History of Mediaeval Science*, Cambridge, Mass.: Harvard UP, 1924.

LEYSER, K.J., 'The Emperor Frederick II', in *Medieval Germany and its Neighbours 900–1250*, London: The Hambledon Press, 1982, pp. 269–76.

MOLAJOLI, BRUNO, *Guida di Castel del Monte*, Fabriano: Gentile, 1940.

MONTEVERDI, ANGELO, 'Federico poeta', in *Atti del Convegno Internazionale di Studi Federiciani: VII° Centenario della Morte di Federico II Imperatore e re di Sicilia (10–18 dicembre 1950)*, Palermo: Universities of Palermo, Catania & Messina, 1952, pp. 351–65.

POWELL, JAMES M., (TRS.), *The Liber Augustalis, or Constitutions of Melfi Promulgated by the Emperor Frederick II for the Kingdom of Sicily in 1231*, Syracuse, NY: Syracuse UP, 1971.

ROMANINI, ANGIOLA MARIA (ED.), *Federico II e l'Arte del duecento italiano, Atti della III° settimana di studi di storia dell'arte medievale dell'Università di Roma, 15–20 maggio 1978*, Galatina: Congedo, 1980, 2 vols.

SAPONARO, GIORGIO (ed.), *Castel del Monte*, Bari: Mario Adda.

THORNTON, HERMANN H., 'The Poems Ascribed to Frederick II and "Rex Fredericus"', *Speculum*, I (1926), pp. 87–100.

— 'The Poems Ascribed to King Enzio', *Speculum*, I (1926), pp. 398–409.

— 'The Authorship of the Poems Ascribed to Frederick II, "Rex Fredericus", and King Enzio', *Speculum*, II (1927), pp. 463–9.

VAN CLEVE, THOMAS CURTIS, *The Emperor Frederick II of Hohenstaufen: Immutator Mundi*, Oxford: Clarendon, 1972.

WILLEMSEN, CARL ARNOLD, *I castelli di Federico II nell'Italia meridionale*, Naples: Società Editrice Napoletana, 1979.

— *Castel del Monte: Il monumento più perfetto dell'imperatore Federico*, Bari: Mario Adda, 1984.

— & ODENTHAL, Dagmar, *Puglia: Terra dei Normanni e degli Svevi*, Bari: Laterza, 1978.

WOOD, CASEY A., & FYFE, F. MARJORIE, *The Art of Falconry. Being the De arte venandi cum avibus of Frederick II of Hohenstaufen*, Stanford: Stanford UP, 1943.

## EPILOGUE

ALIGHIERI, DANTE, *De Vulgari Eloquio*, in *Opere Minori*, ed. P.I. Fraticelli, Naples: Francesco Rossi-Romano, 1855.

DE FRANCOVICH, GEZA, *Benedetto Antelami architetto e scultore, e l'arte del suo tempo*, Milan-Florence: Electa, 1952 (2 vols.).

DEVOTO, GIACOMO, *Gli antichi italici*, Florence: Vallecchi, 1977.

GALASSO, GIUSEPPE, *L'Italia come problema storiografico*, Turin: UTET, 1979.

HOLMES, GEORGE, *Dante*, Oxford: OUP, 1980.

— *Florence, Rome and the Origins of the Renaissance*, Oxford: Clarendon, 1986.

KRISTELLER, PAUL OSKAR, *Renaissance Thought: The Classic, Scholastic, and Humanist Strains*, New York: Harper & Row, 1961.

LARNER, JOHN, *Italy in the Age of Dante and Petrarch 1216–1380*, London: Longman, 1980.

LO NIGRO, SEBASTIANO (ed.), *Novellino e Conti del Duecento*, Turin: UTET, 1968.

MIGLIORINI, BRUNO, *Storia della Lingua Italiana*, Florence: Sansoni, 1978.

MORGHEN, RAFFAELLO, *Medioevo cristiano*, Bari: Laterza, 1978.

OPPENHEIMER, PAUL, *The Birth of the Modern Mind: Self, consciousness, and the invention of the sonnet*, Oxford: OUP, 1989.

PIETRAMELLARA, CARLA, *Il Duomo di Siena: Evoluzioni della forma dalle origini alla fine del Trecento*, Florence: Edam, 1980.

PREVITALI, GIOVANNI, 'La periodizzazione della storia dell'arte italiana', in *Storia dell'arte italiana: Volume primo, Questioni e metodi*, Turin: Einaudi, 1979, pp. 5–95.

PULLAN, BRIAN, *A History of Early Renaissance Italy from the Mid-Thirteenth to the Mid-Fifteenth Century*, London: Allen Lane, 1973.

SETTON, KENNETH M., 'The Byzantine Background to the Italian Renaissance', in *Europe and the Levant in the Middle Ages*, London: Variorum Reprints, 1974, I.

SWARZENSKI, GEORG, *Nicolo Pisano*, Frankfurt: Iris-Verlag, 1926.

ULLMANN, WALTER, *Medieval Foundations of Renaissance Humanism*, London: Paul Elek, 1977.

BARRACLOUGH, GEOFFREY, *The Crucible of Europe: The Ninth and Tenth Centuries in European History*, London: Thames & Hudson, 1976.

BALZANI, UGO, *Le cronache italiane nel medio evo*, Hildesheim/New York: George Olms, 1973.

BARLEY, M.W., (ed.), *European Towns: Their Archeology and Early History*, London: Academic Press, 1977.

BAYNES, NORMA H., & MOSS, H.ST.L.B., *Byzantium: An Introduction to East Roman Civilization*, Oxford: Clarendon, 1948.

BECKER, MARVIN B., *Medieval Italy: Constraints and Creativity*, Bloomington: Indiana University Press, 1981.

BENEVOLO, LEONARDO, *Storia della città*, Bari: Laterza, 1975.

BERTOLINI, OTTORINO, *Roma di fronte a Bisanzio e ai Longobardi*, Bologna: Cappelli, 1941.

BLOCH, M., *La Società Feudale*, Turin: Einaudi, 1962.

BOLOGNA, FERDINANDO, *La pittura italiana delle origini*, Rome: Editori Riuniti, 1962.

BOYD, CATHERINE E., *Tithes and Parishes in Mediaeval Italy: The Historical Roots of a Modern Problem*, Ithaca, NY: Cornell UP, 1952.

BRENTANO, ROBERT, *Rome before Avignon: A Social History*, London: Longman, 1974.

— *Two Churches: England and Italy in the thirteenth century*, Berkeley: University of California Press, 1988.

BREZZI, PAOLO, *Roma e l'impero medioevale*, Bologna: Cappelli, 1947.

BROOKE, CHRISTOPHER, *Europe in the Central Middle Ages 962–1154*, London: Longman, 1964.

BROWN, PETER, *The World of Late Antiquity*, London: Thames & Hudson, 1989.

BRYCE, JAMES, *The Holy Roman Empire*, London: Macmillan, 1873.

BULLOUGH, DONALD, *The Age of Charlemagne*, London: Elek, 1965.

— *Italy and her Invaders*, (Nottingham University Inaugural Lecture), Nottingham: Hawthornes, 1968).

CAPITANI, OVIDIO, *Storia dell'Italia Medievale: 410–1216*, Bari: Laterza, 1986.

CILENTO, N., *Italia meridionale longobarda*, Milan: Ricciardi, 1971.

CONANT, KENNETH JOHN, *Carolingian and Romanesque Architecture 800 to 1200*, Harmondsworth: Penguin (The Pelican History of Art), 1959.

D'ALESSANDRO, VINCENZO, *Storiografia e politica nell'Italia normanna*, Naples: Liguori, 1978.

— *L'Italia nel Medioevo*, Roma: Riuniti, 1985.

DELVOYE, CHARLES, *L'Art Byzantin*, Paris: Arthaud, 1967.

DE STEFANO, ANTONINO, *Civiltà Medievale*, Bologna: Zanichelli, 1955.

DODWELL, C.R., *Painting in Europe 800–1200*, Harmondsworth: Penguin (The Pelican History of Art), 1971.

DUBY, GEORGES, *L'An Mil*, Paris: Julliard, 1967.

[276]

— *Guerriers et paysans VII–XIIe siècle: Premier essor de l'economie européenne*, Paris: Gallimard, 1973.

— *A History of the Private Life, Vol 2: Revelations of the Medieval World*, Cambridge, Mass: Harvard UP, 1988.

ECO, UMBERTO, *Arte e Bellezza nell'Estetica Medievale*, Milan: Bompiani, 1987.

ELZE, REINHARD & FASOLI, GINA (EDS.), *La Città in Italia e in Germania nel Medioevo: cultura, istituzioni, vita religiosa*, Bologna: Il Mulino, 1981.

ENNEN, EDITH, *Storia della città medievale*, Bari: Laterza, 1975.

FARAGLIA, NUNZIO FEDERICO, *Il Comune nell'Italia Meridionale (1100–1806)* Naples: Furcheim, 1882.

FASOLI, GINA, *Scritti di Storia Medievale*, Bologna: Fotocromio Emiliana, 1974.

FAWTIER, ROBERT, *The Capetian Kings of France: Monarchy and Nation 987–1328*, London: Macmillan, 1960.

FICHTENAU, HEINRICH, *The Carolingian Empire: The Age of Charlemagne*, New York: Harper Torchbooks, 1964.

FOSSIER, ROBERT, *Peasant Life in the Medieval West*, Oxford: Blackwell, 1988.

FUMAGALLI, VITO, *Terra e società nell'Italia padana*, Turin: Einaudi, 1976.

— *Il regno italico*, Turin: UTET, 1978.

— *Città e campagna nell'Italia medievale*, Bologna: Patron, 1985.

GEARY, PATRICK J., *Before France and Germany: The creation and transformation of the Merovingian World*, Oxford: OUP, 1988.

GENICOT, LEOPOLD, *Profilo della Civiltà Medievale*, Milan: Vita e Pensiero, 1968.

GIES, JOSEPH & FRANCES, *Merchants and Moneymen: The Commercial Revolution 1000–1500*, London: Arthur Baker, 1972.

GRAND, ROGER & DELATOUCHE, RAYMOND, *Storia Agraria del Medioevo*, Milan: Il Saggiatore, 1968.

HARTMANN, LUDO MORITZ, *The Early Medieval State: Byzantium, Italy and the West*, London: Historical Association Pamphlets, General Series No. 14, 1949.

HASKINS, CHARLES H., *The Renaissance of the Twelfth Century*, Cambridge, Mass: Harvard UP, 1927.

HAVERKAMP, ALFRED, *Medieval Germany 1056–1273*, Oxford; OUP.

HERLIHY, DAVID, *The Social History of Italy and Western Europe 700–1500: Collected Studies*, London: Variorum Reprints, 1978.

— LOPEZ, Robert S., Slessarev, Vsevolod (eds.), *Economy, Society and Government in Medieval Italy: Essays in Honor of Robert L. Reynolds*, Kent, Ohio: Kent State UP, 1969.

HEYD, W., *Histoire du Commerce de Levant au Moyen Âge*, Leipzig: Otto Harrassowitz, 1923 (2 vols.).

HODGKIN, THOMAS, *Italy and her Invaders*, Oxford: Clarendon, 1892–9 (8 vols.).

HUSSEY, J.M., *The Byzantine World*, London: Hutchinson University Library, 1970.

HYDE, J.K., 'Medieval descriptions of cities', *Bulletin of the John Rylands Library*, XLVIII (1966), pp. 308–40.

JENKINS, ROMILLY, *Byzantium: The Imperial Centuries AD 610–1071*, London: Weidenfeld & Nicolson, 1966.

JONES, A.H.M., *The Later Roman Empire*, Oxford: OUP, 1964 (3 vols.).

JONES, PHILIP, 'La Storia Economica: Dalla caduta dell'impero al secolo XIV', in STORIA D'ITALIA, Turin: Einaudi, 1974, vol. II, Part 2, pp. 1, 469–1, 810.

— *Economia e società nell'Italia medievale*, Turin: Einaudi, 1980.

KOTEL'NIKOVA, L.A., *Mondo contadino e città in Italia dall'XI al XIV secolo: Dalle Fonti dell'Italia centrale e settentrionale*, Bologna: Il Mulino, 1967.

LAVEDAN, PIERRE & HUGUENEY, JEANNE, *L'Urbanisme au Moyen Âge*, Geneva; Droz, 1974.

LAWRENCE, C.H., *Medieval Monasticism: Forms of Religious Life in Western Europe in the Middle Ages*, London: Longman, 1984.

LEFF, GORDON, *Medieval Thought: St Augustine to Ockham*, Harmondsworth: Penguin, 1958.

LE GOFF, JACQUES, *Il Basso Medioevo* (Storia Universale Feltrinelli, Vol. II), Milan: Feltrinelli, 1967.

— 'L'Italia fuori d'Italia: L'Italia nello specchio del Medioevo', in STORIA D'ITALIA, Turin: Einaudi, 1974, Vol. II, Part 2, pp. 1,935–2,088.

— *Medieval Civilization*, Oxford: Blackwell, 1988.

— *The Medieval Imagination*, Chicago & London: University of Chicago Press, 1988.

LEIGHTON, ALBERT, C., *Transport and Communication in Early Medieval Europe AD 500–1100*, Newton Abbot: David & Charles, 1972.

LEWIS, ARCHIBALD, R., *Naval power and trade in the Mediterranean AD 500–1100*, Princeton, NJ: Princeton University Press, 1951.

LOPEZ, ROBERT S., 'The Trade of Medieval Europe: the South', in *Cambridge Economic History of Europe*, Vol. II, Cambridge: CUP, 1952, pp. 257–534.

— *The Commercial Revolution of the Middle Ages*, New York: Prentice-Hall, 1971.

— & RAYMOND, Irving W., *Medieval Trade in the Mediterranean World*, London: OUP, 1955.

LOT, FERDINAND, *La fin du monde antique et le début du moyen âge*, Paris: Albin Michel, 1968.

LUZZATTO, GINO, *An Economic History of Italy, from the Fall of the Roman Empire to the beginning of the Sixteenth Century*, London: Routledge & Kegan Paul, 1961.

MACK SMITH, D., *A History of Sicily: Medieval Sicily 800–1713*, London: Chatto & Windus, 1968.

MANGO, CYRIL, *Byzantium: The empire of the new Rome*, London: Weidenfeld & Nicholson, 1988.

MARINO, JOHN A., *Pastoral Economics in the Kingdom of Naples*, BALTIMORE: The Johns Hopkins University Press, 19??.

MARTINES, L. (ed.), *Violence and Civil Disorder in Italian Cities 1200–1500*, Berkeley & Los Angeles: Univ. of California Press, 1972.

MISKIMIN, HENRY A., Herlihy, David, & Udovitch, A.L., (eds.) *The Medieval City*, New Haven: Yale UP, 1977.

MOSS, H.ST.L.B., *The Birth of the Middle Ages 395–814*, Oxford: OUP, 1974.

OAKLEY, FRANCIS, *The Medieval Experience*, Toronto: Toronto UP, 1988.

OTTO OF FREISING, *The Deeds of Frederick Barbarossa and his Continuator, Rahewin*, trs. C.C. Mierow, New York: Columbia University Press, 1953.

PARTNER, PETER, *The Lands of St Peter: The Papal State in the Middle Ages and the Early Renaissance*, Berkeley and Los Angeles: University of California Press, 1972.

PIRENNE, HENRI, *Medieval Cities: Their Origins and the Revival of Trade*, Princeton NJ: Princeton UP, 1969.

PREVITÉ-ORTON, C.W., 'The Italian cities till *ca* 1200', in *Cambridge Medieval History: Vol V*, Cambridge: CUP, 1926, pp. 208–41.

RODOLFO IL GLABRO, *Chronache dell'anno mille*, Milan: Fondazione Lorenzo Valla/ Mondadori, 1989.

ROMANO, G., & SOLMI, A., *Le dominazione barbariche (395–888)* Milano: Vallardi, 1940.

RUNCIMAN, STEVEN, *Byzantine Civilisation*, London: Edward Arnold, 1933.

RUSSELL, JOSIAH COX, *Medieval Regions and Their Cities*, Newton Abbot: David and Charles, 1972.

SETTIA, ALDO A., *Castelli e villaggi nell'Italia padana: Popolamento, potere e sicurezza fra IX e XIII secolo*, Naples: Liguori, 1984.

SOUTHERN, R.W., *The Making of the Middle Ages*, London: Century Hutchinson, 1987.

STEPHENSON, CARL., *Medieval Feudalism*, Ithaca & London: Cornell UP, 1942.

STOREY, R.L., *Chronology of the Medieval World 800–1491*, London: Barrie & Jenkins, 1973.

TABACCO, GIOVANNI, *The Struggle for Power in Medieval Italy: Structures of Political Rule 400–1400*, Cambridge: CUP, 1990.

TIERNEY, BRIAN, *The Crisis of Church and State 1050–1300*, Toronto: Toronto UP, 1988.

TOUBERT, PIERRE, *Les structures du Latium mediéval*, Rome: Bibliotèque des Écoles françaises d'Athènes et de Rome, 1973 (2 vols.).

— *Études sur l'Italie mediévale (IXe–XIVe siècles)*, London: Variorum Reprints, 1976.

— *Histoire du Haut Moyen Âge e de l'Italie mediévale*, London: Variorum Reprints, 1987.

ULLMANN, W., *The Individual and Society in the Middle Ages*, London: 1967.

VASILIEV, A.A., *History of the Byzantine Empire 324–1453*, Oxford: Blackwell, 1952.

VILLARI, PASQUALE, *Medieval Italy, from Charlemagne to Henry VII*, London: T. Fisher Unwin, 1910.

VOLPE, GIOACCHINO, *Medio Evo Italiano*, Florence: Sansoni, 1961.

WALEY, D.P., '''Combined Operations'' in Sicily, A.D. 1060–78', *Papers of the British School at Rome*, XXII (1954), pp. 118–25.

— *The Italian City-Republics*, London: Longman, 1969.

WICKHAM, CHRIS, *The Mountains and the City: The Tuscan Apennines in the Early Middle Ages*, Oxford: Clarendon, 1988.

WOLFF, P., *Storia e Cultura del Medioevo dal IX al XII secolo*, Bari: Laterza, 1969.

WRIGHT, F.A., (trs.) *The Works of Liudprand of Cremona: Antapodosis, Liber de Rebus Gesti Ottonis, Relatio de Legatione Constantinopolitana*, London: George Routledge, 1930.

# INDEX OF PEOPLE AND PLACES